ANGLICAN EIRENICON

ANGLICAN EIRENICON

The concept of Churchmanship in the Quest for Christian Unity

John Fitch

The Lutterworth Press

The Lutterworth Press
P.O. Box 60
Cambridge
CB1 2NT
United Kingdom

www.lutterworth.com
publishing@lutterworth.com

ISBN: 978 0 7188 9212 8

British Library Cataloguing in Publication Data
A record is available from the British Library

Copyright © John Fitch, 2009

First Published, 2009

Table of Contents

For my children and grandchildren

and

in affectionate and grateful remembrance of all
from whom I have learned true wisdom
in the course of a long life.

Preface

Not the least of my problems in writing this book was the choice of its title. To hit on a suitably arresting phrase or word that would neatly and accurately encapsulate my argument, without simultaneously releasing a shoal of red herrings, proved surprisingly difficult. After much thought, I eventually chose the words printed on the title page.

"Eirenicon" is not a word in common or frequent use. Its very unfamiliarity may have sent some prospective readers to their dictionaries. If yours happens to be the *Concise Oxford*, you will find it defined there as "a proposal tending to make peace". That word, qualified by "Anglican" (for that is what I am and what is distinctive about the book) gave me exactly what I was looking for.

I realise, of course – how could I not? – that, in present circumstances, to launch a book with such a title is to invite derision. It will be said: "For Anglicans, of all people, who notoriously can't agree about anything, to offer an eirenicon is a total absurdity." The Anglican Communion, to borrow the title of a book by Stephen Bates published in 2003, is *A Church at War* – at war with itself. And that, if a sensational, is not an unfair description. If the Church of England, mother church of the world-wide Anglican Communion, is *plausibly* to put forward a proposal to make peace, it must surely first address *itself*, try to heal its *own* self inflicted wounds, to bridge its deep ideological/theological divisions. They are reminiscent of the party factions in the apostolic Church of Corinth in New Testament times which shocked St. Paul (see 1 Corinthians 1-3).

A particularly daunting difficulty in the C. of E. today is that we Anglicans have become so inured to our long standing party divisions, that we are only too apt to take them for granted, almost unnoticed, as part of our inherited environment – so much so in fact that we can hardly bear the thought of parting with them, can scarcely imagine Anglican life without them. We have come to cherish what we smugly like to call our "diversity", a word dear to some of our less thoughtful bishops.

But that is not the case with the current rifts in our world-wide Communion. Their gravity first became widely apparent in the bitter shenanigans at the (1998) Lambeth Conference; it was the first time since these ten yearly gatherings from across the world began in 1867 that such scenes have marred their harmony. In the troubled decade which followed, culminating in Lambeth 2008, the patient, prayerful and persistent diplomacy of two sharply different Archbishops of Canterbury has succeeded in preventing formal schism. But the regrettable impatience of a group of conservative evangelical prelates, mostly from Africa, precipitated the next worst thing – a rival, breakaway conference in the Holy Land under the specious slogan of Global Anglican Future – GAFCON. This has created new tensions. All efforts, if only to agree to disagree, deserve the prayerful support of all sensible Anglicans. This book is not intended in any way as a criticism of the efforts of those working for peace.

I am (I hope) not so conceited or foolish as to imagine that where such strenuous efforts, through no fault of their own, have failed, I have found some magic formula, pretentiously dressed up as an "eirenicon", which, hey presto, will do the trick! Instead, what I am offering here is nothing slick or clever, but simply a rather different *approach*, and a long-term one at that, based upon a long lifetime's experience, observation and reflection in the remote rural backwoods of the Church of England.

This new approach will be by way of a gadget and a technique the very existence of which is sure to be new to readers. The gadget is called an ecclesiometer and the technique as well as the *purpose* of using it, ecclesiometry. This, by some accounted the art, by others the science of accurately gauging the churchmanship of an individual or parish, is obviously a matter of precision. You are not obliged to believe in its existence, but if you are prepared to suspend disbelief it will help. You will, I trust, be braced and ready for a gruelling trawl, in successive chapters of the four basic aspects of churchmanship, one by one, enabling us to complete a positive reformulation of churchmanship as an invaluable peacemaking tool.

If that does turn out to be the case, as I believe it will, its uses will not be confined to bringing peace and harmony within the Anglican fold. Our attention must turn as well to the wider ecumenical field. For not only is the Anglican Communion, and, within it, the Church of England at present bitterly divided within itself, and hampered thereby from bearing effective witness to the Gospel, but – if we substitute "deeply" for "bitterly" – so is the entire Christian world.

If we include the Great Schism between the Latin, Catholic West and the Greek and Slavonic Orthodox East, going back with a few breaks to 1054, this has been the case for nearly a thousand years. We in the West look back to the disruption of the sixteenth century Reformation and the later breaks *within* the Protestant world, almost all of which remain unresolved. To Paul's anguished question, "Is Christ divided?" (1 Corinthians 1 v.13) the sad, reluctant reply has to be, "Yes".

In this respect, the last (20th) century witnessed what we must surely see as the decisive turning of the tide. From small but significant beginnings in 1910 with the International Missionary Conference at Edinburgh and the associated work of the Student Christian Movement, *di*vergence began to be replaced by *con*vergence. The Lambeth 1920 Appeal to All Christian People marked a further stage in the development of the Ecumenical Movement, hailed by William Temple as "the great new fact of our era". The largest Christian Communion, the Roman Catholic Church, stood aloof, until with the Second Vatican Council (1962-65) called by Pope John XXIII, this changed and Rome began to cooperate. In the 1970's and early '80's hopes ran high, with a genuine *rapprochement* between the Anglicans and Rome marked by a reciprocal visit at the highest level and the official setting up of the Anglican Roman Catholic International Commission (ARCIC) and the constructive interchanges that followed in succeeding years. It even seemed that the recognised ultimate goal of visible Christian Unity/Reunion, was attainable. For various reasons, in the late 1980's and 1990's these hopes faded. We seemed to have run out of steam, to have reached an impasse. This remains so today. Yet some hopeful signs are not lacking.

In these circumstances a unified Christian churchmanship incorporating the positive essence of each of the four distinctive and *complementary* positions, such as I advocate in this book, could and should be *a* deciding factor in breaking the current ecumenical deadlock and opening the way to *some* form, not of artificial monolithic uniformity, but of genuine visible Christian *unity in diversity*, safeguarding all integrities and undergirded by universal intercommunion.

If this is indeed attainable as a practical possibility by the action of the Holy Spirit of Truth, Wisdom, Reason and Love, a *further* prospect beckons – the eventual coming together of the three great monotheistic "Abrahamic" faiths, Christianity, Judaism and Islam, under the sovereignty of the unique and universal Son of God, the Head of redeemed humanity who laid down his life for us *all* and lives and reigns for all eternity. Such is the argument considered in its complexity and underlying simplicity, of the concluding chapters.

That then is the intended scope of this book. Who are envisaged as its readers? I have endeavoured in writing it as far as possible to avoid technical language – dare I call it jargon? – so often found in academic theology and so off-putting to the general reader, in the hope of making it as widely accessible as possible. You will judge the extent of my failure or success.

In conclusion I wish to express my warmest thanks and appreciation to all who have given me their encouragement. I can now reveal that three or four years ago I completed an earlier version which I called *Beyond a Joke: A Study in Ecclesiometry*. It was an injudicious mélange of the serious and the frivolous that didn't "work". I was trying to be too clever and I had not sufficiently thought through my ideas and their implications. I submitted it to two publishers and they turned it down – to my (subsequent) relief. They were entirely right to do so. I then decided on a further programme of serious reading and hard thinking with the intention of eventually rewriting it as an entirely serious project, but leaving room for light relief. I am deeply grateful to *all* to whom I submitted the original draft, *Beyond a Joke*, for their candid opinions – not least to those who frankly told me they couldn't make head or tail of it!

But some there were who thought it had real possibilities. Among them were my revered old mentor and friend the late Professor C.F.D. Moule, Ronald Blythe, literary critic of distinction and author of *Akenfield* and *Word from Wormingford* and much else, my cousin and godson, John Brian Lott, an old friend Audrey Serreau of Poitiers, France, and Dr. Pamela Tudor-Craig, Lady Wedgwood, friend and art historian. To them all I record my sincere thanks. They are in no way responsible for the present recension, which is all my own work. Pray God it may prove useful.

I cannot conclude this Preface without the warmest and most grateful tribute to Maureen Barsby of Long Melford, Suffolk. From the very inception of this project she has faithfully transformed reams of my untidy longhand into elegant print. Without her unfailing patience and cheerful good humour it could never have got off the ground.

To this I must add a word of warm appreciation for the strenuous efforts of my publisher's editorial staff in preparing my script for publication.

Great Yeldham, 29 December 2008
J.A.F.

Chapter 1
The Anglican concept of Churchmanship

Prologue

A distinguished journalist, John Whale, who died in June 2008, was wont to describe Anglicanism as "the most grown up expression of Christianity". He knew what he was talking about. What led him to that flattering conclusion was undoubtedly his view from the editorial chair of the *Church Times*. This gave him a unique insight into the extraordinary breadth, height, depth and maturity of Anglican diversity, comprehensiveness and mutual tolerance, unparalleled in any other branch of the Christian Church.

That precious, easygoing tolerance, that civilised agreement to differ on so many vital issues, which so impressed Whale (himself born into a contrasting form of ecclesiastical anarchy, his father's Congregationalism), has worn extremely thin of late, transforming the Church of England and the Anglican Communion worldwide from the appearance of a (more or less) civilised ecclesiastical debating society, into something more like a theatre of war, leading many staunch Anglicans to, or even over, the brink of despair. That, at any rate, is one way of looking at our present situation.

It is not, however, the view taken in this book. Its author claims to be as staunch an Anglican as any, though remaining far from uncritical. Born, baptised, confirmed and brought up in the C. of E., serving in its regular ordained parochial ministry for upwards of sixty years and firmly expecting to end his days in its communion and fellowship, he offers a broader, longer term and in some ways a more hopeful, positive and optimistic perspective, though only too aware of its limitations.

As he sees it, far and away the *most distinctive* feature of present day Anglicanism is what until very recently was universally known as CHURCHMANSHIP. If you come to think about it, this word, concept or thing is quite extraordinarily difficult accurately, succinctly and precisely to define – and even harder to replace with something better! In recent years journalists and others have sought to avoid ambiguities and complexities associated with the word "churchmanship", by substituting for it the word "tradition" – as when we often read nowadays of "the evangelical, or catholic, or liberal tradition". This is singularly unsatisfactory. Tradition and churchmanship are not the same thing. This becomes obvious when confronted with such nonsense as "the traditionalist tradition". So, whether we like it or not, we are stuck with churchmanship and must make the best sense of it we can.

Therefore, unappealing as (in cold blood) it may sound, this book consists very largely of an in depth, no holds barred exploration of this vital, unavoidable and irreplaceable, uniquely and distinctively Anglican concept or thing, *and* of the four separate and distinct manifestations into which it has very naturally fallen in the course of Anglican history. These coincide with the four dimensions and spatial directions within which we all live, move and have our being, viz. up, down, backwards and forwards, and sideways, or North, South, East and West. This is a central contention of this book, which stands or falls by it. Diagramatically it can best be expressed, very simply, by a perfect cross within a circle; the main lines of the cross, longitude and latitude, intersecting at the central point, the Cross. (Those who desire a scriptural warrant for everything are referred to Revelation chapter 21, verses 13 and 16).

The author stubbornly believes that this proposed exploration will prove surprisingly rewarding. We should eventually arrive, though some of the journey will inevitably prove hard, rough and tough, at a true, clear and reasonably succinct and precise definition of that notoriously slippery and elusive concept, word and thing. The route to that goal will lead us through a detailed examination, in four successive chapters following this one, of each in turn of the four basic dimensions into which churchmanship will be seen to fall.

This will be followed by a positive and constructive analysis of the whole thing, showing how each of the four dimensions is essential to the fullness of Christian faith and practice, how not just one or two in isolation but *all four*, each in its basic essentials, are *interdependent, interlocking*, and *necessary* to the *fullness* of catholic/universal Christian Truth, Faith and Practice.

For that reason I have ventured to dub not only Chapter 6, but the whole attempt, *Anglican Eirenicon*. Writing this Prologue in the wake of Lambeth 2008 and the GAFCON Conference of conservative evangelicals which preceded and challenged Lambeth, it may seem foolhardy to be in the least optimistic about Anglican unity worldwide. Nevertheless, taking a long term view – as this author does throughout – and bearing in mind the prospects of an agreed Anglican Covenant, it may yet prove justified. Thus Chapters 7, 8, and 9 would appear not too far-fetched in their hopes of an enduring, worldwide unity. In any case, may God's will be done. That, in the long run, is all that matters.

This Prologue, written by the author after the rest of the book, now concludes, leaving him (boldly assuming the first person singular in place of the old fashioned periphrasis) to take up the theme in his own somewhat rambling style. Be patient with him.

Ecclesiometry and Churchmanship

A few years ago, purely for my own amusement, I coined a new word "ecclesiometry", with its cognates, "ecclesiometer" and "ecclesiometrist". As far as I know, they have yet to be recognised by any reputable dictionary. But I live in hope. In any case they will be put to serious use in this book; so that should do the trick!

Ecclesiometry, let me explain, is the art, technique or even (as some would maintain) the science of measuring, assessing and gauging (not churches but) what we Anglicans usually call CHURCHMANSHIP. An ecclesiometer is the instrument, or device, used in order to achieve this. As will emerge in the course of this chapter (towards the end) I myself designed an elementary one, but only on paper. I never got so far as to patent it, much less put it on the market as the Fitch ecclesiometer. An ecclesiometrist is, of course, a person trained and skilled in its use.

Amateur, untrained and unqualified ecclesiometrists abound; in fact one could almost go so far as to say, without exaggeration, that every Anglican, whether a regular churchgoer or not, considers him/herself an ecclesiometrist (though, *as yet*, he or she is pardonably ignorant of that word). An "old chestnut" will suffice to explain what I mean. A stranger to the parish: "How d'you like your new parson?" Parishioner: "Well, 'e do antick; but us likes our parson so when 'e antick, we antick along of 'e." From this it was to be deduced that the new parson was decidedly "High Church", but that all this new ceremonial ("anticking") was going down well in the parish. There was a different reaction in another country church. "I hear your new Vicar's a fine preacher." Parishioner, who happens to be employed as the church cleaner. "Popular preacher, indeed. I've no patience with

'im. We never 'ad all this mud in church afore 'e come." Obviously
a "Low Church" hot gospeller – an evangelical.[1]

Amateur ecclesiometry like that was a bit of harmless fun in
those unsophisticated days. We all indulged in it. It was a staple of
churchy gossip, almost always confined to the vertical axis, "High"
and "Low" with "Central" occasionally inbetween. I acquired the
habit as a schoolboy and it stuck with me. It was based on a system
of easily recognisable "indicators", mostly regarded as infallible.
One was the Clerical Collar Test; the height, or width, of the clerical
collar was in *inverse* ratio to the height or depth of the wearer's
churchmanship. Thus a Rock Bottomer (extreme Low Church man)
wore such a high collar that it usually concealed his chin, or lack of
one. Whereas something resembling a piece of string round a priest's
neck indicated a Spike (colloquial for extreme High Churchman).
Another sure "indicator" was facial hair or its absence. Almost any
kind of moustache, especially aggressive military-style whiskers,
revealed a Low Churchman. Spikes were clean shaven unless they
were exceptionally eccentric and sported beards (like Bishop Gore).
But beards were a problem; hard to classify. Ultra spikes tended to
wear funny hats in church, called birettas. If I remember rightly,
these had a black pom-pom in the middle (or have I dreamed that?).
And instead of a surplice they wore a short white garment trimmed
with lace, called a cotta. This, like the biretta, they copied from
Roman Catholic priests.

Amateur ecclesiometry was not focused only on the clergy, of
course. Its other prong was, and is, based on the evidence of a
church building. For example, the "Candle Test". Six tall candles
on the "high altar", standing not directly on the altar itself but
on a kind of shelf called a gradine with a locked "tabernacle" in
the centre in which (or in an "aumbry" beside the altar) reposed
consecrated bread and wine – the sacramental Body and Blood of
Christ. A flickering sanctuary lamp would hang above or in front of
it to indicate its presence to the initiated devout. There might also
be a prominent Rood or life size Crucifix above the chancel arch
with carved figures of Our Lady and St. John on either side and
perhaps Stations of the Cross on the walls of nave for use in Lent,
and statues of saints by side altars. Finally, a perceptible whiff of
stale incense. All these infallibly signified an "advanced" Anglo-
Catholic church.

The opposite extreme would be equally unmistakable: a bare

---

1. *Punch* 24 Jan. 1924. Classic George Belcher cartoon, reproduced in *The
Reverend Mr. Punch* (Mowbray 1956).

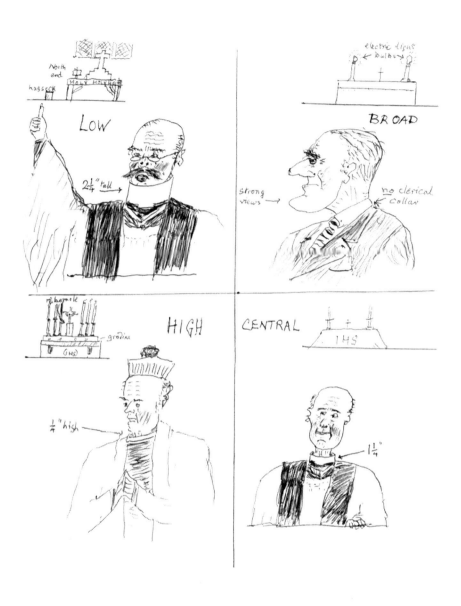

Fig.1. Amateur (Juvenile) Ecclesiometry c. 1935

wooden table under the east window, with nothing more than an aggressively plain brass or wooden cross (not crucifix) in the middle and a prominent kneeler at the north end indicating the required position of the officiating minister. Not a ('popish') candle to be seen, and a pervading smell, not of incense, but of furniture polish!

Most churches were like neither of these; a dignified altar with a decent "frontal" and just two candles and perhaps a small crucifix by the pulpit, indicating middle of the road Anglican – "central" churchmanship, no extremes (see Fig.1) Probably, in days gone by, an aroma of decaying hassocks – the odour of sanctity?

These twin ecclesiometrical prongs seemed originally to focus solely on the vertical polarity of Anglicanism – High and Low with the main body of Central in between.

Gradually another axis came under review, the horizontal. Here we unavoidably come up against problems of nomenclature, ideological labels. We have deliberately avoided them until now. Instead of the old, historic and generally accepted Highs and Lows, the use of which goes back to the late-seventeenth and early-eighteenth centuries, though with subtle alterations of meaning, we have to reckon with what are, in effect, battle cries, ideological slogans used to differentiate and identify rival parties in the established Church. Chief among them are "Evangelical", "Tractarian", and "Catholic" or "Anglo-Catholic" on the vertical axis, and "Latitudinarian", "Broad Church", "modernist", "liberal", "Conservative" and "Traditionalist" on the horizontal axis. It is worth pausing to note that whereas on the old vertical axis degrees of height and depth balanced each other on either side of Centre, although the term "Broad Church" was employed with varying shades of meaning it was never in the same way balanced by shades of Narrowness or Breadth. Possibly this was because it, "Narrow", was considered, mistakenly, to be too derogatory. More will be written about this towards the end of this chapter. Suffice it to say here that, for purposes of strict and impartial ecclesiometry the High/Low, Broad/Narrow system of classification has much in its favour – it is less colourfully partisan, more neutral and impersonal. At least I think so.

It is also worth a passing mention that with the passage of time, the increasingly diverse character of the National Church became more and more noticeable. With it, the prevalence of the amateur, slapdash ecclesiometry on which we have previously commented came to be increasingly reflected in English literature and the media, notably in the Victorian novels of (among others) Thackeray, George Eliot, Trollope and Samuel Butler. Also, more recently in those of

E.F. Benson, Barbara Pym, Susan Howatch and Joanna Trollope; in the light verse of John Betjeman *par excellence* and observant wits and satirists ranging from Osbert Lancaster to S.J. Forrest and Eric Mascall. The C. of E. has always been able to see the funny side of itself. Most, if not all, of this was good-natured and affectionate. Those days seem to have passed beyond recall.

The tribe of Religious Affairs Journalists: their function

These days the subject of and practice of ecclesiometry (despite pardonable ignorance of the term) is kept very much alive and in the eye of an increasingly bemused public by the select tribe of Religious Affairs Correspondents of what used to be, until recently, the respectable broadsheets. A year or two ago the most notable of this tribe were Ruth Gledhill of *The Times*, Jonathan Petre of *The Daily Telegraph* and Stephen Bates of *The Guardian* At the time of writing, Gledhill is still in place, but Petre has been replaced by Martin Beckford and Bates by Riazat Butt. To this list should be added Robert Pigott of the BBC. Their business is to keep the public informed of any significant event or developments in, what in today's rabidly secular culture, is commonly perceived as the outdated sphere of "religion", and of their likely implications for and impact on the wider world we inhabit.

Any journalist worthy of his trade, whether in the Press, radio or television, puts Truth first. He sees his job as intelligent, fair, honest, truthful reporting *plus* clear, objective interpretation and, if need be, comment, in language his readers/listeners/viewers can readily understand. That is the ideal. It can seem an impossibly high one. Still, it remains the ideal and applies as much to the Religious Correspondent as to any other.

To do his job properly in the light of this ideal in the sceptical zeitgeist prevailing today, the Religious Correspondent must be thoroughly conversant not only, but chiefly, with the three great, historically related monotheistic "Abrahamic" faiths, Judaism, Christianity and Islam (to put them in the order of their historic emergence), each in the variant forms in which they are found today, and of the causes underlying these varieties. He/she must also have a working knowledge (at the least) of the *outlines* of the ancient Oriental religions, Buddhism, Hinduism and the Sikh religion, *their* varieties and the history of each in relation to the others and to world history. On top of all this he/she must be thoroughly *au fait* and *au courant* with all the main Christian denominations – Catholic, Protestant, Anglican and Orthodox – their history, their ramifying organisations, memberships, leading authorities and personalities, liturgies, doctrines and ethical teachings and standards, missionary and evangelistic outreach, ecumenical relationships, and, especially, current controversies, schisms and points at issue between and within them. It goes almost without saying that a more than superficial familiarity with the Bible and the work of international scholarship upon it, as well as some acquaintance with the Qu'ran, is indispensable. This list is not exhaustive. In short, the Religious Correspondent, poor dear, must be all but omniscient. Since, even today, omniscience is still a little beyond human reach, what is more important is mature wisdom, sound judgment and a cross-bench mind. As good a role model as any for the Religious Correspondent would be the late Gerald Priestland of the BBC; and he was well aware of *his* limitations.

My purpose in that long, drawn-out digression was to put the ecclesiometrical demands which inevitably impinge on this select tribe of journalists into some sort of perspective. When it falls to their lot to single out some protagonist in a church controversy or debate, perhaps to report or summarise his arguments, it is natural enough to try to identify his standpoint further by attaching a ready made label to his name – "evangelical", "liberal", "conservative", "traditionalist", "charismatic" or whatever, only to incur a bitter complaint that the label doesn't fit, is inappropriate. No such label is ever completely adequate in particular cases. Let us be charitable and credit these hardworking, and mostly conscientious journalists with doing their best in an exceptionally difficult and demanding job. They are accountable, as we all are, to a just and merciful God whose interests are not confined to the "religious" and who has been this way himself in the person of his "Son", but in *their* case also, to the piercing scrutiny of Andrew Brown's weekly column on the media page of the *Church Times*. It always makes good reading. Finally, all Religious Correspondents inevitably have their own, individual standpoints and preconceptions. Some, e.g. Stephen Bates, make no secret of theirs. He is a liberal Roman Catholic with a fiercely Anglican evangelical wife! Ruth Gledhill's father is an Anglican bishop.

Author's Confession

This seems a good point for me to make a confession. In the sixty years that have so far elapsed since I was ordained deacon at Trinity in 1947, I have never once signed up to any churchmanship stance, any partisan point of view. There have been many occasions, such as when I have been offered a new clerical job, or just moved to a new parish, when people have sought to pin a particular label on me and have been baffled when I have replied, "Oh, I'm just C. of E. That's good enough for me." I must also admit that I enjoy the consequent puzzled expression on their faces. What is the explanation? Indolence? Cowardice? Smug self-satisfaction on my part? I *am* (absurdly) a bit conceited and more than a little cowardly, but I don't think either is the explanation. It is simply that I am blessed, or cursed, with an incorrigibly cross-bench mind, I can't help seeing *both* sides of *almost* every question. This has become "more so" as I have grown older. It is not so much a virtue as a habit. And it can make life difficult at times.

There is, however, a little more to it than that. *What* that is must wait until later in this chapter.

A Problem: Defining Churchmanship

It may not have escaped your notice that, up to this point, although I have used the word "churchmanship" many times, I have assumed that its meaning is clear and clearly understood and have made no attempt to define it, still less to examine and unpack the concept underlying the word. The time has now come to tackle what is, once you come to think about it, quite an elusive quest. In fact the argument of this book stands or falls by the result. Have I got it right?

So *what, precisely* and *exactly, is* churchmanship? Most people, when they use the word, as we have been doing, take it for granted that they know what they are talking about. But do we? Immediately you try to find words to express and define it, you become aware of the difficulty. It is, in fact, slippery and elusive in both word and concept.

Let us begin by turning to the word experts, the lexicographers, and their most authoritative production, the *Oxford English Dictionary* (second edition 1989).[2] It gives the primary meaning as "the position, quality or action of a churchman". This is a bit disappointing, but it gives us a start. "Position", yes, as on a chessboard, but "quality" or "action" emphatically no: they seem irrelevant to its real meaning.

2. The usual citations from early known instances of the use of the word are interesting, though irrelevant to its meaning today. The earliest is Somers *Tracts* c.1680 .265: "It is well for the Church that she needs not apprehend any Retrospect into her Behaviour since as Times go with Churchmanship. . . ." The second earliest is more illuminating: *The Growth of Deism* 1696 p. 19: "your Churchmanship will not appear by any Mark so well as by the Hatred you bear to all Dissenters." (There will be further recourse to OED when we come to deal with the BROAD CHURCH.)

Churchmanship's New Testament origins and Church Unity, ideal and actual (past and present)

With "positioning" in mind, let us look more closely at the concept of "churchmanship", the thing itself. Obviously the *word* is not there but the thing it represents most certainly *is*. Christians have been "positioning" themselves, at variance with one another, forming parties, pressure groups, incipient sects, heresies and schisms around plausible standpoints, "on crucial matters of principle", generally coalescing round the name and person of some leader/ spokesman, right from the earliest days. Human nature doesn't change – much.

The Early Church

Consequently, the history of Christianity, that is to say the history of the Christian *Church* (community, brotherhood, family, the "mystical Body of Christ") from its very beginning until now is littered with the stories of disagreements, controversies, splits, heresies and schisms, damaging, threatening, breaking and destroying Christian Unity, which has to be rebuilt slowly and painfully. Heresy, now an unfashionable word, is essentially a *distortion* of *truth*, a kind of *half* truth posing as the *whole* truth. That is why it was, and is, so dangerous to Christian solidarity.

In the first five Christian centuries some such heresies are known by the name of the original breakaway leader (or "heresiarch" as he came to be called). Such were the Marcionites, Sabellians, Montanists, Arians, Nestorians and Pelagians. Others are named after their original distortion of Christian Faith/Truth, e.g. Gnostics, Docetists, Monophysites – all from Greek words (e.g. Gnosis = knowledge, distorted).

The New Testament

These later splits and distortions mostly have their origin in New Testament times, in the unique revelation of God in Christ, in the nature of His work of "redemption" and "reconciliation" through death and resurrection, and the experience of the/His Spirit in the Church and by individual Christians. Apart from the tensions among the chosen Twelve due to the naive ambitions of some of them, and their bid for precedence in the coming "Kingdom" (Mark 10 35-45) there is abundant evidence in Acts, in the letters of Paul, John and Jude, and in Revelation[3] of disruptive forces, both within and outside the brotherhood, threatening the harmony of the Apostolic Community.

3. Acts 15; Galatians 3. 1-5, 4. 8-11, 5. 7-10, 6. 12; Ephesians 4. 30; Colossians 2 8,10; 1 John 2. 22; Jude 8-13, 17-19; Revelation 2. 6,14f; 3. 9. 22. 18f

This is in no way surprising in view of the fundamental issues arising from the transformation in such a short while of a small Jewish sect (or what appeared to be such) into a universal, "catholic" *church*, comprising both Jews and (non-Jewish) Gentiles on an equal basis.

St. Paul

None of this has such direct bearing on the concept of "churchmanship" as the evidence of party strife *within* the young Church at Corinth which features so prominently in the first four chapters of Paul's first Letter to the Corinthians, written from Ephesus in or about A.D. 54, (at least a decade *before* the earliest Gospel).

The occasion which evoked this powerful letter was the deeply disturbing reports reaching Paul, its founding Apostle (Acts 18) and anxious "father" (1 Cor. 4, 15), of the appalling goings on in that lively Christian community of some forty or so members.[4] The one that shocked him most, and with which the letter begins, was the development of no less than four rival factions in that primitive church, each apparently invoking in its support a personal loyalty, including one to Paul himself. "It has been reported to me by Chloe's people that there are quarrels among you my brothers. What I mean is that each of you says, 'I belong to Paul ... I belong to Apollos ... I belong to Cephas ... I belong to Christ'". (We may pause to note here that Cephas was the Aramaic form of the Greek nickname Peter, given by Jesus to Simon Bar (son of) Jona/John, and that Apollos was a brilliant Alexandrian Jewish Christian who had arrived in Corinth after Paul had left; also that, whereas one of these rival factions had had the cheek to claim the "Prince of the Apostles" – not known ever to have visited Corinth – as its patron, the fourth had the supreme oneupmanship to claim Christ Himself.)

After citing that report, Paul exploded. "Has Christ been divided? Was Paul crucified for you?" (1 Cor. 1. 11-13). He was revolted to the depth of his being by these reports. "I appeal to you, brothers and sisters, by the name of our Lord Jesus Christ that all of you should be in agreement and that there should be no divisions among you, but that you should be united in the same mind and the same purpose" (1. Cor. 1. 10). Beyond that direct appeal for unity, his counter attack took two distinct forms.

---

4. This is the careful estimate of Jerome Murphy-O'Connor O.P. in his brilliant and stimulating commentary (1997) in the Bible Reading Fellowship People's Bible Commentary series, to which I am much indebted. The same author's *Paul: A Critical Life* (1998) should also be consulted.

Perceiving that the basic cleavage was between Paulites and Apollosites, he was at pains to point out that there was absolutely no rivalry between them, as both were equally God's willing servants. The difference was simply one of function. "What then is Apollos? What is Paul? Servants through whom you came to believe as the Lord assigned to each. I planted, Apollos watered, but God gave the growth. So neither the one who plants nor the one who waters is anything, but only God who gives the growth . . . For we are God's servants, working *together*; you are God's field, God's building," (1 Cor. 3. 5-9).

This leads Paul on directly to the second part of his counter attack, his conception of the essential nature of the Christian Church, the *ecclesia*, as literally and spiritually the dwelling place of the living, victorious Christ, and therefore in the highest degree *sacred*. Starting from the homely simile of the Church as God's field, farm or garden, he goes on to that of a building, of which the foundation, laid by "the skilled master builder", is Jesus Christ (1 Cor. 3. 10f.). This not entirely satisfactory image leads him on to that of a temple. "Do you not know that *you* are God's temple and that God's spirit dwells in *you*? If anyone destroys God's temple, God will destroy that person. For God's temple is holy and *you* are that temple" (1 Cor. 3. 16f.). He sums up his argument so far in this typically Pauline sarcastic rhetoric: "So let no one boast about human leaders. For all things are yours, whether Paul or Apollos or Cephas or the world or life or death or the present or the future – all belongs to you, and you belong to Christ and Christ belongs to God," (1 Cor. 3. 21-23).[5]

It is, however, towards the end of this long letter that Paul returns to the theme of the essentially corporate and organic nature of Christian living, and this time he has *at last* found the perfect metaphor, no longer the field, garden, building, temple, but the human body. "For just as the body is one and has many members, and all the members of the body, though many, are one body, so it is with Christ. For in the one spirit we were all baptised into one body – Jews or Greeks [i.e. non Jews, "Gentiles"], slaves or free – and were all made to 'drink' of one spirit . . . there are many members yet one body . . . If one member suffers, all suffer together with

5. Jerome Murphy-O'Connor's comment on this passage in his provocative commentary on 1 Corinthians (p. 41) is: "His inability to resist a chance to slide the knife did Paul no good among his readers, but what he wants to get across remains valid. The only reference point for Christians is Christ: to him alone do we belong." Murphy-O'Connor is severe on Paul's use of savage sarcasm.

it, if one is honoured all rejoice together with it. Now *you* are the body of Christ and *individually members* of it" (1 Cor. 12, 12f., 20, 26f.).

With this passage should be compared (i) Romans 12. 4f. where he uses almost exactly the same words, concluding "so we, who are many, are one body in Christ and individually members one of another" and (ii) two crucial passages in the Letter to the Ephesians, where he approaches the same theme from different angles, enriching it even further in the process.

In the first of these Paul is specifically addressing "you Gentiles by birth, called 'the uncircumcision' by those who are called 'the circumcision', at that time without Christ, aliens from the commonwealth of Israel and strangers to the covenants of promise, having no hope and without God in the world" (Eph. 2. 11f.). He then goes on, "But *now in Christ Jesus* you who once were far off have been brought near by the blood of Christ. For he is our peace; in his flesh he has made both groups into one and has broken down the dividing wall, that is, the hostility between us. He has abolished the law with its commandments and ordinances, *so that he might create in himself one new humanity* in place of the two, thus making peace, and might reconcile both groups to God in *one body*, through the cross, thus putting to death that hostility through it. So he came and proclaimed peace to you who were far off and peace to those who were near, for through him both of us have access in one Spirit to the Father", (Eph. 2. 13-17). And from that point Paul goes on triumphantly to conclude this great passage by including his earlier metaphors in the new panorama.

"So then you [Gentiles] are no longer strangers and aliens, but you are citizens with the saints and also members of the household of God, built upon the foundation of the apostles and prophets, with Christ Jesus as the cornerstone. In him the whole structure is joined together and grows into a holy temple in the Lord; in whom you also are built together spiritually into a dwelling place for God", (Eph. 2. 19-22). Paul surely is the world's champion master of mixed metaphors, and how effective they are in combination!

From the very beginning of Ephesians, Paul, or whoever it was who wrote in his name, (if, as seems possible, he was not himself the author) was working towards the great prayer with which the first half of the letter concludes, but which is not strictly relevant to our theme of peace and unity in the church (Eph. 3. 14-21).

The second half begins with Paul returning to this theme in one of the most purple passages in the New Testament. "I therefore, the prisoner in the Lord, beg you to lead a life worthy of the calling to which you have been called . . . making every effort to maintain the unity of the Spirit in the bond of peace. There is one body and one Spirit, just as you were called in the one hope of your calling, one Lord, one faith, one baptism, one God and Father of all, who is above all and through all and in all", (Eph. 4. 1-6). Finally, in the sublime Christological passage in the first chapter of his (almost certainly authentic) Letter to the Colossians, beginning "He [Christ] is the image of the invisible God, the first born of all creation" (Col. 1. 15) Paul writes, "He himself is before all things and in him all things hold together. He is the head of the body, the church, the beginning, the first born from the dead, so that he might come to have first place in everything. For in him all the fulness of God was pleased to dwell, and through him God was pleased to reconcile to himself all things, whether on earth or in heaven, by making peace through the blood of his cross", (Col. 1. 17-20).

This brief overview of Paul's "high" doctrine of Christ-in-his-members would not be complete without reference to the significance of his characteristic use of the expression "in Christ". A typical example is the opening sentence of his letter to the Philippians, in which he addressed "all God's people at Philippi, who are *incorporated* in Christ Jesus." (Phil. 1. 1 in the Revised English Bible translation, which makes its meaning explicit inevitably reminding older Anglicans of "that we are very members incorporate in the mystical Body of Thy Son, which is the blessed company of all faithful people".)[6] Paul clarifies his meaning still further in 2 Cor. 5. 17: "For anyone united to Christ, there is a new creation; the old order has gone; a new order has already begun." (R.E.B. translation).

If we take Paul seriously, and (believer's) baptism does indeed entail union with, *incorporation into* the living Lord Jesus Christ, crucified and risen, *i.e.* his contemporary embodiment in His universal church, "one, holy, catholic and apostolic", there can be no room, and no excuse, for rival parties, dissension, factional in-fighting, conflict and strife.

But, rather than take it seriously, do we not say: Paul was writing in ideal terms? The actuality, given human shortcomings, is far different. We are so inured, after two millennia of Christian dissension, heresies, splits and schisms that we have come to regard it and our consequent ineffectiveness at representing the Prince of Peace in a hostile, divided world, as natural, inevitable, beyond all hope.

6. The alternative post-Communion prayer, otherwise known as the Prayer of Oblation, in the *Book of Common Prayer.*

The Four Gospels

Turning from Paul's letters to the Gospels, we find that, apart from two blatantly anachronistic[7] occurrences of the Greek word *ekklesia* in Matthew 16. 18 and 18. 17, there are no references in our Lord's reported utterances to "the church" in any gospel, because Jesus's teaching focused entirely on the coming of God's *Kingdom* in His own day.

However, in Matthew and Luke (only) he teaches his disciples to pray, using the outline formula we know as the Lord's Prayer; it takes a slightly different form in the first and third gospels – Luke's version is briefer, more terse.[8] (It is absent from Mark and John). Its opening words "*Our* Father" teach all who use it to see themselves not as isolated individuals but brothers and sisters in the "family" of God, siblings one of another in the bond of mutual love and brotherhood, with unlimited and unconditional readiness to forgive as a condition of being forgiven our sins by our heavenly Father. Jesus is consistently reported in all the Synoptics (as in John 13) as constantly dinning into his disciples/apostles the urgent need to follow his example of service (an echo here of the four servant songs in Isaiah 42-53). (Mark 9. 35ff. and 10.42-45; Luke 22. 24-27).

Mark reports Jesus saying, "Have salt in yourselves and be at peace with one another", (Mark 9. 50).

The Fourth Gospel: St. John

But it is when we come to the fourth Gospel, bearing the name of John, that we have the most explicit teaching on the ideal nature of the Church, and in each case it takes the form of words (in two cases teaching, in the third, prayer) composed by "John" and placed upon the lips of Our Lord.

The first instance of John's liberality with creative licence is in Chapter 10, sayings characteristic of this gospel – not paralleled in the first three, the Synoptics. Here Jesus, using the introductory "I am" which may be a deliberate echo of the sacred name of God (Exodus 3. 13-15) describes himself both as the Good Shepherd and as the door or gate of the sheepfold. The language put on his lips is strongly reminiscent of that used by the prophet Ezekiel in relation to ancient Israel, the Old Covenant "People of God" (Ezek. 34) but, of course, refers to the New Covenant Israel, the all-embracing, i.e.

---

7. By "anachronistic" I mean that Jesus could not possibly have spoken of "my church". This concept (church) post dates his Resurrection. It was added to this saying later, by the evangelist. (Matthew)
8. Matthew 6. 9-13; Luke 11. 2-4

catholic Church – "other sheep I have which do not belong to this fold" – the Gentiles. "I must bring them also and they will listen to my voice. So there will be one flock, one shepherd" (Verse 16). This is one of the most precious chapters of the Bible.

The second instance is in Chapter 15, part of the long Johannine discourses at the Last Supper. Again, it is an "I am" passage. Jesus *is* "the True Vine". The vine throughout the Old Testament is the recognised symbol of Israel – the O.T. "Church". (See especially Isaiah chapter 5 and Psalm 80 verses 8-13). So Jesus *is* God's People personified. "I am the vine, you are the branches". Jesus's disciples, his "branches", must "abide" in him. Only so will they be able to be fruitful – and flourish. In other words there is no such thing as individual Christianity. The Christian must actively belong to the Body, the Church. Thus does St. John (whoever he was; in this world we shall never penetrate the mystery of his true identity) reinforce, in Christ's name, the teaching of St. Paul.

Finally we approach, with reverence, fear and trembling, the third and perhaps the greatest of these Johannine passages, chapter 17, often called "The High Priestly Prayer" in recognition of the fact that in this wonderful composition, placed by the evangelist on the lips of our "Great High Priest after the order of Melchizedek" (Hebrews 4. 14 and 5. 5f.), in which He offers and consecrates Himself as the all sufficient sacrifice on behalf of us, His sinful people. It takes the place of the simple Synoptic narrative of Our Lord's agonised prayer in the Garden of Gethsemane (but in no way contradicts it) "Father, for you all things are possible. Remove this "cup" [of sacrifice and suffering] from me. Yet not what I want, but what you want", (Mark 14. 36). (R.S.V.)

In the course of this long prayer, Jesus is made (by "John") to ask that those the Father has given Him "may be one as we are one" (verse 11). Some verses later (20-23),

> on behalf of these, but also of those who *will* believe in me through their word, that they may all be one. As you, Father, are in me and I am in you, may they also be in us, so that the world may believe that you have sent me. The glory that you have given me I have given them, so that they may be one, as we are one, I in them and you in me, that they may become completely one, so that the world may know that you have sent me and have loved them even as you have loved me.

I have dared to extract from this complete composition only those sections which are directly relevant to the New Testament witness to the theme of *Christian Solidarity* – Christ and Christians in His Body the Church.

Probably no two people will react in quite the same way to these typically Johannine monologues. To me they faithfully represent the consecrated human mind of our Saviour at the supreme crisis of his earthly life and ministry, *as interpreted* (I believe, correctly) for posterity with uncanny, God-given insight, long after the event itself, by John who, whatever his precise historical identity, was uniquely qualified, equipped and (if you like) inspired to find the right, simple words in which to express the almost inexpressible mystery of the Divine Identity. This, or something like it, seems to me the only credible explanation, not only of this unique prayer, but of the entire Gospel which bears John's name. Among others, the nineteenth century poet Robert Browning, author of *A Death in the Desert*,[9] seems to have been of the opinion that John's Gospel was the product in extreme old age of John, the son of Zebedee and brother of James, following a long lifetime of reflection and meditation on the life, teaching, death and resurrection of Jesus. This seems plausible, but certainty eludes us. I wonder what you think?

New Testament evidence summarised

This cursory review of the New Testament evidence as to *both* (i) the *essential, ideal* nature of the Christian Church as clearly conceived in the minds of St. Paul and St. John and vividly expressed in the correspondence of the former and the gospel compositions of the latter, and hinted at (?) in the Synoptics, and (ii) the *actual* conditions prevailing in the apostolic churches of which we have record, is now complete. What does it tell us and how is this relevant to our theme of "churchmanship"?

(i) The evidence for the ideal (as we should call it) vision of the Church in the minds of Paul and John could not be stronger or more clear. It is indisputable. Though using different figures of speech (the human body and its "members", Paul; the vine and its branches, John) they both conceived of the Church as *an organic extension of the risen life of Jesus, so that the baptised faithful were literally incorporated in Him*. For both, the ideal *was* the actual; the inevitable consequence being fierce stress on the absolute necessity of unity, concord and agreement among Christians and consequent horror at discord, rivalry, infighting, and factional partisanship in churches.

9. Printed in full in the *Oxford Book of Christian Verse*. ed. Lord David Cecil (1940)

Whether this concept in the minds of Paul and John originated in that of Our Saviour himself cannot be known. It is bound to be a matter of conjecture and of the balance of probability. But it may be conceded that Paul and John were both in a better position to know His mind than we are, and that their clear agreement favours this supposition.

(ii) As for the actuality in the New Testament churches, the evidence is mixed. Not all the churches of which we have knowledge in the New Testament were like that of Corinth. Far from it. Those of Philippi, Thessalonica and Rome were warmly commended by Paul (Phil. 1. 3-11; 1 Thess. 1. 2-10 and Rom. 1. 7-12), as were those of Smyrna and Philadelphia by the John who wrote *Revelation* (Rev. 2. 8-11 and 3. 7-13). But there is no reason to believe that Corinth was unique in its rival factions, and disorderly conduct, which incurred such severe apostolic rebuke. The Galatians were notorious backsliders and the Colossian Church, which Paul had never visited in person, but with which he had precious links through Philemon and Onesimus, clearly needed to be kept up to the mark and warned against the machinations of fussy conservatives (Col. 2. 16-23). Four of the Asia Minor churches addressed by John got it severely in the neck from him (Rev. 2. 12-29 and 3. 1-6 and 14-22).

The fact is that the apostles were up against stubborn human nature. This was not lost on Paul, who, despite his idealism, was capable of being a sensible, hard-headed realist, as when he wrote in 1 Corinthians, "When you come together as a church, I hear that there are divisions among you; and to some extent I believe it. Indeed there have to be factions among you, for only so will it become clear who among you is genuine..." (1 Cor. 11. 18f.). On the face of it this seems disconcertingly to contradict much of what he had written earlier in the same letter. It is almost as if he were climbing down off his doctrinaire high horse, like a thoroughly pragmatic Anglican! It is this gift of flexibility, this many sidedness which makes him so fascinating to study and as we shall see a little further on when we consider his missionary/evangelistic strategy – "all things to all men" (1 Cor. 9.20).

What then, provisionally, are we to conclude from all this? I suggest that, as with our Lord's strict teaching about marriage (Mark 10. 5-9, with which compare Matt. 19. 8f.) we must strictly uphold the ideal, while making due allowance for human frailty, thus opening ourselves, as we have done, to the charge of inconsistency, or worse, hypocrisy. Total consistency is a luxury only affordable by the most determined martyr and most of us run-of-the-mill Christians do not seem to be cut out for that.

A little light relief

After this, it is time (you may think, more than time) for a little light relief.

Several years ago, when turning over matters ecclesiometrical in my head, it occurred to me that some useful light might be thrown on the basic nature of churchmanship by a judicious comparison with the valuable researches of the late Stephen Potter on the kindred subjects of Lifemanship, Gamesmanship and Oneupmanship. That dates it, and me, a bit. I was thinking particularly of Potter's seminal treatise, *Notes on Lifemanship*, published by Penguin as long ago as 1950 at the modest price of two shillings and sixpence (half a crown) paperback. My own copy, a prized possession, is a little battered from constant use. It has a distinguished cover illustration by Nicolas Bentley. In our enlightened days this will almost certainly lay it open to the serious charge of blatant élitism. I wonder if any of my readers have ever come across it? If so, they must be nearly as senile as I am.[10]

The very title Potter chose, *Lifemanship*, so evocative of the universal scope of his ingenious theories, inevitably suggests close kinship to *Churchmanship* and to my mind it is one of the not-so-minor tragedies of twentieth-century English literature, and indeed philosophy, that, for some obscure reason, Potter never got round to the application of his philosophy to "Churchmanship". For, had he done so, daily life, to say nothing of thought, in the C. of E. and indeed the Anglican Communion worldwide, at all levels from the domestic and parochial to the archiepiscopal and synodical, would have been immeasurably enriched. The Life/Churchman basic one-up principle would have been clearly enunciated with examples cited, and illustrated, as in *Lifemanship*, from the experience of leading exponents such as Odoreida and Gattling-Fenn with the actual conversational gambits, ploys and counters they had perfected.

Seriously, depending on your view of human nature, and especially of ecclesiastical human nature, it may, or may not, surprise you to realise that "churchmanship" and "lifemanship" (in its aspect of oneupmanship) are not so far apart as you might have thought.

The principles of both are timeless. Indeed we have already noticed two instances in the New Testament. Those two disciples, James and John, the sons of Zebedee, were trying out a very crude

10. Should any reader hail from Somerset, he will surely be acquainted with the statue of the great Lifeman himself; it stands outside his former H.Q. at 680, Station Road, Yeovil (and is illustrated as the frontispiece to *Lifemanship*). It should also appear in the forthcoming revised edition of Pevsner's *Somerset*.

ploy when they (or their mother, Mrs. Zebedee, on their behalf) sought to "bag" two top posts in Jesus's future Cabinet. No wonder the other disciples were miffed. Who wouldn't have been? The other example, of course, is the rival factions forming in Corinth, each named after distinguished church leaders, while one group (early evangelicals?) had gone one better than the rest, claiming the *highest* authority – "*I* am of *Christ*". Similarly today one occasionally comes across people who call themselves "committed Christians". To them an effective counter is, "Oh, I am only an *un*committed Christian", thus effortlessly going one up on both modesty and humility. *Plus ça change, plus c'est la même chose.*

That interval of light relief is now *almost* over, unless we extend it still more briefly to include a reference to three lively surveys of the Church of England, published in the final decade of the twentieth century. They were Michael De La Noy's *The Church of England* (1993), perhaps the most thorough; Ysenda Maxtone Graham's *The Church Hesitant: A Portrait of the Church of England* (also 1993), the liveliest and most entertaining; and Monica Furlong: *The C of E: the State its in* (2000), possibly the most perceptive, as it is the most recent. Sadly, Furlong and De La Noy have since died.

All three are fair minded, largely orientated to the divisions over the ordination of women, illuminating on the varieties of theological colleges and their distinctive ethos, and very much alive to the wide varieties of Churchmanship (described by Maxtone Graham as "the Spectrum", a term which has since gained wider currency, as has the misuse of the term "tradition" (evangelical, catholic, liberal) to make partisanship or organised party strife, sound more respectable.)

These three "surveys", all by intelligent lay folk, taken together have real value still, but, sadly, all three now have a slightly period flavour. The Anglican scene is even less attractive today.

New light on Churchmanship

In this penultimate stage of our exhaustive pursuit of an accurate but at the same time realistic understanding and definition of this slippery concept of churchmanship, we cannot avoid turning to an important new book specifically devoted to that very subject, but, perhaps due to its quizzical review by John Pridmore in the *Church Times* of 6 Jan 2006, less widely read than it deserved to be.

Published by Ashgate, Aldershot, in 2005, it is entitled *Evangelicals etcetera: Conflict and Conviction in the Church of England's Parties.* Its author is Kelvin Randall. On the flyleaf we are told that he is "an Anglican Vicar and Clergy Trainer at Southampton and is also Researcher at the National Centre for Religious Education, University of Wales, Bangor, U.K." From this it is no surprise that an enthusiastic blurb appears on the back paper cover from the pen of Professor Leslie J. Francis, also of the University of Wales at Bangor, or that Randall's extensive bibliography includes no less than sixty books or articles by the prolific Leslie J. Francis[11] either alone or in collaboration with others (pp. 224-227). Bangor is his power base and Randall and Francis would both claim to be, among other things, serious, scientific sociologists of religion. Randall's findings from numerous recent "surveys" among mostly young Anglican clergy on a variety of subjects ranging from extraversion/introversion, stable/neurotic, liability to "burn out", happy/unhappy, masculine/feminine, to priorities for ministry, patterns of belief and behaviour, are set out in methodical detail in the bulk of the book, together with elaborate classifications of the self-claimed churchmanship of the participants/victims.

Whatever value we may attach to these findings, I suspect that for most of Randall's readers the main interest of the book lies in its opening chapters. The first of these (pp. 1-43) claims to set out impartially, "the origin" and history "of churchmanship differences", from which much may be learnt. It is followed (pp. 44-63) by a fascinating review of ways in which churchmanship differences have been, and are still being, measured, in other words "pure ecclesiometry", with a few diagrams of what are, in fact, primitive ecclesiometers and their rationales – although, of course, without using that word.

I was delighted to learn from this chapter two things – first (Randall p. 44) that the Anglican pioneer of ecclesiometry was the Revd. W.J. Coneybeare who in an article on *"Church Parties"* published in the *Edinburgh Review* in 1853 (vol. 98 pp. 273-342) "recognised that there were not two, or even three, but nine parties in sight. They are commonly called the Low Church, the High Church and the Broad Church parties, but such an enumeration is the result of an incomplete analysis. On a closer inspection, it is seen that each of these is again triply subdivided into sections which exemplify respectively the exaggeration, the stagnation and the normal development of the principles which they severally claim to represent . . ." (op.cit. p. 273).[12]

But what gave me even greater pleasure was the discovery (Randall

11. Francis, a graduate of both Oxford and Cambridge, had begun his Anglican ministry as curate of Haverhill to its energetic Vicar Eric Graves in the 1970s. I remember him there.
12. On wider grounds a claim to be THE pioneer of ecclesiometry could be advanced for Jonathan Swift: *A Tale of a Tub* (1704)

pp. 47ff.) that my ecclesiometer had in outline been anticipated by one M.G. Daniel in 1968.

According to Randall, Daniel (1967) was the first to see the need for, and make use of, a second dimension as well as the standard Catholic/Evangelical axis. His was a sociological study arising from interviews with 96 clergymen serving in the Greater London Council area and ordained in 1955, 1960 or 1965. He was concerned to discover whether or not the new currents of theological thought in the 1960's were changing the clergy's self-image. His conclusion was that churchmanship was the main criterion for determining the clergy's reaction to new ideas. Daniel is quoted by Randall as writing: "The factor determining which alternative a clergyman will choose is *the particular religious ideology which he already holds – that nexus of beliefs and interpretations which in the Church of England is called churchmanship*" (Daniel, *Catholic, Evangelical and Liberal in the Anglican Priesthood* in D. Martin (ed.) *A Sociological Year Book of Religion* SCM 1968 vol. 9 pp. 232-249 (My italics)).

Here, then, incidentally, in the passage italicised, we have an attempted definition of churchmanship. We will consider it later, when reaching a final conclusion.

To resume a summary of Daniel's method of assessing churchmanship, "he plotted" individual "positions on two axes representing sources of authority". He wrote that "in practice, churchmanship positions usually appeal to the authority of the Bible (evangelical), or of the church (catholic) in the first place, and after that to tradition (conservative), or to human reason (liberal)" (Daniel, unpublished dissertation, 1967, cited by Randall).

To illustrate this understanding of churchmanship which in its basic simplicity is substantially the same as mine, Daniel constructed a chart (reproduced in Randall p. 48 Fig. 2.1) in the form of a cross; its vertical section below the point of intersection with the horizontal axis is inscribed "evangelical" and is based on the BIBLE, its upper section is, of course, "Catholic", and above it is CHURCH. The horizontal arms are, to the left "Conservative", based on TRADITION and the right "liberal" based on REASON.

Ideally, I would have liked to be able on facing pages here to illustrate the Daniel diagram opposite my putative ecclesiometer. If this were possible, the comparison would be obvious and immediate – as would, I hope, the advantages of my inclination towards simplicity. This would be criticised by Randall (and others) as *too* simplistic. He and his fellow researchers desiderate a *third* axis – that of Pentecostalism/ the Charismatic movement. While frankly admitting my personal ignorance of this more recent phenomenon I would argue that it is historically, like its eighteenth-century predecessor (to the study of which and its precursors and antecedents, Ronald Knox devoted his seminal work *Enthusiasm*, 1950, O.U.P) closely akin to aspects of Evangelicalism, and that the overriding merit of the Daniel/Fitch model is its underlying simplicity, which is truly basic, fundamental, rooted in the ultimate reality of unchanging (and unchangeable) Christian belief/ experience in a constantly changing world.

We are now, at long last, clearly within sight of "the object of our journey" and of the end of this chapter. If the route has at times been wearisome and repetitive the fault is entirely mine and I apologise. I am neither a professional theologian nor a logician – that is only too obvious. It has too often been a case (hopefully) of *solvitur ambulando* – thinking it out as we go along. Still, we *must* get it right in the end.

An elusive concept, hard to define

In attempting to define such a vague, elusive concept as churchmanship I may have been attempting an impossibility. We have, in passing, glanced at several attempted definitions, none of them entirely satisfactory. Let us have one final attempt, bearing in mind all the considerations we have encountered along the way.

I have now come to believe that some if not most of our difficulties have arisen from a confusion between two separate and conflicting senses in which the word and concept is sometimes used. One is idealistic, the other factual.

(i) Is there not a sense in which churchmanship embraces the *totality* of Christian faith, experience and commitment? "The faith once delivered to the saints" (Jude 3), the unchanging and unchangeable faith to which the Scriptures bear witness, and to which the Catholic Creeds give classic expression, that unswerving faith "which has been believed everywhere, always and by all" which the Vincentian Canon proclaims, *together with and alongside* the *interpretation*, often radical, of that unchanging faith by the unquenchable "Spirit of truth" (John 15. 26 and 16. 13) in successive generations of our ever changing and developing world, but restrained from falsehood and excess by traditional wisdom?

I believe that in the minds of those familiar with this concept, there is some such arrière pensée, to which I have perhaps assigned too definite a content, and that it is only in the light of such an ideal, however vague or precise, that the much more familiar, secondary usage makes sense. I will now attempt to define that.

Churchmanship defined – at last!

(ii) The peculiarly Anglican concept of churchmanship is the deliberate choice or identification of one or more of *four* distinctly separable, but essentially complementary and interlocking aspects or elements of Christian belief/commitment, seen and emphasised as being of *supreme* importance over against the others, and used as a label for his/her "churchmanship". This use of the expression is inevitably in conflict with the ideal, inclusive first sense.

The four separable but complementary aspects, elements or strands of the properly indivisible whole are those commonly known these days as (i) evangelical (ii) catholic (iii) liberal and (iv) conservative (or traditional). In earlier times, and still perhaps by the less sophisticated, they were called (i) Low Church (ii) High Church (iii) Broad Church and (iv) (should have been called) Narrow Church – a phrase with, properly, no derogatory overtones (see Matthew 7. 13).

In writing the above I have, of course, in mind the two axes of my ecclesiometer, as foreshadowed by Daniel, 1967. The vertical axis, evangelical, catholic, represents the basic unchanging Christian faith. The horizontal axis, liberal/conservative equally clearly represents the guidance of the Holy Spirit of Truth, in both its positive, radical and its negative, restraining, moderating, traditional aspects.

There is, thus, a slight difference between the rationales of M.G. Daniel's chart and my putative ecclesiometer constructed to exemplify the foregoing definition, but it is not substantial. I am happy to accept his formulae as *in substance* no different from mine. Both are essentially four square. For those who value a Biblical analogy, I would refer them to Revelation 21.16.

Finally – my proposal

If, therefore, I may claim M.G. Daniel as an ally, the proposal now put forward as a formula for advancing both Anglican, and wider Christian unity is simplicity itself. Maintaining that for twenty first-century Christian orthodoxy the four aspects or elements represented by the words evangelical, catholic, liberal and conservative/traditional are *all equally essential and interlocking, interdependent, complementary, and ultimately inseparable*, two things follow.

1. for any individual Anglican, or group of Anglicans to isolate or overemphasise any one or more of these at the expense of the rest is to *distort* true Christianity and to *undermine* Christian Unity. And,

2. It is incumbent upon all Anglicans to think, work and pray to enter more and more deeply into the *fullness* of the Christian heritage of faith and truth, and to open themselves at every point to the influence of the Spirit of Truth, praying that He would overcome all prejudice.

It may be said that this is no more, or less, than a plea for old fashioned Central Churchmanship. If by Central Churchmanship is meant scoring an ecclesiometrical BULLSEYE by aiming one's thought and prayer at the point of the intersection itself, the CROSS in the middle of the Ecclesiometer (or Daniel's Diagram) I should be only too happy to agree.

I have long had reason to suspect that Central Churchmanship in this best sense of the term, is, and certainly was, far more widely prevalent in the C. of E., especially among its upper echelons and among the sensible laity, than most people would suppose. Among the latter I suspect that, just as in politics the ideal position for a successful politician is slightly to the left of centre, the same, by and large, is true of the Church. English people for the most part, least of all Anglicans, are not intellectuals, still less amateur theologians. Most shrink from any form of extremism.

As for the upper echelons of the clergy, such as bishops and archdeacons, having constantly to deal with strongly opinionated, partisan clergy of all shapes and sizes, there would be a strong temptation to an easy flexibility. That kind of lazy, unprincipled "central Churchmanship", the line of least resistance, (on which a certain Archbishop of Canterbury is said to have possessed a season ticket), is the last thing I am advocating. I disassociate myself from it.

It is perfectly *possible* to embrace all four "positions" simultaneously. I say that because I do it myself. No supple feat of intellectual gymnastics is required. But it does help (and here is a useful tip) constantly to bear in mind the axiom variously ascribed to S.T. Coleridge and F.D. Maurice: "Men are mostly right in what they affirm and wrong in what they deny".[13]

In the next four chapters we will look at each "position" in turn.

---

13. A.R. Vidler *"The Church in the Age of Revolution"*. (Penguin 1961) p. 84.

Part 1
Churchmanship's Four Standpoints

Chapter 2
Low Church/Evangelical

In case any reader is unclear as to exactly what constitutes (Anglican) evangelicalism, it seems desirable to begin this chapter by attempting a fair and accurate definition. The word "evangelical", of course, derives from "evangel", the original Greek New Testament word translated "Gospel" – old English "God'spel" – literally Good News. Evangelicals characteristically lay particular stress on the necessity of personal conversion, whether dramatically sudden or gradual, in response to the genuine preaching or proclaiming of the Gospel of Jesus Christ; and thereafter of salvation by faith in the atoning life and death of Jesus, on account of our sins, for all mankind. Evangelicals especially revere the Bible as "God's Word" containing all things needful for salvation, and on its total reliability as the ultimate criterion of Truth. Evangelicals are evangelistic, mission-minded, eager "to share Jesus" with everyone. This gives them an earnestness which some, even fellow Christians, can find off-putting!

There is no disputing the fact that the Evangelicals are at present, and have been for the last quarter century at least, the dominant party in the Church of England. Yet that statement calls for immediate qualification in at least one respect. For, far from being an identifiable, monolithic, united party, evangelicals today are sharply and deeply divided among themselves on issues of our day, such as the ordination of women (particularly to the episcopate) and attitudes towards homosexuality, and, in both of these, on the nature and extent of the authority of the Scriptures. This latter raises in an acute form the longstanding cleavage between "liberal" and "conservative" evangelicals. For this reason, we shall find that, in this and succeeding chapters, overlaps are unavoidable.

A little history

Evangelicals, or Low Churchmen, as an identifiable element within the C. of E. have a history of nearly three hundred years – or more if the sixteenth and seventeenth century Puritans are deemed proto-evangelicals. But for practical purposes, the modern evangelical movement began with the Wesley brothers, John and Charles, and the conversion of the former in a Moravian meeting house in Aldersgate Street, London on 24 May 1738. (It is on this day every year that the brothers are commemorated in our *Common Worship* Calendar). And it was then that John took as his aim and object for the rest of his life "to promote as far as I am able vital, practical religion and by the grace of God to beget, preserve and increase the life of God in the souls of men". This he did by means of his indefatigable tours on horseback throughout the length and breadth of England. He had no lack of followers among the clergy and although, contrary to his stated intention of remaining in the Church, his unilateral action in purporting to ordain new ministers led to the Methodist secession. It was the influence of later evangelicals of the calibre of Charles Simeon (1759-1836), Fellow of Kings and long-time energetic vicar of Holy Trinity Cambridge, who ensured that the main body of evangelicals, clerical and lay, remained loyally within the Anglican fold.

The movement recorded some outstanding achievements especially in its early years, many largely owing to lay initiative and generous financial support. They include the establishment in 1799 of the Church Missionary Society, soon to overtake the century-older Society for the Propagation of the Gospel (1701) in both size and scope and to become far and away the largest Anglican missionary agency for work mainly within the rapidly expanding British Empire. The CMS, with heroic pioneer-martyrs like Henry Martyn on its roll, could count amongst its accomplishments the abolition of the slave trade (1807) and of slavery itself within the empire (1833), as well as the series of Factory Acts aimed at ameliorating the worst excesses of the Industrial Revolution, pioneered as they were by the evangelical seventh Earl of Shaftesbury, Anthony Ashley Cooper (1801-1885).

These wholly beneficial initiatives were however accompanied by others, more partisan and divisive, which had the effect of creating something of a church within a church, especially when countered by similar developments on the opposite – i.e. Tractarian/Ritualist/ Catholic – side of the fence. The first of these was an evangelical weekly newspaper, *The Record*, founded in 1828: on its original

staff was the Reverend John Henry Newman! The Church Pastoral
Aid Society, established in 1836, was aimed at recruiting a reliable
evangelical ministry and raising funds for that purpose. It is still
going strong. Charles Simeon, a man of means, had used some of
it to buy advowsons to various influential benefices, to which, when
they became vacant, he could present clergymen known for their
sound evangelical outlook. Thus was constituted the Simeon Trust
based on exemplary pastoral principles, ensuring the continuity of an
evangelical ministry in its parishes in perpetuity. One such benefice
was Bath Abbey. In its wake a number of similar Trusts, such as the
Martyrs' Memorial Trust and the Hyndman Trust were set up, not all
of them on such exemplary lines.[1] All are still in existence, although,
with the steep decline in the number of clergy and the consequent
unions of benefices and setting up of team and group ministries, their
influence is much reduced – sometimes with one turn of presentation
in five or six.

With the same intention, evangelical theological colleges,
Wycliffe Hall, Oxford (1872), and Ridley Hall, Cambridge (1881)
were established – both still flourish. Evangelical sons of evangelical
clergy were not forgotten, with the foundation of public schools such
as Dean Close, Cheltenham and Monkton Combe near Bath. It thus
became perfectly possible for an evangelical clergyman's son(s) to
pass safely through the whole system from the cradle to the grave
without fear of contamination from undesirable influences. A similar
network exists on the opposite side of "the fence", which is thus,
theoretically, rendered a sort of Maginot Line. Unfortunately for
its creators, like the Maginot Line, it was only too easily breached.
A well-known instance of this in the early twentieth century was
the Knox family. The leading Evangelical Edmund Knox, Bishop
of Manchester, had three clever sons. E.V. became a distinguished
editor of *Punch*, but of his two clerical brothers, Ronald, the brilliant
satirist and parodist, turned Papist, while Wilfred, an expert on St.
Paul, was distinctly Anglo-Catholic, much to their father's mystified
chagrin.

The battle against Fundamentalism

The key to understanding the history of Anglican evangelicalism in
the last century and a half is the unremitting struggle of its more
enlightened proponents to emancipate the movement from the dead
hand of Fundamentalism with which, for too much of this time, it has
in the popular mind been closely identified. Before the beginnings of

1. See C. Smyth: *Simeon and Church Order* (1940) CUP

judicious scholarship in the scientific, literary and historical analysis ('criticism') of the Scriptures in the early nineteenth century, all evangelicals, indeed almost all serious Christians, were what we should call Fundamentalist in their general assumptions about the direct divine inspiration of the Scriptures and their literal freedom from error as the divinely ordained vehicles of the revelation of God.

The publication of *Essays and Reviews* in 1860, and the writings of Bishop Colenso, marked the dawning of a new understanding of the Bible amidst violent controversy. It was not until the unimpeachable scholarship of men such as Lightfoot, Westcott and Hort came to be generally accepted that an increasing number of genuine evangelicals began to see that the hand and voice of God was no less discernible in the newly enriched awareness of the genesis of the Bible than in the old.

As I shall explore in further depth in following pages, the struggle is not over yet, with its latest manifestations in the battles over homosexuality in today's Church. A factor which tends to create confusion in the popular mind is the deep rooted and longstanding tradition (or unthinking habit) of describing the Bible as "the word of God". This is currently enshrined in and risks being perpetuated by the new rubric in *Common Worship* directing the reader of Scripture in public worship to proclaim immediately after the reading: "This is the word of the Lord". It may indeed be unquestionably His word, but not invariably or automatically. I can think of passages in both Testaments where, if I were the reader, I would be extremely reluctant to obey that unfortunate rubric. For instance, Genesis 6:5-7; 2 Kings 2:23f; Acts 5:1-11; 2 Thess. 2:1-12 and Rev. 14:14-end. What the Bible does tell us clearly is that in Jesus Christ, the word of God became flesh (incarnate) and "dwelt among us" (St. John 1 v.14) and that "Long ago God spoke to us through his prophets, but that in these last days he has spoken to us by a Son whom he appointed heir of all things, through whom he created the world and that He is the reflection of God's glory, the exact imprint of His very being." (Hebrews 1. 1f.)

In other words God uniquely made Himself known to mankind in the living person of His son Jesus, rather than in ancient books. To speak of the Bible as God's word does carry a risk. He does indeed communicate with all who will listen in the pages of the Bible read with understanding and humble intelligence. It is best to see Christ as "the human face of God", and to seek the guidance of His loving and powerful Spirit. Fundamentalism never escapes the danger of lapsing into idolatry – putting the Bible in the place of God – Bibliolatry. This is to be avoided like the plague: its influence is insidious.

"The Fullness of Christ" (1950): a superb (Liberal) Evangelical report

It is a prime contention of this book that, sooner or later, and the sooner the better, if they are to survive, *genuine* evangelicals (among whom I desperately hope to include my very unevangelical self) have *got* to come to terms with the Bible *as it really is*, and to renounce once and for all the total absurdity of Biblical fundamentalism of any and every kind (which is a form of idolatry). This includes the falsehood that the Bible is, in some sense, "the word of God". It is not. No sensible Christian, who knows, loves and reveres his Bible would deny for one moment that God, who is in the living Christ and in His Holy Spirit, does very often speak directly to us as we read or hear the words of Scripture, but this is not automatic or mechanical, and some, often extended, passages in the Bible tell us nothing true about God. The books of the Bible, in all their astonishing diversity were written by human beings all as fallible as we are.

Today it is common form for those most vociferous in claiming to speak for "evangelicalism" to denounce what they call "liberalism" as loudly as the former Cardinal Ratzinger, now Pope Benedict XVI, and his revered predecessor ever did. *It was not always so.*

Half way through the last century seventeen Anglican clergymen, called upon by the then Archbishop of Canterbury, Geoffrey Fisher, to represent the current evangelical standpoint, presented him with a wise and thoughtful report entitled *The Fullness of Christ: the Church's Growth into Catholicity* (SPCK 1950). The circumstances were as follows. Fisher, himself a quintessential Central Churchman, had, shortly after taking over at Lambeth from William Temple, who had died unexpectedly from gout towards the end of the Second World War, addressed a number of searching questions, first to a representative group of distinguished Anglo-Catholics and, after receiving *their* considered response in the report entitled *Catholicity: A study in the Conflict of Christian Tradition in the West* (Dacre Press, 1947), to the aforesaid group of Evangelicals, who therefore had the considerable advantage of being in a position to respond to *Catholicity*.

At this point, I had better, in honesty, interject a confession. When the reports were published, I dutifully bought them both, together with

the third in the series, a report of a group of *Free* Churchmen entitled
The Catholicity of Protestantism, which, to my shame, remains on
my shelf unread. I struggled with *Catholicity*, which attracted much
notice at the time, but, frankly, though I suppose I thought of myself
as a kind of High Churchman at the time, I found it heavy going,
disappointing and unrewarding. I set *The Fullness of Christ* on one
side for future reference but did not read it through until *many* years
later, when I found it deeply impressive. Its seventeen co-authors
included two of the highest distinction, both of whom only died in
2008 and 2007 respectively. They were the younger of the two brilliant
Chadwick brothers, Henry, successively Dean of Christ Church,
Oxford and Master of Peterhouse, Cambridge, and internationally
in the top rank of Church historians; and C.F.D. Moule, sometime
Lady Margaret's Professor of Divinity, Cambridge, whose reputation
as a meticulous New Testament scholar of total integrity was held in
universal regard. Among their colleagues were Donald Coggan (later
Archbishop successively of York and Canterbury), Stephen Neill,
Geoffrey Lampe and Max Warren, all outstanding men of learning
and experience.

I have read much of it again in preparation for this book, and am
more than ever impressed by its wide-ranging wisdom and breadth
of judgment. I would love to see it reprinted now and am strongly
tempted to quote extensively from it, especially because it has
been completely forgotten and will never be reissued. Fisher in his
introduction refers to "these three documents, all so admirable in
spirit and substance". He shrewdly adds this comment:

> There is not complete agreement…if there were, one
> could be certain that it would be short lived. No age of the
> Church, no school of theologians, no single Church, has
> ever comprehended the "wholeness" of the Christian Faith
> without any falsity of emphasis or insight …

What refreshing common-sensical realism, so typical of this
headmaster-primate to whom historians have not been kind, but
who in his matter-of-fact way accomplished more for the cause of
Christian unity than he is generally given credit for.

The Report itself is superb in its breadth of vision. "Only the whole
human race, as redeemed [in Christ] is wide enough to express the
richness of his representative and comprehensive humanity." This
means that the Church, at every stage of its development, is aware of
its own imperfection. Further, it recognises that it is called to move
onward into the fullness that has not yet been revealed until "we all

attain unto the unity of the faith, and of the knowledge of the Son of God, unto a full grown man, unto the measure of the stature of the fullness of Christ" (Eph. 4). "This is not a promise to the individual: it is a portrayal of the destiny of the whole human race" (p. 2). "Confession of faith in the Catholic Church is always proleptic, it looks forward in faith to a fullness which has not yet been made manifest" (p. 4).

But it is when it comes to the place of reason in religious understanding that it makes such refreshing reading today; particularly when it treats of "liberalism".

Having noted with approval the expression given by Richard Hooker, "to this reverence for reason which has remained a characteristic feature of Anglican theology", it goes on:

> but orthodox Christianity has always held that reason, for its right use, needs to take account of all fields of human experience; that it needs to recognise its own limitations in dealing with a cosmos of which it knows so little and to seek the cleansing and illumination of the Holy Spirit; for inasmuch as the whole of human nature is infected by sin, reason is not exempt from that infection. This means that it must distrust a logic which, on the basis of limited premises and limited data, reaches conclusions against which the moral and religious judgment rebels; that it must be ready to accept as part of its own limitation the impossibility of fully and satisfactorily schematizing the whole universe; and that it cannot hope to go far on the road to truth unless it acts from within that discourse and contact with God which the Christian religion gives. The Christian use of reason gives a place for understanding as well as logic; it is not ready to disbelieve simply because it does not fully comprehend, since it knows that its failure to comprehend may be due to its own limitations and not to the faultiness of the proposition in question; and it does not separate rigidly between understanding the truth and living according to truth. "The Spirit" remarks Richard Baxter, "is not given to make our religion reasonable, but to make sinners reasonable, in habit and act, for the believing it." "Where is it," he asks elsewhere, "that the Spirit giveth light but into our own understandings; and how perceive we that light, but by the rational apprehensions and discourses of those understandings? By which you may see that the Spirit and reason are not to be disjoined, much less opposed. As

reason sufficeth not without the Spirit, being dark and asleep;
so the Spirit worketh not on the will but by the reason". *It is
to this proper Christian attitude to reason that we shall apply
the term "liberalism"*, and it must be distinguished from the
distortion of it – which we shall call *"rationalism"* – as clearly
as the proper Christian emphasis on spiritual experience has
to be distinguished from the distorted emphasis which we
have denoted in the term "pietism". (p. 46)

In a footnote (p. 47) at this point the Report adds a further
distinction:

> The term "liberalism" besides being used as above to denote
> the right use of reason as contrasted with obscurantism
> is sometimes employed, especially on the continent, to
> denote that radically sceptical attitude which we have
> called "rationalism" or (in some of its manifestations)
> "modernism". Though the dividing line between the two
> attitudes is not easy to define with precision, we believe
> that they are in essence radically different tempers of mind
> which ought not to be confused. In customary English usage
> the term "liberalism" applies to the former rather than to the
> latter, and the noticeable contemporary tendency to make
> it also include the latter may cause confusion of thought.
> There is a risk of condemning reason as such along with
> the wrong use of it by lumping them together under a single
> title. *Thus the impression is created that the right alternative
> to scepticism is not reasonable faith but an obscurantist
> dogmatism.*[2]

In a historical review of the effects of Biblical criticism on the various
Christian traditions, Catholic and Protestant, the Report goes on to
note that it is to

> "protestants" together with a notable school of Anglo-
> Catholic theologians [i.e. Bishop Gore and the *Lux Mundi*
> school of Liberal Catholics] that most of the credit must
> go for incorporating the new knowledge in the Church's
> thought, and making it the means by which the Church's
> understanding of the truth of the gospel, so far from being
> ultimately undermined, is now seen to have been enriched,
> purified, and deepened. The genuine Christian liberalism
> which welcomes all new knowledge and upholds the use

2. Unless otherwise noted, all italics are, as here, my own.

of reason in understanding the revelation of God has been powerfully reinforced and vindicated. It is beginning to demonstrate, not without success, that while some received ideas of authority and revelation have to be drastically revised in the light of scientific and critical knowledge, the concept of revelation is itself fully valid; that while the Bible is not verbally inerrant it is none the less authoritative; and that the new knowledge is a positive aid towards its fuller understanding and appreciation.

The verbal inerrancy of Scripture is seen to be no more essential to the authority of the Bible upheld by "protestantism" than the infallibility of the Pope is essential to the authority of the Church upheld by "catholicism". Not all the problems have been solved. Tension still remains. But the recent return to the biblical theology on the part of "protestantism" [i.e. that of the school of Karl Barth] ably assisted by some of the Anglo-Catholic tradition [i.e. Hoskyns] is a sign that the Church is on the road to resolution of tension and growth in the truth. While the liberal element, at least within "protestantism" has been vindicated, the rational influence of a negative minded modernism has already receded, and seems unlikely to gain a place within either tradition save as an insignificant eccentricity on the part of a tolerated minority. (pp. 48f.)

The chapter of the Report from which these lengthy extracts have been taken begins drawing to a close with a historical review which includes a notably generous assessment of the achievement of Liberalism. This again deserves to be quoted.

Liberalism can claim affinity with the emphasis on reason characteristic of Hooker and of the Cambridge Platonists. The true work of Liberalism has been to influence and modify for good both the Anglo Catholic and Evangelical wings of the Church of England; by doing this in such a way as to win general acceptance for the reasonably assured conclusions of scientific and historical study it has placed the Church of England immeasurably in its debt. It is to be distinguished from the alien elements of modernism, with which it is frequently confused. This modernist element, with its emphasis on rationalism and scientific humanism, has not succeeded in winning a place for itself other than as a tolerated minority opinion in the Church of England. (p. 54)

This chapter concludes with the observation that

> Anglicanism now represents a combination of "catholic" and "protestant" traditions which is new in Christendom. The modern Anglican Communion differs from the Church of England of the sixteenth to eighteenth centuries in theological character quite as much as in size and organization. It has been led out of a mild and tolerant protestantism, which allowed for rather more of the "catholic" and liberal elements than was common in the more rigid continental protestantism, into a position in which two traditions . . . recognisably "catholic" and "protestant" yet manage to live together in one body. The experiment of co-existence is thus a modern one, and it is too early to judge yet of its success. Only in recent years has it been widely recognized as an experiment that is being made and ought to be made, and recognition of this has only recently become a major factor in preserving the bond of unity.
>
> Hitherto unity has been preserved by what may be thought to be providential accidents of history.
>
> The comprehensiveness of Prayer Book and Articles; the lack of any precise definition of the significance of history; the Establishment; the tolerant English spirit insofar as it has encouraged the C. of E. to relax the stringency of the Declaration of Assent and to tolerate a great deal of ecclesiastical disorder rather than initiate heresy hunts and excommunications; the balance of parties, none of which has been able to achieve dominance; the existence of a large and influential body of "central churchmen", who would be unwilling to identify themselves clearly or exclusively with any one of the main schools of thought – all these "accidental" factors have helped. But while these factors have opened the way for the experiment to be made they cannot secure its success, and some of them are already ceasing to operate as once they did. The overt repudiation in some quarters of major elements in the doctrine and liturgy of the Book of Common Prayer is a feature of the contemporary situation which means a real loosening of the bonds of unity and as such is gravely disquieting. *The experiment will succeed only if it is accepted as right on its own merits and if that judgment is a true judgment.* Certainly in recent years there has been a growing tendency to regard it as right. There are responsible leaders in both schools of thought who reject the old partisan policy of trying to seize control and exclude

each other as much as possible from influence in the church, and who equally refuse to regard the differences between the traditions as unimportant. There is a growing effort to enable the Church to hold the two traditions in tension not merely as "two sides of the shield" which are complementary to each other, but as traditions which at certain points conflict but which must be held together if we are to be led into a resolution of the conflict and a fuller integration in our apprehension of truth. Meanwhile, the experiment is being made; and while it is too new to pronounce certain judgment upon it, it is a highly significant factor which cannot but influence our judgment on the general question of the possibility of synthesis between the "catholic" and "protestant" traditions and of their co-existence in one Church. (pp. 54ff.)

The breadth, widsom and sheer maturity of this remarkable Report has tempted me to quote from it more extensively than I intended. Mainstream evangelicalism was unequivocally liberal *then*. What has become of the liberal evangelicals *now*? And what has occurred in the fifty-seven years since the publication of that enlightened Report? Before attempting to answer those questions and leave the Report behind, I want to extract one further section, a brief one this time, to illustrate its wise teaching on the Bible.

For neither Bible nor Church do we claim infallibility. That would be to ignore God's method of dealing with men and to posit an over-ruling to the fact of human ignorance and fallibility which would do violence to man's personality and freedom. Inspiration means rather that God takes men as they are and uses the facts of their personality and historic environment as a means of bringing to bear the personal influence of His Spirit upon their personalities. Thus the apostles had a unique opportunity to know and understand the revelation given in Christ because of his calling of them to be eyewitnesses and to enter into personal friendship with him on earth. The writers of the New Testament books were either apostles or men who historically stood in a closer or more immediate relationship to them than was possible for later generations. The Bible stands as the authoritative record of the revelation given in Christ because God used these historical circumstances and the natural gifts of the individuals selected by him as apostles or as recorders of the apostolic teaching, in order to give a permanent and sufficient exposition of the historic facts and their meaning. (p. 62)

I make no apology for such lengthy quotation from an outstanding document more than a half-century old now, if only because it comes as a salutary reminder of a mainstream evangelicalism which was not afraid to embrace a moderate liberalism and to publicly disclaim association with an obscurantist Bibliolatry unworthy to be labelled by the honourable and positive adjective "conservative".[3]

Why did Evangelicals become less "liberal", more "conservative"?

The question naturally arises: what caused mainstream Anglican Evangelicalism to change its outlook from broadly liberal to broadly "conservative" in the course of the second half of the twentieth century?

Before attempting an answer, two generalisations are worth bearing in mind. First, that any large body of opinion, such as that described as Evangelical, is certain to comprise within it, at any given time, a range of varying points of view. Second, that those singled out in 1948 to represent the Evangelical viewpoint were for the most part academics, and as such more likely to be liberal in outlook.

That said, a number of factors, over the years, contributed to a change in the climate of opinion. Of those, one greatly preponderated, and will be identified after the others have been sketched.

In the immediate aftermath of the Second World War, the publication of another C. of E. report, *Towards the Conversion of England* (1945), temporarily monopolised the attention of most professing Anglicans. It set out the detailed findings and proposals of the Archbishops' Commission on Evangelism, whose Chairman was the veteran Evangelical Bishop of Rochester, Christopher Chavasse. These proposals, notoriously including evangelistic advertising campaigns in the national Press and the strategic deployment of the Church Army, proved, like the Decade of Evangelism half a century later, a pretty damp squib.

One longer-term indirect outcome was, however, a series of highly organised, lavishly financed revivalist campaigns led by the professional American evangelist Billy Graham, a Southern Baptist. The earliest and one of the most successful of these was the Greater London Crusade held at Harringay in 1954, and lasting three full months. Graham's total sincerity, winning personality, evangelistic competence and persuasive eloquence were alike unquestionable. His theology, just as unmistakably, was a homely brand of Biblical fundamentalism for

---

3. I am tempted to replace the adjective "conservative" with "reactionary" or "obscurantist".

which (as indeed for the vast majority of his audience) a century and a half of devoted Biblical scholarship might never have occurred. This did not pass without notice in academic circles, as witness more than one lively controversy in the correspondence columns of *The Times* (the first of which was published as a pamphlet entitled "Fundamentalism" in the spring of 1955 and makes for fascinating reading). The *lasting* effect of these crusades is debatable. In later decades somewhat similar campaigns were conducted by a young home-grown Anglican evangelist, David Watson, later based in York at St. Michael le Belfry just outside the Minster. A very public-school descendant of a notorious eighteenth century Bishop of Llandaff, Richard Watson, he had reacted against the teaching of theology when a Cambridge undergraduate and had been deeply influenced by the Cambridge Intercollegiate Christian Union (CICCU) which had earlier been closely involved in the Billy Graham organisation. He inspired enormous affection and his early death from cancer was deeply and widely felt. It is noteworthy that in his later books, his earlier fundamentalist point of view had mellowed into a far less critical stance on Biblical scholarship.

These successive crusades/campaigns had undoubtedly brought encouragement and renewed enthusiasm to the Evangelical constituency in the Church of England as, more recently, has the Alpha movement originating at Holy Trinity, Brompton in London's West End. Before shining the spotlight on that I shall first briefly record two significant earlier developments within Anglican Evangelicalism in the period under review. I shall then turn to a series of events which combined to polarise opinion and frighten many Anglicans with the spectre of radical scepticism masquerading as "liberalism" and giving it a thoroughly bad name.

First, for the sake of historical completeness, two developments *within* the Evangelical constituency – developments moving in opposite directions. From early days the Church Missionary Society was a flagship of Anglican evangelicalism. Of its great achievements the whole of the world-wide Church – to say nothing of its evangelicals – had every reason to be proud. But there was some dissidence within. This came to a head in 1922 when some of its missionaries and erstwhile supporters, in reaction to the Society's policy of openness to modern Biblical research, broke away from CMS. to form the Bible Churchmen's Missionary Society (BCMS). Their standpoint, although I disagree with it, deserves respect, for the very real and sincere "Biblical" faith their members exemplify and the simple character it informs and inspires. BCMS still continues on its way.

There was not long afterwards a move in the *opposite* direction, i.e. by *Liberal* evangelicals desiring "to free evangelicalism" from what they regarded as "an unduly 'conservative' interpretation of Christianity, to welcome the help of science and criticism in the search for truth and to infuse more dignity and beauty into worship" (article ad hoc in *The Oxford Dictionary of the Christian Church*). In 1923 what had been a small private group was launched as the *Anglican Evangelical Group Movement* with the first two Bishops of Chelmsford among its leading members. "Its members were pledged to study the social and economic implications of the Gospel and to work for effective unity among all Christian people" (op. cit.). Through group study and retreats they aimed to deepen their spiritual life. The heyday of AEGM influence was between 1923 and 1939 under the leadership of Vernon Storr. Attempts to revive the movement after 1945 were not entirely successful. It formally ended its existence in 1967. Perhaps there is a case for reviving AEGM or something like it to reassert the Liberal Evangelical identity today. If anything, its place may be taken by "Fulcrum".

Following that parenthesis, we turn to the series of events beginning in the turbulent 1960s, which, cumulatively, had the effect of exposing what to many Anglican contemporaries seemed a disturbing and unwholesome aspect of liberal thinking, provoking a strong "conservative" reaction. (To older Churchmen this had a notorious precedent in Bishop E.W. Barnes and his infamous book *The Rise of Christianity* (1947), but by the sixties that was largely forgotten.)

In 1963 the comparatively calm waters of post-war Anglicanism were rudely disturbed by the first of a succession of powerful theological explosions. This was the publication of a Student Christian Movement paperback by the suffragan Bishop of Woolwich, John A.T. Robinson. Its title was *Honest to God*, and, as a result of all the Press publicity it received, and all the subsequent controversy, it had to be reprinted many times. It rapidly (and unexpectedly) became a best seller. Mostly written in hospital where the bishop was being treated for a painful slipped disc, it developed what seemed revolutionary ideas about the "image" of the Divine as glimpsed through the "Man for others" Jesus of Nazareth. These ideas were, for the most part, a rather indigestible distillation of the Bishop's recent delvings into three influential German theologians, Bonhoeffer, Bultmann and Tillich, still (then) largely unknown in this country outside academic circles. The furore was immense. Michael Ramsey, by then Archbishop of Canterbury, waded in with a highly critical pamphlet *Image, Old and New*, but later admitted that he had misjudged Robinson. It became evident that he was not alone in this; many there were who expressed their gratitude to the author for clarifying much that had been obscure to them, enabling them to make contact with "the Ground of our being" in a new and realistic way, both in prayer and in daily life. Among these, evangelicals were few. For the most part they were deeply shocked and shaken.[4]

Honest to God prepared the way for further explosions, some, less shattering, originating in the University of Cambridge. Here a group of Anglican theologians, led by the open-minded but profoundly orthodox Alec Vidler, Fellow and Dean of King's, and editor of the monthly journal *Theology,* struck out a daring new line with a series of books called *Objections,* the first of which was *Objections to Christian Belief* (1963). Originally a brief course of open lectures in the university, Vidler wrote that its aim was

> *not* to provide answers to objections to Christian belief. There is a spate of books which set out to do that. We hold that it is more important to try to plumb the depth of the objections, without complacently assuming that answers are readily available. Above all in a University, Christians must seek to understand the fundamental doubts to which their faith is exposed in this age . . . These lectures were intended to contribute to that kind of understanding. They were thus intended to be disturbing rather than reassuring. Belief in Christianity, or in anything else, if it is to be mature, must want to face the worst that can be said against it, and to evade no difficulties . . . Christians should listen attentively to all who submit their beliefs to an acute and sensitive criticism. But the objections are likely to be perceived and felt even more keenly by people who, maybe for many years, have been living with one foot in Christian belief and the other resolutely planted in the radical unbelief of the contemporary world, so that they are, as it were, torn between the two. If there is to be a profound recovery of Christian belief – or a profound rejection of it – it will surely come out of such an experience rather than out of an awareness of only one side of the question. (op. cit. pp. 7-9)

This was a bold and courageous strategy indeed and inevitably left

4. I recall that my physician, parishioner, and critical, or rather quizzical, friend, Bruce Ogilvie, presented me with a copy – on prescription as it were and commanded me to read it in small, but frequent doses, and I did.

itself open to damaging criticism from the less adventurous, but it was surely right. In the slim volume referred to, moral, psychological, historical and intellectual objections were stated and discussed in turn by Donald MacKinnon, H.A. (Harry) Williams, the editor, Vidler (himself an historian) and J.S. Bezzant. The last quoted in conclusion the saints day hymn "they wrestled hard, as we do now/with sins, and doubts and fears" adding, "this is so often precisely what we do *not* do. We wish to make religion an escape from the conflict, a haven of refuge even from trials of faith, and tend to enjoy the contempt for others which only a sense of religious superiority can give, forgetting that it is he who shall *endure* to the end who shall be saved."

"These lectures," comments Paul Welsby,[5] "attracted gatherings of over a thousand undergraduates and for several weeks the published work was a topselling book, translated into several languages."

The publication of these two controversial books in one year, 1963, was guaranteed to frighten evangelicals and other cautious or timid believers into deep suspicion of all that smelt of theological liberalism, as of covert sceptics selling the pass. Their fears were not entirely groundless. As well as moderate liberals like Vidler and his associates, whose basic orthodoxy was beyond question, there were others, ordained Anglicans, who were not in that category. Foremost among them was Don Cupitt, long-time Fellow and Dean of Emmanuel, ironically a college which, from its foundation in 1584, had been a renowned stronghold of first of Puritanism and later of Evangelicalism. Cupitt is brilliantly clever, a philosopher rather than a theologian, and his views grew progressively more extreme as time went on, until he ended by renouncing "belief in God" altogether. He lost no opportunity of airing his radical opinions, particularly on air, first in the TV series (partnered by Peter Armstrong) *Who Was Jesus?* (1977). Later that same year he leapt on a second opportunity at publicity when he took part in the symposium edited by John Hick called *The Myth of God Incarnate* which created the final and perhaps most spectacular in the series of theological explosions referred to above. It would be tedious to list the minor outbursts in between.

The list of distinguished Anglican theologians who participated in the notorious *Myth* was wide-ranging, including both Maurice Wiles and Dennis Nineham, who occupied the Regius Chairs of Divinity at Oxford and Cambridge respectively, but who have both remained within the Anglican fold. Also of their manner of thinking was Leslie Houlden, while Michael Goulder, like Cupitt, has become an atheist

---

5. *History of the Church of England 1945-1980* p. 15

or agnostic. The purpose of the book was to question the historicity (if such a word can be so applied) of the concept of Incarnation, regarding it rather as a "myth", the precise meaning of which term was carefully analysed and explained in the relevant essay by Maurice Wiles.

The furore aroused by this compilation was, naturally, mostly confined to professional theologians such as E.L. Mascall, who attacked it from the orthodox Anglo-Catholic side, and two leading Evangelicals: my old mentor, the Liberal Evangelical Professor C.F.D. Moule whose major work *The Origin of Christology* was published in the same year, and Sir Norman Anderson, a distinguished layman whose stance was more "conservative". As a footnote Cupitt's involvement in this early stage, it is worth noting that his subsequent career would involve the publication in 1980 of, his book *Taking Leave of God,* which set out to define his philosophical atheism. Later still he would produce his influential though destructive BBC TV series *The Sea of Faith.*

When, on top of all this very public theological questioning in the field of Christian Doctrine, the equally explosive events in the ethical field for which the sixties seem most to be remembered were added – the advent of "The Permissive Society" and "The Sexual Revolution", the *long term* effects of which are only now being experienced – the strength of the "conservative" reaction against all appearances of theological and ethical/moral liberalism can well be imagined.

The Influence of John Stott

To most sapient readers of this chapter, it must seem amazing that I have got so far without so much as a single mention of one whose name is more closely intertwined with the evangelical cause, even now in his old age (and mine) than any other. John R.W. Stott is described by another outstanding churchman of our day, David L. Edwards, as "apart from William Temple the most influential clergyman in the Church of England during the twentieth century". That was not flattery, but the considered opinion of a wise, judicious and knowledgeable historian and to be taken with full seriousness (*Essentials* by Edwards and Stott. Hodder 1988 p. 1).

Stott came from a privileged background. His father, Sir Arnold, a leading Harley Street physician, sent him to Rugby and Trinity College, Cambridge, where in addition to gaining Firsts in Modern Languages and Theology, he promptly threw in his lot with CICCU, a group with which, along with the Inter-Varsity Fellowship and Press, his subsequent life was to be so closely identified. He discovered a vocation to Holy Orders, for which he prepared at Ridley Hall, where he was taught by (among others) C.F.D. Moule, then its vice principal.

Following ordination, he served an immensely energetic curacy at All Souls, Langham Place in which parish he was born and brought up, eventually being appointed Rector in 1950. His ministry at Nash's elegant West End Church, next to Broadcasting House, for the next twenty years became little short of legend, followed by a further spell as its revered Rector Emeritus. He rapidly built up a huge and loyal regular Sunday (total) congregation of around a thousand. His powerful, meticulously prepared, Biblically based preaching ensured that All Souls became, in the words of David Edwards, "more than any other, the shop window of the Conservative Evangelical revival". There were others, of course, including Holy Trinity Brompton, later to be world famous as the birthplace and H.Q. of Alpha, with "Sandy" Millar as vicar, and St. Helen, Bishopsgate in the City under Dick Lucas, but All Souls was clearly pre-eminent in London evangelicalism.

And its Rector soon became recognised, not only in the Anglican Communion, but internationally, as the more or less unchallenged leader and spokesman of Evangelicalism. He took the Chair at not only the important National Evangelical Anglican Congresses at Keele 1967 and Nottingham 1977, but was a key figure in the historic Lausanne Congress on World Evangelisation in 1974, when Billy Graham was the host. Indeed, It was Stott who drafted the Lausanne Covenant and wrote the official commentary on the agreed statement, also chairing several international conferences arising from it.[6]

Not only was he an outstanding preacher and speaker, but also a genuine man of God to whom so many owe so much. He had an extraordinarily wide and profound knowledge of the Bible and grasp of the history of Christian doctrine, and a powerful gift as an incisive and, within limits, logical and persuasive writer. Outside his religious interests, but not entirely separate from them, he is an extremely knowledgeable, and lifelong, birdwatcher. Stott has, in addition, written much. His major work, *The Cross of Christ* (Inter-Varsity Press 1986, reprinted many times, with useful study guide 1989), is a devotional exposition of the substitutionary "theory" of The Atonement and repays careful study. It is discussed in *Essentials.*

John Stott's influence on at least two generations of evangelicals can scarcely be exaggerated. Along with the other potent factors

6. All this information I owe to David L. Edwards and John Stott: *Essentials: A liberal-evangelical dialogue* (1988) and to Edwards' generous estimate of Stott pp. 1-22 q.v.

previously mentioned, he has been a prime mover in changing the climate of opinion from the positively Liberal evangelicalism so marked in the *Fullness of Christ* report of 1950 to the distinctly "Conservative" (reactionary?) atmosphere of today, or at least of yesterday. John Stott is now eighty-seven and his day is over, but his influence lingers.

Essentials: A Liberal/Evangelical Dialogue (1988)

I have already referred more than once to a book called *Essentials* (1988). It came about as a result of an invitation, or challenge, from David L. Edwards, without doubt one of the most intelligent, shrewd and fair-minded clergymen in the Church of England, to John Stott. The two have a great deal in common – as well as also coming from a privileged public school background, much of Edwards's distinguished career has, like Stott's, been based in London.

Edwards, a prolific author, historian and journalist (whose perceptive book reviews have long been a feature of the *Church Times*) is essentially a Central Churchman. In *Essentials* he lays claim to allegiance to *both* the Catholic and Evangelical wings of the C. of E., but he writes deliberately from the point of view of a *moderate* Liberal.[7] The foremost impression that emerges is the admirable intention of establishing two important facts in open dialogue with John Stott, viz. (i) exactly what are the differences between the so-called "liberals" and the so-called "conservatives" and (ii) what are the areas of convergence and chances of agreement and mutual understanding between them. Stott accepted the invitation and agreed the procedure. Edwards was to challenge Stott in successive chapters on what he (Edwards) considered the main points of divergence and Stott was to have the right and space to respond. Thus Edwards was guaranteed the first word and Stott the last. The civilities between them were duly observed but both hit hard.

I read the book twice, with the closest attention, to make sure I did not misunderstand any of the arguments. Following the second reading I wish to record one impression, as well as my admiration for the spirit in which the dialogue was conducted; it could so easily have deteriorated into an intellectual punch-up. The manner in which each presented their arguments did them both credit. The point that struck me was that both men – Edwards the more successfully – were striving

---

7. Edwards was at one time presiding genius of The Modern Churchman's Union. He read History at Magdalen College, Oxford after which he was elected a Fellow of All Souls, then as now one of the highest intellectual awards in England.

to be moderate, to eschew extremes. Stott explicitly disclaimed being a "fundamentalist". Anyone who sincerely wants to know exactly what is at stake in this vital conflict cannot do better than study this book. As will be apparent, my sympathies are with Edwards, but I consider that Stott makes some excellent points on matters of detail.

This, obviously, is a juncture where there is bound to be an overlap with territory more proper to later chapters, but, that admitted, to avoid the danger of unnecessary repetition I propose here to outline the main areas of conflict as usefully pinpointed by Edwards, who, before writing a single word, was at pains to read everything written and published by Stott, whom he is scrupulous to quote in full in areas of disagreement.

Importantly, Edwards prefaces this list (op. cit. page 30) by writing that "the questions and criticisms which I shall submit as a contribution to this dialogue will boil down to the suggestion that there are some conservative Evangelical ideas which, whether or not they are valid, are essential if one is to believe the gospel revealed in the Bible . . . They are religious convictions which have often been thought to be the 'God-breathed' truth and to be absolutely essential, fundamental, 'non-negotiable' in any dialogue". He adds, "When I explore them, I hope I shall be sensitive enough to realise that I am trading on sacred ground." He then quotes Stott as referring to

> these convictions, when he passionately defends . . . the contemporary Evangelical emphasis on the Bible and the Cross, and on the finality of both. It is not because we are ultra-conservative, or obscurantist, or reactionary or other horrid things we are sometimes said to be. It is because we love Jesus Christ and are determined, God helping us, to bear witness to his unique glory and absolute sufficiency. (Stott, *Focus on Christ*, 1979, p. 32)

On this, Edwards comments:

> Nevertheless, I am compelled to ask whether the insistence on these ideas has not become a handicap in the communication of the gospel. Rightly or wrongly, these ideas are widely believed to belong not to the gospel itself, not to Christ's glory and sufficiency, but to a dead or dying culture. I long to persuade conservative Evangelicals that if only they can regard these ideas as optional (not necessarily as wrong) they will find that they can communicate the biblical gospel in terms which are far more intelligible, meaningful and credible.

They can build bridges between the word and the world, so that their hearers, who at present are puzzled or repelled, will think what in their hearts Evangelicals are thinking about God, Jesus and the human situation. Evangelicals have the spiritual strength to do this, with very great benefit to the Church and the world. They have the holiness, the determination and the energy which we liberals often lack; we are better at criticising. (op cit. p. 31)

The main points at issue between "conservatives" and "liberals"

With this passionate conviction (equal to that of Stott surely) and disarming humility as a preface, Edwards lists the points at issue:

> I shall be asking (1) whether the Hebrew and Christian Scriptures are infallible or inerrant; (2) whether Christ died in order to propitiate the wrath of God by enduring as a substitute for us the punishment we deserved; (3) whether in order to believe in God as a Christian it is necessary to believe in all the miracles reported in the Bible; (4) whether the Bible authoritatively offers us detailed teaching about our behaviour or about the future; (5) and whether it is necessary to respond to the Christian gospel before death in order to be saved by God.

He concludes with a quotation from a recent (1983) book *The Future of Evangelical Christianity* by one Donald Bloesch: "It it my position that the future belongs to that branch of Christendom that is willing to make itself expendable for the sake of the evangelisation of the world to the greater glory of God." (op. cit. p. 7)

We shall return to these themes, but from a different angle, appropriately, in the following chapter on Broad Church liberalism. With that we take leave of John Stott and David Edwards, for the time being at least.

Nicky Gumbel and Alpha

Today in the world of Anglican Evangelicalism the long reign of John Stott as its undisputed spokesman and quasi-Pope is over; centre stage now is the still comparatively youthful, dynamic figure of Nicky Gumbel. Gumbel is known almost world-wide as the originator of Alpha, and author of the many times reprinted paperback best seller *Questions of Life*, on which that renowned course is based. It was first published in 1993, when Gumbel was the young curate of another fashionable London West end Church, Holy Trinity, Brompton, colloquially, and affectionately, known now to thousands as "H.T.B.". His vicar there was "Sandy" Millar, whom he has at long last succeeded as vicar, on the former's resignation and subsequent consecration as a bishop with wide ranging responsibilities in East Africa. The longstanding friendship and collaboration between these two men was close and some of the credit for Alpha and its remarkable success story must be Millar's.

It is not without significance that Alpha's début and initial impetus coincided with the reign at Lambeth of George Carey, whose emphatic evangelicalism leaned more to the "conservative" than to the "liberal" and whose energetic sponsorship of the Decade of Evangelism was a leading feature of his archiepiscopate (1990-2002). His warmhearted and uncritical support of Alpha was emulated by most diocesan bishops, whatever their churchmanship, perhaps on the shallow axiom "if you can't beat 'em, join 'em".

Although the Alpha course, since its inception c.1993, has been widely used for evangelistic purposes in a broad spectrum of Anglican parishes and by clergy of more than one brand of churchmanship throughout the Anglican Communion (and even beyond, in some Roman Catholic dioceses with their bishops' blessings), and although its originators (I believe) disclaim for it party bias, its origins, presuppositions and flavour are unmistakably Evangelical – and "conservative" at that. It must also be beyond question that, at a time when the Christian faith and Church is under exceptionally severe attack, there is much that is *excellent* in Alpha. Strengths may be found not only in its highly professional organisation and flair for publicity, but also in the actual material of its teaching and manner of its presentation, both in the book and in the course based on the book. This makes it all the more regrettable that, by its doctrinaire refusal to face certain vital facts about Jesus and the Bible, it has laid itself open to serious criticism and greatly weakened its long term effectiveness. This, along with its phenomenal "success" and popularity, makes it seem at the least ungracious to articulate those criticisms. Still, this risk must be taken, though it must be emphasised that there is no intention whatsoever to impugn the basic sincerity and integrity of Alpha's authors and presenter.

Where to begin this distasteful task? Perhaps there is no better place than near the beginning of the course, since this was the moment at which, when I attended a local sample course in response to a friend's invitation, I was immediately alerted to what I considered a false note and felt I could no longer in honesty continue to attend. I tried to explain my action in a letter to our hostess, a good friend. In chapter 2/Alpha session 2 under the deceptively innocuous heading, "What did Jesus say about himself?" Gumbel lists four of the great "I am" sayings *attributed* to Jesus in the Gospel of John. They are, in order of appearance, "I am the Bread of Life" (John 6. 35 and 48); "the Light of the World" (8.12); "the Resurrection and the Life" (11.25); and "the Way, the Truth and the Life" (14.6). (There are others but Gumbel does not mention them.)

These four "sayings" are treated by Gumbel as if they were *unquestionably* spoken by Jesus about himself (as "claims") and are adduced, with breathtaking naïveté, as conclusive, knockdown evidence that he *"was/is* who he claimed to be". Now, it is a *fact* that no serious present day student of John's Gospel, or indeed a reasonably level-headed Bible reader with a good knowledge of all four gospels (and even a modicum of common sense), comparing these supposed utterances of Jesus with most of those recorded in the three Synoptic Gospels (Mark, Matthew and Luke) where He says so little about himself, could possibly believe that they originated from the same speaker. There is an *utterly* undeniable difference between the comments in John in terms of style and subject matter from those utterances with a plausible claim to be something like authentic recorded words of the Master. Simply taking the first example, "I am the Bread of Life" in its context in that *extraordinary* sixth chapter of John, if one believed that all those recorded sayings actually originated on the lips and tongue of Jesus, one would have to conclude that he was a crazy megalomaniac – not the Jesus depicted by Mark, Luke or Matthew. Try reading that chapter through carefully and see if you are not compelled to agree.

What then is the explanation? Surely, something like this. These great "sayings" were composed by the evangelist John and artificially – though according to a perfectly legitimate literary convention of the time – put upon Jesus' lips, ascribed to him, to express who *he, John,* passionately believed Jesus really was. *Like that they make very good sense.* Put very simply, the real, historical Jesus did not "make those claims" and would never have dreamed of doing so. But they were certainly made by John – and I, along with most if not all Christians, believe they are *true of Jesus.* He *is indeed* the Bread of Life, the Light of the World, the Way, the Truth, the Resurrection and the Life. He was also the Good Shepherd who laid down his life for us, his flock of sheep. But it would have been completely out of character for the Synoptic Jesus of historical *fact* to have brashly made these claims for himself.

As compared with the Synoptics, the fourth Gospel, John, despite a deceptive, superficial appearance of simplicity, is extremely complex and subtle. To take it as the literal truth is to miss its point *completely.* It is *not* to be taken as a *historical* document, (as the Synoptics reliably *are)* but as a profound theological meditation of a devout disciple of Jesus. (That is not to say that *parts* of it, e.g. the Passion and Resurrection narratives *may* well be true and reliable *history;* it is a baffling book, but, properly understood, one of the most precious ever written!)

A final note to put this in an historical perspective; few if any Biblical scholars would question what I have written above. Most of it is common sense, unprejudiced observation and analysis. But it is also true that before the days of historical and literary analysis of the Scriptures, clergy, theologians and the ordinary lay Bible reader *all* accepted without question that *all* the sayings (and actions) attributed to Jesus in *all four* gospels were authentic. At least that is what they *thought* they believed: common sense must have caused the more thoughtful readers considerable perplexities.

What Gumbel and all his fellow so-called "conservatives" have done, in their timid reluctance to face facts, is to "put the clocks back" a couple of centuries. If botanists will forgive me, Gumbel when dealing with the Bible is truly Gumbelliferous – reading him or listening to his tapes, we are all in the deep shade of the early nineteenth century. His early-Victorian attitude to and understanding of the Bible pervades his entire book and the Alpha course from start to finish. It is, however, in Chapter 5/course session 5 ("Why and How should I read the Bible?") that his unquestioning fundamentalism becomes *explicit.* We should look very closely at his carefully chosen words (*Questions of Life* p. 69f.).

He begins by quoting, as all fundamentalists (such as Jehovah's Witnesses) invariably do, 2 Timothy 3. 16f. which he correctly but literally translates: "All Scripture is God-breathed and is useful for teaching, rebuking, correcting and training in righteousness, so that God's servant may be thoroughly equipped for every good work." On this he comments "the writer is saying that Scripture is God speaking. Of course he [God] used human agents. It is 100 per cent the work of human beings. But it is also 100 per cent inspired by God (just as Jesus is fully human and fully God)".

To this I reply:

1.   Assuming that the writer of the second letter to Timothy (who, of course, in writing of "all Scripture" is alluding to the *Old* Testament, the "Bible" of Jesus and his disciples) *did* mean exactly

what Gumbel says – i.e. that Scripture is God speaking and therefore literally true in every detail, infallible and inerrant (to use expressions dear to fundamentalists) and nowhere self-contradictory[8] – then he was wrong. If you doubt this, look up and read, for example, Exod. 4. 24; Exod. 11. 4-6; Num 31. 1-18; Deut 20. 10-18; Deut 21. 18-21; the whole of Joshua chapter 7; 1 Sam. 15. 1-33; 2 Sam. 6. 6f; Psalms 58, 139. 19-22 and 137. 7-9; Nahum 1. 2. Is *this* the God revealed in Jesus Christ? Obviously NOT.

2. The Bible abounds in obvious human errors and contradictions. If you, or Gumbel, doubt this, check the following few examples all from the New Testament, most of them from the Gospels.

i) The words of Jesus at the Last Supper. Mark 14. 22-25; Luke 22. 17-20; 1 Cor. 11. 23-25; Matt. 26. 26-29. (The institution of the Eucharist is not even mentioned in John at all).

ii) Jesus' reply to the High Priest: Mark 14, 62; Matt. 26 64· Luke 22. 67f; John 18. 19f.

iii) The death of Judas Iscariot. Compare Matt. 27. 3-10 and Acts 1. 16-19.

iv) Burial and Resurrection of Jesus: 1 Cor. 15. 3-8; Mark 15. 42-47 and 16. 1-8; Matt. 27. 58-end and 28; Luke 23. 49-end and 24; John 19. 38-20 (whole chapter).

v) The Ascension. Compare Luke 24. 30-end and Acts 1. 6-11, (both by the same author).

3. Many other examples from both Testaments could be given. These are the *facts*. I for one, with my training in history, am *glad* that the Bible *does* show ample signs of human error and contradiction. It is to me *strong* evidence of its authenticity and general reliability. Were it not so, I should be deeply suspicious that it had all been "tidied up" or faked.

In the light of all of this, would not Nicky Gumbel be well advised to save himself from future embarrassment and Alpha from legitimate criticism (from disillusioned intelligent participants) by inserting an entire extra session/chapter headed "What actually is the Bible and why should Christians (and others) study it in the confidence that it is reliable?"

He could then use that extra session to "come completely clean" on the Bible's historical origins and the gradual process of its formation, and, in the Old Testament, its immense range and variety as the entire surviving literature of Yahweh/God's unique ancient people, Israel. Furthermore, and even more to the point, he would thereby be able to explain the total contents of the New Testament as bearing

8. But a greater Biblical scholar than Gumbel or me, Prof. C.F.D. Moule, has a different interpretation as will be seen in the Chapter 11 (p. 246f.).

authentic human witness to that God's unique "son" – his life, teaching, ministry, death and resurrection and to the gift of his spirit embodying the living Jesus in his "Body", the universal (=catholic) Church – God's appointed agency for proclaiming the Gospel.

Gumbel probably thought that anything like this would be deemed dry and boring by many of his audience and therefore best left out, in the interests of (a false) simplicity. Such a thought is surely mistaken. As it stands, the unprejudiced observer is given the impression *either* of almost unbelievable naïveté on Gumbel's part *or* of a deeply regrettable lack of candour. Because of Alpha's undoubted popularity and "success" such criticism has been muted or restrained, but the facts are as stated above.

This, while understandable, is all the more regrettable since Alpha is, generally speaking, admirable. If, instead of originating in a rather narrow *segment* of the Church, it had been more broadly based in the thought and prayer of the Church *as a whole* at once evangelical, catholic, liberal and (in the *true* sense) conservative, while still retaining all Gumbel's refreshing enthusiasm and undoubted evangelistic genius, what a *tremendous* force for good it would have been. As it is, no one would doubt for a moment the abundant evidence of the genuine, if limited, impact it has been able, surely under God, to make – still less to grudge its "success".

If only. . . .

There are in existence alternative courses in evangelism, such as *Emmaus*, of which one hears good reports. But as I have no actual experience of any of them, I am in no position to comment.

N.T. (Tom) Wright, Bishop of Durham

This long chapter is still far from complete. The line up of post-war Anglican Evangelical *leaders*: Christopher Chavasse, Donald Coggan, John Stott, George Carey and Nicky Gumbel still lacks one, the latest, whose *public* début about the turn of the century/ millennium may not prove the least significant.

The name of N.T. (Tom) Wright, Bishop of Durham since 2003, and outstanding Biblical scholar, critic and historian, is even now only beginning to impinge on the national awareness. A proud Northumbrian by birth, from a traditional Anglican clerical background, he was formerly quite unknown outside the academic circles in Oxford, Cambridge and Montreal in which, as a younger man, he worked and taught. Wright is a prodigiously prolific author, and an all-rounder. Besides his manifold New Testament studies, he gained his credentials as a meticulous historian in collaboration with and succession to another outstanding scholar-bishop, Stephen Neill[9] in *The Interpretation of the New Testament 1861-1986* (OUP 1988) bringing it up to date after Neill's death (c. 1984).

In spite of energetic involvement in sport and other student activities, Wright had pulled off Firsts both in Greats and Theology at Oxford. As an undergraduate he had been deeply influenced by active membership of OICCU (the Oxford equivalent of CICCU) of which he was elected President. Its deep positive commitment to discipleship of the Living Christ obviously meant far more to him than the strictly conservative evangelicalism, verging on fundamentalism, by which it was coloured. This was totally out of accord with open, unprejudiced Biblical scholarship into which he threw himself without reserve in his academic career. (In later years he was to define his own approach as "critical realism", as distinct from "naïve realism".) The broad minded quality of his churchmanship in those days enabled him, as Fellow and Chaplain of Worcester College, to celebrate a weekday "mass" in chapel wearing eucharistic vestments, singing plainsong and using incense. If challenged on this point by OICCU colleagues he would cheerfully observe that, since on good Biblical authority, incense is offered in heaven (Rev. 8. 3-5) we might as well get used to it here on earth! Such broad mindedness in an OICCU president must be without precedent – more's the pity! Wright is also on record as having found party strife in the C. of E. "most unbiblical". (What would he think of the evidence from 1 Corinthians in my chapter 1 above, one wonders.) In *Who's Who* NTW cites his recreations as music, hill-walking, poetry, cricket and golf. He is a lifelong supporter of Newcastle United F.C. and a devoted family man.[10]

His particular theological interests centred on Christology (i.e. the actual core identity of Jesus) and were therefore early focussed upon His historical life, ministry, teaching, passion, death and resurrection, and especially upon His personality and developing "mindset" and "worldview", so far as these are accessible to us.

Wright's natural aptitude, indeed zest for controversy – fruitful and constructive, rather than sterile – stimulated by the publication

9. S.C. Neill, sometime Bishop of Tinnevelly in South India, author of *A History of Christian Missions* (Penguin 1964) and *A History of the Ecumenical Movement 1517-1948*. Neill was a signatory of *The Fullness of Christ* (1950), a quintessential Liberal Evangelical, and like Wright, a polymath.

10. For these and other anecdotes, I am indebted to an article by Glyn Paflin in *Church Times* 5 Nov. 1993 (based on an interview with NTW)

of such viciously perverse, superficially plausible pseudo-scholarly books as *Jesus* by the brilliant atheist A.N. Wilson (1992) led him to write a number of lively, cogently argued little books such as *Who was Jesus?* (S.P.C.K 1992) to set the record straight. He also took part in similar broadcast discussions. By that time, and indeed for long before, his feet were firmly set on what it has become fashionable to call "The Third Quest" of the historical Jesus.[11]

N.T. Wright: Christian Origins and the Question of God

All NTW's other achievements, in scholarship, in writing and in his Durham episcopate, remarkable as they are, pale into insignificance beside his majestic project, as yet (2009) incomplete, of a five or six volume series on *Christian Origins and the Question of God*. Conceived originally as four or five volumes (viz. 1. Introduction. 2. Jesus: His life, ministry, intentions, passion, death, resurrection and exaltation. 3. Paul/Acts. 4. The Gospels and the Evangelists and, possibly, 5. The Question of God), in the process of writing vol. 2, it became increasingly obvious that *The Resurrection of the Son of God* would have to form a third, separate (and in fact the largest so far) volume. (The author acknowledges this in his preface to vol. 3.) This massive volume, the latest so far to appear, was published (by SPCK) in 2003, the year in which its author was appointed Bishop of Durham. (The inevitable consequence was a corporate groan from the Bishop's eagerly impatient public – would his conscience and the strain of the

---

11. This derives from a landmark book by the renowned Alsatian Biblical scholar/musicologist/saint Albert Schweitzer, the title of the English translation of which was *The Quest of the Historical Jesus* (1910). In this book Schweitzer, whose own work had led him to the conclusion that Jesus mistakenly believed the end of this world to be imminent, listed and reviewed the successive 19th century "liberal" lives of Jesus (i.e. "the first Quest") such as the outstanding one by D.F. Strauss (1835) translated by George Eliot, and the notorious sceptical *Vie de Jésus* by E. Renan, and concluded that "he [Jesus] comes to us as one unknown" and that to reconstruct his life was an historical impossibility). This view was shared by influential theologians of the mid-20th century such as R. Bultmann ("we can now know almost nothing concerning the life and personality of Jesus") R.H. Lightfoot ("we trace in the gospels but the outskirts of his ways") and G. Bornkamm ("No one is any longer in the position to write a life of Jesus"). This was largely the pessimistic outlook when I read Theology at Cambridge in the 1940s. I frankly admit my own difficulty, as a trained historian, in making convincing historical sense of the New Testament evidence for Jesus and I further confess that I did not try hard enough! That was deeply culpable and effectively vitiated my preaching and evangelistic ministry.

inevitable burden of episcopal duties delay the completion, or even the *continuation* of the project, *sine die.* My hunch as one of the groaners was that somehow the time *will* be found for everything, not (one hopes) at the expense of abounding health and vitality.)

To give some idea, to those who have not even seen the three volumes published so far, of the sheer size and scope of this mammoth undertaking, the *total* number *so far* of pages of *actual text*, excluding bibliography, index etc. at a rough average of 550 words a page is 1,899. On top of this there is a total so far of over 6,000 footnotes. To ignore these altogether is to risk missing out on some choice examples of scintillating Wrightean wit. Statistics such as these might convey an impression of monumental scholarly dry dullness. Nothing could be further from the truth. Wright is a master of lucidity, logic and disciplined, orderly presentation, and although the unphilosophical and non-specialist reader will at times feel out of his depth, if with grim determination and furrowed brow he/she will doggedly persist, that perseverance will ultimately be rewarded.

The first volume in the series, entitled *The New Testament and the People of God* (SPCK 1992), is introductory to the whole series and should be read, pondered, and absorbed *in full.* Despite the felicity of Wright's English, it is by no means all easy reading for the non-specialist – especially the chapter on epistemology (the philosophy of knowledge) and the author's deliberate repudiation of the now discredited but, until recently, fashionable and widely accepted positivist and/or phenomenalist methods of reading the historical sources. Wright invariably gives convincing reasons for his methodological choices.

Early in the book (pp. 7ff.) he enumerates the four successive stages in the ways in which the Bible and the New Testament in particular have been approached, read and understood. The first was the pre-critical, prevailing from the earliest times until the beginning of "the Enlightenment" c.1700. This was the way of "prayerful Christians who believe the Bible to be Holy Writ", ask few if any questions about its value as authentic history "and listen for the voice of God as they read the text. This pre-critical approach," says Wright, "aims to take the authoritative status of the text seriously, but would today be criticised on (at least) three grounds, corresponding to the other three ways of reading: it fails to take the text seriously historically, it fails to integrate into the theology of the New Testament as a whole, and it is insufficiently critical of its own presuppositions and standpoint." (p. 7)[12]

With the coming of "the Enlightenment" and the beginnings of

12. The pre-critical approach roughly approximates to what most people today describe as fundamentalism.

modern "science", this pre-critical attitude began to give way to increasingly rigorous historical criticism, exemplified in the work of the pioneer German scholar Reimarus (1694-1768) and in D.F. Strauss' *Life of Jesus* (1835) translated into English by George Eliot. This movement was spearheaded in the twentieth century most notably by Bultmann (1884-1976), whose name is virtually synonymous with his radical "demythologization" programme resulting from his profound historical scepticism and leading to his theological critique which has had great influence. The entire "Enlightenment" approach, embracing *both* of Wright's second (historical) and third (theological) categories, corresponds to the "liberal", "modernist" phase of Biblical scholarship and comprises of all the established techniques from textual criticism to the (later) source, form and redaction criticism. Be it noted, in passing, that all these forms of New Testament (and especially Gospel) analysis derive ultimately from applied commonsense and observation and all have contributed in their several ways to our understanding and interpretation of ancient Scripture. All are explicitly endorsed and brilliantly utilised by Wright and their continuing validity affirmed by him.

At the same time, whereas the pre-critical approach asked few if any questions, liberal modernism, from its sceptical base in history, asked a great many, all searching, some deeply disturbing. They range from, "How far can we be sure that we have in the gospels the authentic teaching of Jesus in his own words and how far have they been developed, or even invented and placed on his lips by a later generation of Christians?" to "Was Paul and not Jesus himself the founder of Christianity as we know it?" The latter represents a view notably expounded by the great German scholar Harnack (1851-1930), held by many today with little or no learning, but (one hopes) convincingly and definitively to be exploded by the present Bishop of Durham.

As that Bishop observed, back in 1992,

> This world [sc. that of professional New Testament scholarship] has changed beyond all recognition in the last few years. The rise of *post*modernist literary criticism has made the essentially *modernist* disciplines – of investigating the early [sc. Christian] community that handed on traditions, of trying to uncover complex literary sources, of unpicking what precisely the evangelists were doing with these sources – look decidedly passé. The new emphasis in gospel studies

is not on the creative evangelist so much as on the text itself.
(p. 25)

Granted that we are now well into the "postmodern" era, what exactly *is* this new*ish* "literary criticism" so characteristic of it, and which Wright describes as the fourth (and final?) approach to the New Testament and particularly to the gospels?

Using ideas and words (jargon?) unfamiliar to us of an older generation, who, in our youth had to master the techniques and methods first of form criticism, then of redaction criticism, this newish "approach" insists on beginning with an examination of the process of reading itself. (What are we doing when reading this text? What do I bring to it by way of presuppositions and how (if at all) am I changed by reading it? Can such a reading co-exist with authority, history or theology?) "Perhaps because of these problems, post modern literary theory has not yet [written in 1992] made many inroads into mainline Biblical scholarship, but there is every reason to suppose that it will shortly do so." So Wright avers on p. 9. It will not be his fault if this forecast fails to come true!

This brief paragraph summary of mine is, no doubt, a gross caricature of the real thing, due to pressure on space. For a clear exposition see Wright *op. cit.* Chapter 3. "Literature, Story and the Articulation of Worldviews" pp. 47-80. Beginning by pinpointing the (hitherto largely unrecognised) prevalence and importance of "story" (whether primitive and myth-like or developed and sophisticated) in the lives, both corporate/social/national or individual, of *all* human beings, this theory sees "story" reflected in group/corporate/national "worldviews" (cultures, religions) and in the "mindsets" (outlook, habitual stance) of individuals. Other words of this particular jargon, such as "praxis" (life style), "symbol" (characteristic feature or institution of a particular "worldview" e.g. in New Testament Judaism, the Temple, the Sabbath, circumcision) are all frequently deployed by NTW.

In this introductory volume, he defines a major part of his task as the integration of literature, history and theology, something not previously attempted. He defines his basic method as "Critical Realism" as over against naïve realism, and (outmoded, obsolete) positivism. And, discussing his philosophy of history, he frankly writes of the necessity of proceeding by way of hypothesis and verification, setting out the qualifications of "a good hypothesis, and the criteria for its verification" (e.g. dissimilarity, double similarity and multiple attestation). He is unashamedly pragmatic, quoting not

once but again and again: "the proof of the pudding is in the eating".
All this is to be found in Part II of the book: "Tools for the Task".
Parts III and IV are devoted to context viz. respectively, Part III First
Century Judaism within the Greco-Roman World (pp. 145-338) and
Part IV The First Christian Century (pp. 341-464).

Having devoted so many pages to this introductory volume I shall
go to the opposite extreme of brevity with its (so far) two successors
– simply because to summarise them is (for me at least) impossible.
The second volume is *Jesus and the Victory of God* (SPCK 1996).
Here, with permission, I shall content myself by reproducing the
blurb (from his own pen?) on the back cover.

> In this eagerly awaited second volume N.T. Wright offers a
> penetrating assessment of the major scholarly contributions to
> the current quest for the historical Jesus. He then sets out in
> fascinating detail his own compelling step by step account of
> how Jesus himself understood his mission: how he believed
> himself called to remake Israel, the people of God, around
> himself: how he announced God's judgment on the Israel of his
> day, especially its Temple and hierarchy: and how he saw his
> own movement as the divinely ordained fulfilment of Israel's
> destiny. This revolutionary message, articulated in parables and
> acted out symbolically in healings and celebratory meals, drew
> Jesus to Jerusalem – where, as he came to realize, his vocation
> demanded that he would die the death he had announced for
> the people. In obedience to this vocation, Jesus had come
> to realize that he was claiming to do and be what, in Jewish
> thought, only God can do and be. . . .

I will, despite what I wrote above, add just two observations, the first
factual, the second by way of personal testimony.

1. As a conscientious historian, Wright made two correct
preliminary decisions. They were to exclude (a) the two opening
chapters of Matthew and Luke's gospels (i.e. their birth and infancy
narratives) and (b) the Fourth Gospel, that ascribed to "John", on
the grounds that they, all three, are not strictly *historical* sources.
This decision in no way committed him to any judgment about their
intrinsic value or veracity.

2. Whereas, as I have indicated in footnote eleven to this chapter,
partly through culpable laziness, I had always previously had difficulty
in making historical sense of the life, vocation and ministry of our
Lord, I find Wright's painstaking reconstruction 100% credible, and
I am correspondingly grateful. The proof of the pudding was indeed,

for *this* gourmand, in the eating! How I wish this had happened at the outset of my own modest ministry, rather than at the end. What a difference it would have made. *Mea culpa* but *laus Deo*!

The third, and, so far, final volume in the series is *The Resurrection of the Son of God* (SPCK 2003). For the same reason as for its predecessor, I confine myself to the wording of the blurb, which does what I cannot do.

> N.T. Wright takes us on a fascinating journey through ancient beliefs about life after death, from the shadowy figures who inhabit Homer's Hades, through Plato's hope for a blessed immortality, to the first century, where the Greek and Roman world (apart from the Jews) consistently denied any possibility of resurrection. We then examine ancient Jewish beliefs on the same subject, from the Bible to the Dead Sea Scrolls and beyond.
>
> This sets the scene for a full scale examination of early Christian beliefs about resurrection in general and that of Jesus in particular, beginning with Paul and working through to the start of the third century. Wright looks at all the evidence and asks: Why did the Christians agree with Jewish resurrection belief while introducing into it – across the board – significant modifications?
>
> To answer this question we come to the strange and evocative Easter stories in the gospels and ask whether they can have been late inventions. Wright seeks the best historical conclusions about the empty tomb and the belief that Jesus really did rise bodily from the dead, recognising that it was this belief that caused early Christians to call Jesus "Son of God". In doing so they posed a political challenge as well as a theological one. These challenges retain their power in the twenty first century.

* * * * *

Having completed this (hopelessly inadequate) survey of the first half of Wright's tremendous project so far published, I would like to put some observations on it in the form of questions.

1. Do you share my feeling that the massive volume of *The Resurrection of the Son of God*, like its predecessor, is nothing short of superb? It is hard to see how anyone other than the most captious pigheaded sceptic can find reasonable fault with it, or fail to be impressed (and probably convinced) by Wright's cogent arguments

and the sheer weight of evidence adduced in what must by any reckoning be the most baffling and complex problem in all history. The adjective that springs to mind is "definitive".

2. If and when the whole of this vast project comes to fruition with the publication of the three (?) remaining volumes (I, alas, shall not live to see it), and assuming the remaining volumes (as is to be expected) live up to the promise of their predecessors, and it has been received and *absorbed*(!) by its (very limited) readership, assessed by the scholarly world, and (hopefully) acclaimed thereby, may not the *entire series* come *in due time* to be accorded classical status as the *definitive* last word on its subject both within and beyond what remains of Christendom? Is that wildly unrealistic? If not, for that to happen, it will surely need to be made *far* more accessible to the widest possible public. Who better to undertake this task of a simplified "popular" précis than its author (if he is not completely exhausted by that time)? For the volumes on Jesus something on the lines of Wright's *The Original Jesus* (Lion 1996) is suggested. Do you agree?

3. The intellectual, spiritual and devotional repercussions of the entire undertaking when complete and accessible in "popular" form are incalculable. For the first time ever, an entirely *credible* reconstruction of the *actual, historical* origins of the Christian Church, in the contextual life, "mindset", vocation, mission, passion, death and resurrection of Jesus Messiah, and the birth, early growth and development of a truly Catholic (universal) and Apostolic (missionary) Brotherhood (i.e. Church) transcending all human barriers, will be available *alongside* the canonical Scriptures of the Old and New Testaments – something entirely without precedent! Is that not the case?[13]

4. The inclusion in the overall title of the whole multi-volume series, of the words *"and the Question of God"* is sure to puzzle would-be readers and cause their eyebrows to be raised. In his Preface to the first volume (pp. xvi f.), Wright explains, beginning by justifying his idiosyncratic usage of "god" instead of "God" throughout the series."The modern usage, without the article and with a capital," he says,

seems to me actually dangerous. This usage, which

13. To get some idea of the form these repercussions might take, the article *The Quest for the Real Jesus* by Professor Francis Watson in *The Cambridge Companion to Jesus* (ed. Markus Bockmuehl, CUP 2001) is strongly recommended, along with much in the rest of that admirable compilation.

sometimes amounts to regarding God as the proper name of the Deity, *rather than as essentially a common noun, implies* that all users of the word are monotheists and, within that, all monotheists believe in the same god. *Both these propositions seem to me self-evidently untrue.* It may or may not be true that our worship of any god is translated by some mysterious grace into worship of one god who actually exists, and who happens to be the only god. This is believed by some students of religion. It is not, however, believed by very many practitioners of the mainline monotheistic religions (Judaism, Christianity, Islam) or of the non-monotheistic ones (Hinduism, Buddhism, and their cognates). Certainly the Jews and Christians of the first century did not believe it. They believed that pagans worshipped *idols*, or even *demons*. It seems to me, therefore, simply misleading to use "God" throughout this work. I have often preferred either to refer to Israel's god by the biblical name YHWH (notwithstanding debates about the use of this name within Second-Temple Judaism)… and I think it quite likely that many of those who come to a book like this with the firm conviction that "Jesus is God" and equally well many of those who come with the firm conviction that he is not, may hold views on the meaning of "god", or "God", which ought to be challenged in the light of the New Testament. The christological question as to whether the statement "Jesus is God" is true, and if so, in what sense is often asked as though "God" were the known and "Jesus" the unknown: this, I suggest, is manifestly mistaken. If anything the matter stands the other way round.

This is of crucial importance to the understanding of Wright's argument throughout the series and seems likely to form the subject of the concluding volume.

5. The supreme, and I believe *unique* importance of this multi-volume series, when eventually complete and suitably abridged, in the field of Christian *apologetics* will be further considered in the next chapter – that on the subject of Broad Church Liberalism. The reason for this is my belief, right or wrong, that Evangelicals *(per se)* are primarily concerned with evangelism, spreading the gospel, and Liberals *(per se)* are primarily concerned with apologetics, explaining and interpreting the gospel in terms understandable by

the man on the Clapham omnibus. The line between the two is often a fine one, and indeed they are better off when that line is allowed to dissipate altogether and a happy combination result.

Bishop Wright is in no doubt about considering himself an evangelical – that is why he and his works feature so prominently in this chapter. No one would dispute that. There is also no secret about his early enthusiastic allegiance in his Oxford days to the Oxford Intercollegiate Christian Union, (OICCU), which is totally identified with *Conservative* evangelicalism, although the evidence is that his OICCU membership, and indeed presidency, was admirably broad minded. His subsequent academic career in the mainstream of Biblical scholarship, and his espousal of critical realism, seems impossible to reconcile with the dogmatic, if moderate, conservative evangelicalism of the likes of John Stott. Ecclesiometrically it is impossible, likewise, to *resist* classifying the present Bishop of Durham with the older generation of distinguished Liberal Evangelical scholarship alongside C.F.D. Moule, an old friend of his.

In 2003 Bishop Tom, as he was by that time, along with Tim Dakin, the latest in a distinguished line of moderate "liberal" evangelical General Secretaries of the Church Mission (formerly Missionary) Society, took the initiative in founding a specifically evangelical group called *Fulcrum*. In accordance with my life long policy of abstention (lazy aloofness?) from all Church party groupings, I resisted the temptation to join it and in consequence practically all my knowledge of it is conjectural. The choice of name is a useful clue. "Fulcrum" is defined in the Concise Oxford Dictionary as having two meanings. "1. (Mech.) Point against which lever is placed to get purchase or on which it turns or is supported. 2. means by which influence etc. is brought to bear." Without looking it up, I should have risked defining it as "a point of balance", a telling assumption if it is at all representative of what others less inclined to have recourse to a dictionary would think. All of which, together with the surely significant fact that among Bishop Tom and Tim Dakin's confederates or supporters appears to be Mrs. Rowan (Jane) Williams, the wife/consort of the present Archbishop of Canterbury[14] and an eminent Biblical scholar in her own right, strongly suggests that this group is indeed "a means by which influence is brought to bear". That influence should, I hope and trust, prove a sound, moderating, wise influence, sensible in its practical and pragmatic tendencies (proof of the pudding . . .) and indeed broad minded – in

14. With Oliver O'Donovan, one of the dedicatees of *The Resurrection of the Son of God*. O'Donovan is a leading academic evangelical today.

other words moderately "liberal". All of which I find immensely reassuring.

Post-script: Most recently Bishop Tom has produced a first rate series of commentaries on all the letters of St. Paul. Under the general title *Paul for Everyone* and published by SPCK, they illustrate Wright's extraordinary gift for intelligible exegesis of Paul's difficult writings.

* * * * *

There are other eddies in the current tide of Anglican evangelicalism which are less reassuring. As an identifiable "movement" within the Church of England it remains deeply divided within itself. As part of the Stott legacy it is still largely synonymous *in the popular mind* with the "conservative" outlook. For some of its adherents this tendency is confirmed in a hardline reaction to current Anglican controversies. This finds particular expression in a pressure group called *Reform*. From a standpoint of Biblical fundamentalism, its members are explicitly committed to uncompromising opposition to all forms of homosexuality and to the ordination of those so orientated. They were also opposed, on similar grounds, to the ordination of women, whose ministry they will not accept, and naturally remain opposed to any prospect of women bishops.

The current controversy concerning homosexuality and the threat of schism in the Anglican Communion it represents will be considered at length in a later chapter.

AN EXCURSUS
Anglican Protestantism

A further important aspect of Low Church Evangelicalism that has thus far been ignored is its Protestantism, its anti-Roman polemic. We Anglicans who consider ourselves evangelicals generally bracket ourselves as Protestants too. In one sense we have no choice. By the very fact of our membership of the C. of E. or one of its sister churches in the Anglican Communion, we are simultaneously both Protestant *and* Catholic, whether we like it or not! We are catholic in its basic original sense of universal, simply because the Anglican Communion rightly claims to be part of the unhappily divided, universal catholic church of Christ. When, at the Reformation, we separated from the continental church of the Roman obedience, we did not leave the universal Christian brotherhood. So we remain Catholics, but not *Roman* Catholics. And we are Protestants for the same reason, i.e. simply because we are not Roman Catholic. Thus, as a simple matter of *fact*, the most pro-Roman Anglo-Catholic is a Protestant, willy nilly; and the most rabidly anti-Roman evangelical is a Catholic!

Some, but not all, Roman Catholics will dispute this. They believe, wrongly as Anglicans consider, that "the Catholic Church" comprises those, and *only* those in communion with the Bishop of Rome, the Pope. Thus they automatically exclude, not only us, but also the Eastern Orthodox, who, apart from brief spells in the later Middle Ages, have been out of communion with Rome ever since the Great Schism of 1054. (It is possible that this may, happily, no longer be the case, since recent popes, including John Paul II, have made strenuous and largely successful efforts to "mend fences" with the Orthodox owing allegiance to the Œcumenical Patriarch at Constantinople [Istanbul]. But this does not include the Russian Orthodox who remain virulently anti-Roman, and unwilling to welcome the Pope on a visit to Russia.)

So, I am a Protestant and, *as things stand*, a convinced one. As a matter of principle, I could not possibly join the Roman Catholic church *as it is now* – unlike Ann Widdicombe, John Selwyn Gummer, Bishop Graham Leonard, the Duchess of Kent and Tony Blair, all of them presumably former convinced (?) and loyal Anglicans. I do not question their sincerity, but I do question their judgment.[15]

Four obstacles to Reconciliation with Rome

For there are, for a start, at least four strong reasons preventing convinced Anglicans from even considering "going over" to Rome. Three of these originated in the nineteenth century and one in the twentieth.

1. Anglican Orders

The first is that in 1896 Pope Leo XIII issued a "Bull", *Apostolicae Curae*, condemning our Anglican Orders (ordinations to the ministries of bishop, priest and deacon) as absolutely null and utterly void. In other words, he declared that those ordained by Anglican bishops are not really deacons, priests and bishops at all. In 1897 his judgment was successfully contested in a learned and detailed Latin *Responsio* by the then-Archbishops of Canterbury and York, and the last word remained with them. It was unanswerable. I have no doubt whatever

15. The road between Canterbury and Rome sees traffic in both directions. One very notable defector from Rome to the C. of E. was the Belgian patristic scholar Amand de Mendieta. v. his *Rome and Canterbury, A Biblical and Free Catholicism* (1962). Another was Emile Cammaerts, also a Belgian.

that my ordinations as deacon and priest are entirely valid, and could not pretend otherwise.

2. and 3. New Marian Dogmas

Furthermore, Rome has *added* three "dogmas" to the orthodox Christian Faith as set forth in the historic creeds, Nicene and Apostles'. In this sense a dogma is defined as "a religious truth established by Divine Revelation and defined by The Church'" (*Ox. Dict. Chr. Ch.* art. "dogma"). Thus defined, it becomes a duty of "the Roman faithful" to accept and believe it. Two of these dogmas concern the Blessed Virgin Mary. The first, promulgated by Pope Pius IX in 1854, is the Dogma of her supposed Immaculate Conception; the second, by Pius XII in 1950, is that of her supposed *bodily* "Assumption" into heaven. Both were widespread "pious" beliefs among simple and credulous folk and, as such were more or less harmless. What was deeply objectionable, seeing that there is no warrant for them in Scripture, Reason, History or Plain Common Sense, was to purport to make them obligatory articles of belief for all loyal Catholics.

4. Papal Infallibility

The same applied to the third, Papal Infallibility, imposed, after prolonged controversy, at the First Vatican Council in 1870, much to the delight of its sponsor, Pius IX. This preposterous claim (defined as when the Pope as the Church's divinely appointed spokesman speaks *ex cathedra*, i.e from his throne) lies at the very heart of our Protestant controversy with Rome. Unless or until it is clearly rescinded there can be no possibility of reconciliation or reunion. That may, indeed does look realistically to many as a sheer *im*possibility, but I have (good) grounds for believing that it is *not* impossible. I have written more on this subject in Chapter 8. See especially pp. 190 ff.

Infallibility is in itself, in any shape or form, a concept fundamentally alien and insidiously dangerous to Christian faith and belief. This is true whether it be applied by Roman Catholics to their Church and Pope, by (some) Protestants to the Bible, or even, beyond Christendom, by Muslims to the Qur'an or Communists to the writings of Karl Marx. All are forms of fundamentalism.

A few pages back I quoted some profoundly wise words from the specifically *Evangelical* report *The Fullness of Christ* (1950). They are well worth repeating: "For neither Bible nor Church do we claim infallibility. That would be to ignore God's method of dealing with men, and to posit an overruling of the fact of human ignorance and fallibility which would do violence to men's personality and

freedom". To that quotation should be added another: "The Church of
Rome" it has been said "presumptuously claims for itself infallibility.
The Church of England is more modest and only claims that it is
right".[16]

I wrote just now that the concept of infallibility is insidiously
dangerous. This is because it holds a powerful attraction for weak,
lazy minds craving a false kind of certainty, a short cut, to save
themselves the trouble, exertion, sheer hard work of using the brain
the Creator has given them. They seek an infallible readymade
answer. But God, who has given each of us a mind of our own, has
also given us the responsibility to use it even at the risk of error. But
to save us from error and confusion he offers us the free guidance of
his Holy Spirit, the infinitely precious insight of what St. Paul calls
"the mind of Christ". (1 Cor. 2:16; Philippians 2. 5-10)

Those who make claims for infallibility usually refer to the words
attributed to Jesus in John 16:13. "When the Spirit of Truth is come,
he will guide you into all Truth". That is indeed a most valuable
text, and insight, and deserves to be pondered and treasured by all
Christians. In so doing we must make a very clear distinction between
Truth and Infallibility. They are not the same thing – far from it. Truth
is infinitely larger and it is Truth that we should seek, with the sure
guidance of the Spirit, which is neither automatic nor mechanical. If
we will allow him to, the Spirit will work in natural cooperation with
what Paul calls "our spirit" (Romans 8:16), meaning our free and
natural minds and personalities.

We must never give up seeking Truth which is infinite, divine,
and therefore above and beyond us (Isaiah 57:15 – some of the most
illuminating, yet baffling words in the Old Testament). Faith, seeking
God who is the ultimate Truth, is an adventure and like all adventures
it involves risk – an existential "betting your life" on Truth. If a
Newmarket tipster offers you "a dead cert for the 2.30", be wary of
him. Infallibility is "a dead cert".

Before temporarily taking leave of infallibility, let me take the risk
of hinting at what is to come in a later chapter – a kind of trailer, or
preview. It is good news for Protestants of similar mind to myself
that an outstanding *Roman Catholic* thinker, theologian and scholar
– who is also, to judge by the great books he has written, every bit
as good, if not better an evangelical than any of us – published a
deceptively short book as long ago as 1970 with the title (translated)
Infallibility? An Inquiry. It is a thorough "demolition job". In it he

16. A.E.J. Rawlinson and Charles Smyth: *The Genius of the Church of
England* (SPCK 1947). That pamphlet, too, deserves reprinting.

pulled the infallibility rug very neatly from under the Pope's feet. The Pope was not pleased! The then-Secretary of the World Council of Churches, the Dutch Protestant Visser t'Hooft wrote: "As I read it [the book], I felt more and more as if I had an atom bomb in my hand. For if these ideas are taken up in Catholicism, an entirely new situation will arise. Then Protestantism will no longer have any important reason for protesting". The author's name will no doubt be familiar to you: Hans Küng, a German Swiss, longtime Professor at Tübingen University in Germany. We shall meet this formidable man again in Chapter Eight.

Before closing this Protestant chapter I propose (despite the positive-thinking slogan) to concentrate our attention on two more of the less attractive aspects of the Roman Church that we can, and should, continue to protest about. Moving from the four specific topics of contention above, these issues turn towards fundamental aspects of Roman Catholicism that, one could argue, provide the framework upon which those constructs arose. The first is that extraordinary institution, the Papacy. It has been in existence for long enough for us to get used to it, perhaps to take it for granted, but, like all ancient institutions, it has despite appearances changed and developed over the centuries. The second, following on, is the Roman Church's ancient tendency towards controlling, directing, and defining the intellectual stances, indeed the very thoughts of its adherants and, so far as possible, its opponents

The unreformed Papacy

"The Papacy is no other than the ghost of the deceased Roman Empire, sitting crowned upon the grave thereof. For so did the papacy start up on a sudden out of the ruins of that heathen power". That is how it looked to Thomas Hobbes, the Malmesbury philosopher thought by most of his contemporaries to be a dangerous atheist, as, in 1651, he sat writing *Leviathan*. There was some truth in what he wrote. The Temporal Power of the Popes, with a whole swathe of Central Italy under their direct, but not strikingly efficient, rule, lasted for centuries. They traced its origin to the bogus so-called *Donation of Constantine* until that document was exposed as a fake. It ended in 1870, when the troops of Napoleon III, there to prop it up against the forces of the Risorgimento, were withdrawn to fight and be defeated by Bismarck, and it was absorbed into united Italy. It was revived in the minuscule form of the Vatican City under the 1929 Lateran Treaty negotiated by Pope Pius XI with Mussolini. It issues its own stamps and all foreign states desirous of diplomatic relations with it have their ambassadors accredited to the Holy See. (The British one always used to be, and probably still is, invariably a Protestant.) The Pope appoints a Cardinal Secretary of State to deal with "foreign affairs" and matters of protocol.

The Papacy is an absolute monarchy whose incumbent is elected for life. The last Pope to abdicate was in the thirteenth century, Celestine V in 1294. After doing so, he was promptly arrested by his overweeningly ambitious successor, the infamous Boniface VIII, and sent to prison where he died two years later. Despite being later canonised as a saint, his example is regarded with disfavour.

The Popes live and do their business amidst surroundings of unrivalled Renaissance and Baroque splendour with Swiss Guards in colourful fancy dress to protect them. On special occasions they emerge, robed all in white, on to the balcony overlooking the great, theatre-like piazza to survey and be seen by enormous crowds of the faithful and the curious and to bless the city and the world. All this is well known, and expected, and few would wish it otherwise. Much the same though in a very much lower key applies to Lambeth Palace and its principal tenants. But, one wonders, what sort of signal does it give?

Popes are incredibly busy and hard working. Their Court (the Curia) and the elaborate bureaucracy, including expert advisers and hangers on, is a huge administrative machine with tentacles world wide, all centralised in Rome. The Popes from time to time, as and when they see fit, publish Bulls and Encyclicals (letters in the customary flowery language favoured by the Vatican) addressed to the Church and the world in highly authoritative terms on all manner of subjects, moral, social, doctrinal.

How does all this match the apostolic and post-apostolic community reflected in the New Testament? "Their Holinesses the Supreme Pontiffs", styling themselves "Vicars" (i.e. deputies) of Christ and "servants of the servants of God", think of themselves as exercising a "Petrine" ministry, in remote but immediate succession to Simon bar Jonah (= Simon Johnson) nicknamed Peter, "the Rock", by his Master. In support of their claims, in which they no doubt implicitly believe, they trot out the well worn Gospel texts: Matthew 16:18 (You are Peter and upon this Rock I will build my Church. . . . I will give you the keys of the Kingdom . . . and the powers of binding and loosing); Luke 22.31f. (Simon I have prayed that your faith fail not...When once you have turned again, strengthen/stablish your brethren); and John 21. 15-21 (Simon son of John *do* you love me? . . . Tend my lambs; Feed my sheep).

In the light of modern critical scholarship and setting these texts in their original context, what do we make of them? It is a fair question. To the naïve (and most people, understandably, are and always were naïve in such matters) they sound most impressive and are taken as conclusive proof that Jesus envisaged or even instituted the Papacy! But to the common sense mature Biblical student/historian they carry no such implication. Comparing the accounts in the three synoptic Gospels of the same incident, the words added by Matthew to the earlier, more reliable, account in Mark 8. 29-33 (and the parallel in Luke 9.20) in which Matthew makes Jesus speak of "my Church" are *obviously* anachronistic and reflect later circumstances. As for the texts from Luke and John, if authentic they simply imply that Our Lord recognised Peter's natural leadership of the Twelve – nothing more than that.

Granted that the evidence of St. Peter's tomb under the (rebuilt) basilica that bears his name *may* impress, *there is no evidence whatever that, even if, as is probable, he was in Rome and martyred there, he was ever in any sense its first bishop.* Even so, the very antiquity of the claim and the extraordinary longevity of the institution may, perhaps should, command respect.

And what of the popes themselves? They were not all bad, or good, and there were some genuine saints among them. Perhaps the most outstanding was Gregory the Great (Pope 590-604), the first of that name, and the one who sent the reluctant monk Augustine to Kent in 596/7, as we should remember, ultimately to become the first archbishop of Canterbury, armed with the famous Gospel book now in the (Parker) Library of my old college. I have two books in my possession; one is by Mathias Prideaux, Fellow of Exeter College, Oxford and a contemporary of Hobbes. It was published at Oxford; my copy is the fifth edition of 1672. Entitled *An Easy and Compendious Introduction for Reading all sorts of Histories etc.* Chapter VIII begins with "The Life of our Saviour" and continues most instructively with the lives of all the Popes from St. Peter to Urban VIII (d.1644) who was still reigning when the book was written. As an exercise in papal muck raking it would please "Doctor" Paisley or the most rabid Ulster "Prod". There was plenty of scope. The Popes are usefully placed in successive historical categories – they seem to get progressively worse. The categories are (1) Hierarchs Apostolical (all the Apostles); (2) Good Bishops; (3) Tolerable Archbishops; (4) Patriarchs; (5) Usurping Nimrods; (6) Luxurious Sodomites; (7) Ægyptian Magitians; (8) Devouring Abaddons; (9 and finally) Incurable Babylonians including poor Urban VIII.

The other volume is modern viz. Peter de Rosa: *Vicars of Christ: The Dark Side of the Papacy* (Corgi, 1988). The author, Mr. or Signor de Rosa, is apparently an ex-priest, and this is perhaps to be seen as another exercise in muck raking, more sophisticated but not purely propagandist. It certainly tries to be fair and makes interesting reading, especially about more recent times. The reader is advised in all cases to check up on both the bad and good by referring to the more objective accounts in the current edition of the excellent *Oxford Dictionary of the Christian Church*, though even that, like the Bible and the Popes, is not infallible!

Intellectual coercion

The final topic for scrutiny is the long, discreditable history of intellectual coercion, bullying, persecution, censorship in the Roman Catholic Church. I do not intend to go into much detail (readers may be relieved to know), nor to go back further than "the Holy Office" as it was called, surprisingly enough, until Paul VI's reform of the Inquisition in 1968. The famous, or rather infamous, case of Galileo Galilei (1546-1642) is sufficiently well known. That appalling misjudgment has only recently been corrected – a feather in the cap of John Paul II. (It is one of the troubles of this deeply ingrained habit of "economy with the truth" that it is so painfully difficult to do a graceful about turn, to put things right and to apologise.) We should be deeply thankful that the good Lord has given us a patron saint of U turns in St. Paul. We all have to do it some time in our lives. It is good for us, and the more practice we can get the better. A prayer to St. Paul will help enormously. The Index of Prohibited Reading is another example of timid and frightened censorship at work. *Index Librorum Prohibitorum* is its proper Latin name. Its history appears to go back to 1557 and it came, naturally, under the aegis of the Holy Office (of the Inquisition). It is good to know that in 1966 "the Index ceased to have the force of ecclesiastical law, with attached censures, but at the same time the Congregation of the Doctrine of the Faith stated that it retains its moral force" (*Ox. Dict. Chr. Ch.*). Dare I comment?

When Professor Küng wrote his *Infallible?* he declined, on principle, to seek an *"imprimatur"* – knowing he would be unlikely to obtain one! This customary permission for a Catholic book to be published, together with a *nihil obstat*, did nothing to stop Küng's "atom bomb" from being translated and published far and wide.

It is devoutly to be hoped that the penny, or the euro, has at last dropped in the successor to the Holy Office, the Congregation of the

Doctrine of the Faith and all kindred Vatican officialdom, that the days of this sort of thing are numbered. I do not need to be reminded that the rationale of persecution, inquisition, censorship was the salvation of souls in peril of heresy, if need be by fire – *auto da fé*.

I hope that I have now written sufficient to establish my credentials as "a convinced Protestant" *as things now stand*. But no one would be more delighted if all this changed, leaving no further reason to protest.

Summing up

Putting both parts of this chapter together, I sum up my own position as follows:

I gladly take my stand as a Low Churchman, a (liberal) evangelical Protestant, affirming my faith, inadequate though it is (God forgive me) in God the Ultimate Reality, Source and Creator of all that is good, and loving, "Father" of all mankind. And I affirm my faith in Jesus of Nazareth, His Incarnate "Son", who has been called "the human face of God", the Head and Pioneer of restored Humanity. "God was in Christ reconciling the world to Himself" (2 Corinthians 5. 18f.) at the cost of his most precious life, laid down in sacrificial love, obedience and forgiveness for me and all mankind upon the cross, the "Good Shepherd laying down his life for his flock". I believe that He died and was buried and that "on the third day" he was raised from the dead, in the power of the Spirit, triumphant over evil, sin and death. I believe, too, that He achieved this as "the second, the new Adam" never to die again, the Pioneer of the human race, and that through his Spirit, he offers to all humanity the grace and power to follow where He has led the way.

Furthermore I believe that the Bible, being both the Scriptures of the Old and New Testaments, bear true, authentic and unique historical witness to God-in-Christ. This in mind, Christians should thankfully avail themselves of *all* the means that God has provided to enable us to understand and apply them, not least the dedicated work of sound scholarship, both literary and historical "criticism" (i.e. analysis), the application of patient common sense, and throughout all else, openness to the guidance of the Holy Spirit.

Finally, as a Protestant, while recognising and accepting the shared responsibility of all who claim to be Christians for the continuance of the grievous disunity we have inherited from past generations, I sadly acknowledge that, in present circumstances, I as an Anglican am separated from communion and fellowship with my brothers and sisters in Christ of the Roman Catholic, Orthodox and other churches.

I am thankful for progress towards reunion in the Ecumenical Movement in the last century and I long and pray and work for its completion, with God's help, in, hopefully, the near future, so that, visibly united once more, we can bear much more effective witness in mission and evangelism, especially to Jewry and Islam.

All this I seriously believe is involved in the stance of a Low Churchman today. But, even so, as such *it is incomplete*. From the Low Church standpoint we gaze straight down (or more precisely, up) the longitudinal axis of Truth to the opposite High Church end. In so doing we pass the central cross. And *they* there look "down" (I suppose *literally* but not *actually*) at us, wistfully as we to them. Or so we should. *For we belong together.* We need them (the *truly* Catholic Church *is part of the Gospel* – John makes Jesus say "*I am the True Vine and you are the branches*" (John 15. 1 and 5). And even further, "they" need "us" – every bit as much. Without "them" we are incomplete. And without "us" "they" are incomplete. This talk of "us" and "them" is nonsense. We are ultimately one, as shall be seen. In the meantime, however, I turn my attention to the Broad Church.

Postscript: a personal note

Although in many ways (as those who know me well realise) I am myself admittedly very *un*evangelical, I still desperately hope that my grievous shortcomings in that respect will be graciously overlooked at the Last Judgment, and that this penitent sinner will be pardoned by the gracious mercy of God in Christ. (For those still curious, footnote eleven to this chapter may go some way to elucidate the mystery.)

Chapter 3
Broad Church/Modernists/
Post-modernists/Liberals

We proceed in an anticlockwise direction round the dial of my putative ecclesiometer. Following that necessarily long drawn out exploration of evangelical low churchmanship at its base we eventually arrive at its easternmost extremity.

Here we have a little problem of nomenclature. In order to tally with the ecclesiometer, I have deliberately given pride of place in the chapter heading to the admittedly old fashioned, if not archaic, term "Broad Church". This is followed with "modernist", as the former Broad Churchmen were generally known when I was a boy; then (more for fun than anything) I add that absurd expression "post modernist" which is what the *avant garde* tell us is where we are now. I only *end* with the word which is now a term of opprobrium for many from Rome to the present day equivalent of Geneva – "liberal". But "liberal" is the in-word in most general use by both friend and foe for what this chapter (and a considerable part of its predecessor) is about, and therefore I shall use it in future, except where it is inappropriate historically.

But first I must confess to a certain fondness for the expression Broad Churchmanship, and not only for pedantic ecclesiometrical reasons. The *Oxford English Dictionary* (second edn. 1989) tells us that it was first used in conversation in or about 1848 and, on the authority of no less a Broad Churchman than Benjamin Jowett, formidable Master of Balliol, Oxford, attributes its invention to that quizzical poet and man of letters, Arthur Hugh Clough. It is obviously a natural extension of the much earlier "High" and "Low" Church" parties and was made use of by the aforementioned W.J. Coneybeare in his 1853 *Edinburgh Review* article on Church Parties. It also has the merit of a verbal link with what Dryden called "your sons of latitude" – the "Latitudinarians" of the late-seventeenth and eighteenth centuries, the Broad Churchmen's intellectual and spiritual forebears.

To dally for a moment longer with Broad Churchmanship properly so called, if Clough is reliably credited with originating the term, it is hardly in doubt that its positively *final* appearance in English Literature is due to an equally quizzical poet, John Betjeman:

> Broad of Church and broad of mind
> Broad before and broad behind
> A keen ecclesiologist
> A rather dirty Wykehamist.

This opening stanza of *The Wykehamist* appeared in Betjeman's *Continual Dew* (John Murray 1937). A little earlier than that, surely, was the libellous tag: "High and crazy; Low and lazy; Broad and hazy".

Nowadays the expression "Broad Church" still survives but in a different connotation. It is commonly found in the media to describe, no longer a *Church* party, but a *political* party, as when the Tories or Labour are said to be "a broad church", i.e. inclusive or comprehensive of members of widely differing standpoints and backgrounds. This accords with the useful definition offered by the *Oxford English Dictionary*: "A designation popularly applied to members of the Church of England who take its formularies and doctrines in a broad or liberal sense, and hold that the Church should be comprehensive and tolerant, so as to admit of more or less variety of opinion in matters of dogma and ritual."

A Broad Church/Liberal pedigree

Before attempting to define in more detail where we moderate liberals stand today and where we draw the line with radical sceptical rationalists, I would like for a moment to return to the definition of "broad church" given above. With that basic outline in mind, together with the moderate liberal's intimate relationship with basic evangelicalism as it emerged from the last chapter, and with basic Catholicism (to anticipate the next one), I propose to indulge my preoccupation with history by sketching in outline our Broad Church pedigree as I see it.

To make the point that we Anglicans lay no claims to a monopoly of the characteristic liberal stance, I divide this "pedigree" into two: (i) from the beginning of Christianity up to the sixteenth century Reformation and (ii) from then up to recent times *within Anglicanism*. Especially in part (i) this is a highly controversial exercise and one of my criteria for inclusion is a ready capacity for adventurous, even eccentric thinking, risking accusations of heresy.

Dare I begin by suggesting that our Lord himself was the archetypal Broad Churchman, never afraid to shock his hearers into thinking for themselves and acting accordingly, going behind man made "tradition" to the root of a matter? And naturally his less "conservative" disciples followed His example – Paul had to rethink everything in the light of his conversion: his letters are the result. And what of that learned Jew from Alexandria who was "mighty in the Scriptures" (Acts 18. 24f; 1 Cor. 3. 4f.), Apollos? There is a real possibility that he was the author of the subtly argued Epistle to the Hebrews.

In early Church history I would point to two other polymaths also from Alexandria, that stimulating centre of neo-Platonism, Clement (second century) and the very great scholar, critic and spiritual writer, Origen (c.185-254), both of whom wrote in defence of Christianity against its pagan critic, Celsus. That points to another characteristic (as I see it) of the moderate liberal stance, the fact that from earliest times they proved stalwart apologists for the Faith against its detractors. A possibly even greater scholar than Origen was the formidable St. Jerome (Hieronymus) (c.340-420). To him we owe the Vulgate, the translation of the entire Bible from its original languages into Latin. He acted as secretary to Pope Damasus, and, after travelling widely in the Middle East, settled in Bethlehem where he spent the last thirty-four years of his life as an ascetic. He had all of the genuine scholar's acerbity in controversy, on which he thrived. He was a contemporary of St. Ambrose and the latter's protégé, the towering figure of St. Augustine of Hippo. Was the latter a proto-liberal too? He seems, in some ways, a *most* unlikely candidate but his famous *Confessions* could give him eligibility. I ought to have included at least one of the *Greek* Fathers from this early period. How about *either* St. Athanasius of Alexandria, so valiant for orthodox doctrine, and so clear thinking, *or* St. John Chrysostom (the golden mouthed), tactless and fearless against the Constantinople establishment of his day, another of Jerome's contemporaries?

From that time on, until the Renaissance and dawn of the Reformation a millennium later, we must confine ourselves to the British Isles and need to be extremely selective. I bid for four only. My first is St. Columba (c.521-597) the "dove" of the Church who after a dispute about copyright, sailed in a coracle from Derry to Iona, the cradle of British Christianity. He represents all adventurous monks. Leaving aside the great St. Cuthbert, my second choice is that other great Celt, John Scotus Eriugena (c.810-877), a truly original thinker. For the third and fourth, partly for personal reasons but emphatically on merit, two outstanding Franciscans, first that stubbornly independent polymath the Suffolk-born Robert Grosseteste[1] (c.1170-1253) Bishop of Lincoln. (Probably I ought to have included his predecessor at Lincoln, the great St. Hugh who like Grosseteste, feared no one.) But I could not omit that prototype scientist, Roger Bacon (c.1220-1292).

The *serious* intellectual pedigree *must*, surely, begin with Desiderius Erasmus of Rotterdam (c.1467-1536), no saint but the quintessential father figure of all true Broad Church liberals, brilliant Renaissance scholar, wit, man of letters and Christian humanist. No Englishman, yet, because he spent much of the middle period of his life in Cambridge, where he was the first to teach Greek, we could almost claim him as a *naturalised* Englishmen. He became a friend of John Colet, Dean of St. Paul's and very much of his way of thinking, and of Thomas More and John Fisher, both of whom were to perish as Catholic martyrs in the year he died. Jerome incidentally was Erasmus' favourite of the Latin Fathers. "Though he had himself paved the way for the Reformation by his merciless satires on the doctrines and institutions of the Church, his scholarly character, which abhorred violence and sought tranquillity, prevented him from joining the Protestants, and threw him back on the tradition of the Church as the safeguard of stability." (art. Erasmus in *Oxford Dictionary of the Christian Church* (3rd edn. 1997)). Had Henry VIII been more of his civilised way of thinking, the English Reformation would have taken a very different course, and More and Fisher been denied their martyr's crowns.

After Erasmus I would bid to include the judicious Richard Hooker (c.1554-1600), a rare cross-bench mind among Elizabethan Anglicans in that age of understandably polarised opinions, and, in his book *Of the Laws of Ecclesiastical Polity*, the architect of the rationale of the Anglican Church Settlement. William Chillingworth (1602-1644), a friend of Archbishop Laud, whose *Religion of Protestants a Safe Way to Salvation* (1638) defended reason and free inquiry in doctrinal matters and "the Bible only as the true religion of Protestants". Having converted to Rome and returned to the C. of E. he must be included.

Many, if not most, historians would probably begin a *specific* Broad Church/liberal pedigree with the Cambridge Platonists, notably Benjamin Whichcote, Ralph Cudworth and Henry More in the mid-seventeenth century, and their successors the aptly named Latitudinarians. A sympathetic contemporary of the Cambridge Platonists and a great and good man in his own right, John Ray (1627-

1. As an Honorary Canon of St. Edmundsbury Cathedral from 1975-87, I occupied the stall named after him.

1705), prolific pioneer naturalist parson, father of English botany, and author of the deservedly best selling *Wisdom of God in the Works of Creation*. The fine *Life of Ray* by his devoted twentieth-century disciple, Charles Raven, amply makes the case for his inclusion. I would also include that singular medico, Sir Thomas Browne (1605-1682) of Norwich, president of the Royal College of Physicians and author of *Religio Medici* and other works, a devout Anglican who fits easily into no category.

I must try hard not to be greedy, but two outstanding eighteenth-century Anglican divines have a strong claim to be included. They are Joseph Butler (1692-1752), bishop successively of Bristol and Durham and author of the justly famous *Analogy of Religion* (1736), which finally put paid to the Deists, and William Whiston (1667-1752), wildly eccentric but brilliantly erudite translator and editor of Josephus, the Jewish historian.

With the nineteenth century we enter the Broad Church era proper and names come thick and fast, beginning with Richard Whately (1787-1863), successively Rector of Halesworth, Suffolk and Archbishop of Dublin. He wrote a celebrated skit on rationalist criticism, *Historic Doubts relative to Napoleon Buonaparte,* and was the leading light of the "Noetics" at Oriel College, Oxford, a constant irritant to the early Tractarians. Other "Noetics" were the egregious Spanish émigré whose name was quaintly anglicised as Joseph Blanco White (1775-1841); the great Thomas Arnold (1795-1842), Headmaster of Rugby; Mark Pattison (1813-1884); and Julius Hare (1795-1855). I almost forgot Thomas (Tom) Hughes (1822-1896), author of *Tom Brown's Schooldays* and of the fine hymn "O God of Truth whose living word" (English Hymnal 449). It deserves to be revived and sung as the liberal Broad Churchman's battle hymn.

Preoccupation with the Noetics has led us to bypass two distinguished candidates. Samuel Taylor Coleridge (1772-1834) Romantic poet, naturalist, and profound thinker, whose conviction that Christianity is primarily ethical led him to believe in the possibility of a unification of Christendom on a wide basis of common tenets, earning him the title of The Father of the Broad Church Movement. If Coleridge was the father, and that could well be disputed, was one of his (legitimate?) offspring Frederick Denison Maurice (1805-1872), and what of the Christian Socialists? Among *its* children, whose legitimacy no one would dare question, were the contributors to *Essays and Reviews* (1860), foremost among them the outstanding names of Frederick Temple (1821-1902), later Archbishop of Canterbury (and earlier a successor of Arnold and Tait as Headmaster of Rugby); and Benjamin Jowett (1817-1893), to whom we have had occasion to refer already.

All these Broad Church radicals were sturdy Victorian individualists. There was no Broad Church party as such. It was not until 1898 that there was founded "for the advancement of liberal religious thought" to bind men of their way of thinking together what was called simply The Churchmen's Union. In 1928 this was changed to The Modern Churchmen's Union, and again, in 1987 to conform to political correctness, to the Modern Church People's Union. Its presiding genius at one time was David L. Edwards, sometime Fellow of All Souls, Oxford, whom we met at length in the last chapter in lively dialogue with John Stott.

Amongst leading "modernists" in what may be considered the heyday of the movement c.1920-1970 was E.W. Barnes, Bishop of Birmingham (Ramsay MacDonald's first Church appointment) and author of *The Rise of Christianity* (1947) – an extraordinarily unsatisfactory book which caused great scandal. Three Deans may also be included: Hastings Rashdalt of Carlisle; "the Gloomy Dean", W.R. Inge (1860-1954), a brilliant intellect and writer on mysticism; and W.R. Matthews, a wise and level headed theologian who succeeded Inge as Dean of St. Pauls. Between them they presided over London's Cathedral from 1911 to 1967. Others were H.D.A. Major, for many years Principal of Ripon Hall, Oxford, the only professedly "modernist" Anglican theological college, his collaborator and successor at Ripon R.D. Richardson (1893-1989), and finally *his* successor, Geoffrey Allen[2] (later Bishop of Derby), who prepared the way for Ripon's successful amalgamation with the prestigious and traditionalist High Church Cuddesdon.

Almost certainly, the outstanding representative of the *moderate* "Liberal" tradition today is the Very Reverend David L. Edwards aforementioned. Whether he would describe himself as a *post-modernist* I know not. As for the *im*moderate "Liberals" (or however else they should be described), reference will be made to them later in this chapter. After all, we should never forget that "liberal" and "conservative" (the subject of chapter 5) are ultimately both adjectives.

So much (more than enough, you may think) for my putative Broad Church/liberal pedigree. Of course it is open to criticism, but if at least its main constituents are agreed, I hope you will concur that, at

2. Allen offered me a job on the staff there. I turned it down on the realistic (rather than mock modest) grounds that both spiritually and theologically I was not up to it.

the very lowest estimate, it is a respectable one. Few obvious saints perhaps, no women, not many men of action, but plenty of sages and academics and an abundance of common sense!

Continental theological Liberalism

In order to widen the perspective and enable us to see this Anglican Broad Church liberalism in relation and *contrast* to its Continental opposite number, it will be as well to glance briefly at contemporary developments in Western Europe, both Protestant and Catholic.

The background of both was the aftermath of the eighteenth-century Enlightenment with *savants* such as Voltaire, Rousseau and the Encyclopédistes mocking established Christianity as outmoded.

In Protestant Germany the influence of Kant and of Hegelian idealist philosophy was paramount, extinguishing what remained of the wholesome positive Christian orthodoxy of Leibniz (1646-1716). Whereas Lessing, Kant and Hegel himself all professed in some sense to be Christians, in practice the Christian theology taught in such universities as Tübingen, Jena, Berlin and Gottingen was heavily influenced by the sceptical traditions inherited from Reimarus and F.C. Baur and evidenced, for example, in D.F. Strauss's reductionist *Life of Jesus* (1835). German thoroughness and industry produced some examples of massive erudition, but the almost universal "Liberal" orthodoxy in regard to Christian origins took the unquestioned form that Christian dogma and Church organisation derived wholly, not from the simple teaching of Jesus the Galilean peasant, but from Paul, who had developed the Jesus of history into the Christ of faith. This was the theory at the heart of the teaching of Adolf Harnack, the immensely learned historian of Christian doctrine (1851-1930) who personified German Liberalism at the turn of the century. Indeed, such was his influence and prestige that he was ennobled by the Kaiser in 1914, permitting him to prefix the coveted "von" to his surname. Behind Harnack, a little to one side, loomed the sinister ghosts of Nietzsche, Feuerbach, Schopenhauer and Marx, exponents of one form or other of atheism and dialectical materialism. Nothing further from (moderate) liberal Broad Churchmanship could be imagined.

Meanwhile in Roman Catholic Western Europe the new "modernist" label was having powerful continental resonance in Catholic Modernism, the *avant garde* movement *within* the Roman Catholic Church around the turn of the twentieth century. Outstanding among its adherents were the pioneering French Biblical scholar, Alfred Loisy, the German mystical/spiritual writer, Baron Friedrich von Hügel, who spent most of his life in England, and the English

Jesuit theologian, George Tyrell. This movement, described by its critics as "the synthesis of all the heresies", came increasingly under suspicion at Rome where it had been given some countenance by Leo XIII in his declining years. His successor, the "ignorant peasant" Pius X, condemned it outright in 1907 and imposed an "Anti-Modernist" Oath on all RC clerics at their ordination. Until comparatively recently, severe restrictions were imposed on RC Biblical scholarship with stultifying effect. For example, scholars were forbidden to assert the priority of Mark to Matthew and Luke. The consequent isolation of would-be RC scholars from the rest of the learned world, which still existed in my time at Cambridge, is now fortunately a thing of the past, but RC scholars are still cautious![3]

Modernism and the Thirty Nine Articles

Returning to modernism within the *Anglican* church, in the earlier years of the last century it had been largely concerned with questioning the supernatural features of Christian belief in its traditional form. Its main targets were miracles and particularly the Virgin Birth (or, as it is currently styled, the Virginal Conception of our Lord) in the light of the New Testament critically examined, intrinsic improbability, and the known character of God. The *reality* of the Incarnation was not in question. On the doctrine of the Atonement, Hastings Rashdall expounded it subjectively, discounting its objective presentation in the New Testament. This "exemplary" view echoed that of Abelard in the twelfth century.

In the background of all the more daring Broad Church thinking lurked a persistent nagging question. Clergymen were obliged by law at their ordination and on taking up every new Church appointment to "subscribe and assent to" the Thirty-Nine Articles[4] of Religion, the Book of Common Prayer, and the Ordinal, as well as declare that they "believe" the doctrine of the Church of England as therein set forth to be "agreeable to the Word of God". Indeed, this declaration was often not only made publicly and solemnly, but in many cases repeatedly. How far, then, if at all, were clergymen so committed at liberty, both in law and in conscience, to engage in free and unfettered

3. The excellent commentary on St. Luke's Gospel by the Dominican, Dom Henry Wansbrough (Bible Reading Fellowship) is a fine example of RC Biblical scholarship today.

4. It is said that Winston Churchill, when Prime Minister, chipped either Archbishop William Temple or his successor, Geoffrey Fisher, "They tell me, your Grace, that at Lambeth [Palace] you have forty bedrooms. How is it that you only have 39 articles?"

enquiry and debate on such doctrinal matters as referred to above, and others of the kind?

This was a serious question because compulsory assent to these archaic Articles placed an intolerable and unnecessary burden on so many consciences, (including mine). A serious answer did not arise until 1968, when a report of the Archbishop's Commission on Christian Doctrine on *Subscription and Assent to the 39 Articles* was published.[5]

Discussion following its publication led eventually to the formulation of a new and much more widely acceptable Declaration of Assent which, having duly passed through General Synod and received the Royal Assent, became law in 1975, replacing the procedure laid down in the Clerical Subscription Act of 1865. It seems hardly credible now, more than a quarter of a century later, that at my institution and induction to my first two benefices in 1951 and 1970 respectively I was obliged not only to make the old, archaic declaration laid down in the Act of 1865, but also in the course of the following Sunday's services to read the 39 Articles in full to the congregation in order to reaffirm my assent and to have this formally witnessed by the two churchwardens – the whole performance taking almost two hours. An inauspicious start to one's new ministry indeed! This was called "reading oneself in". It might so easily have had the effect of reading the congregation out, never to return!

Because the wording of the new, or not so new, Preface and Declaration of Assent deserves to be as widely known as possible they are printed in full in an Appendix to this chapter.

The Broad Church liberal stance today

Following that necessary digression, it remains for me to summarise as best I can what seems to be the characteristic stance of the moderate Broad Church liberal today.

Two elderly men of integrity and brilliant intellect represent that stance better than anyone else: David Edwards and John (Lord) Habgood, Archbishop of York from 1983 to 1995. Both write with genuine authority and total clarity, somehow managing to avoid technical language in a manner that emulates the very broadmindedness and inclusiveness they preach. A third, younger man of equal distinction, Rowan Williams, the current Archbishop of Canterbury, has or at least until recently had an uncanny – and

5. By SPCK. The Report is a notably thorough and even-handed examination of the problem, which did the Commission great credit. Its recommendations, slightly modified, were not acted upon until as recently as 1975.

unfortunate – gift for obscurity in writing and utterance which too often leaves his audience baffled as to his precise meaning. He is a hopeless communicator, despite his impressive appearance.[6]

Edwards' point of view found generous expression in the preceding chapter, at least on the purely Biblical/theological front. We therefore turn now to Habgood. His background was scientific and agnostic if not atheist until he came to full Christian conviction in his time at King's College, Cambridge. It is, perhaps, out of these critical beginnings that the emphasis on credibility which would come to define his writings as a churchman grew. "The biggest challenges facing the churches today concern the credibility of the gospel" he wrote in his *Confessions of a Conservative Liberal* (SPCK 1988). He continues: "This is not just an intellectual matter: credibility has to be demonstrated as much by what the churches do as by what they say. But it has an intellectual dimension to it and if I concentrate on that it is because that is where most of the recent argument has been, and where some of the toughest work still remains to be done."[7] Those words are every bit as true today as when they were published in 1988.

Christians and the churches to which they belong are under relentless heavy attack by militant secularists/atheists/sceptics on all fronts, from the explicit advances of the media, to the unspoken implications of the spirit of the secular pluralist age in which, willy nilly, we live. What is at stake is credibility, the credibility of the (still deeply divided) church and its often deeply discreditable history of persecution, intolerance and bigotry. At risk is the credibility of the gospel itself, of the Bible, and the Creeds. When the integrity of those building blocks of the faith is called into question, the credibility of practicalities built upon them must follow: Christian ethics, be they in the fields of relationships international, national, racial, and above all personal, or in the field of human rights and responsibilities, or in the application of modern science and technology – the immensely complex fields of medical and sexual ethics for example.

In all these fields credibility, the believableness of the *basic* Christian beliefs and understandings, is entirely defensible at different levels. At the highest intellectual level on which (for example) the wise, experienced and subtle mind of John Habgood is engaged, highly specialised knowledge – as of medical ethics – must be deployed. At a more "popular" level the lively, rapier-like wit and gifts of

6. This is now largely compensated by the recent (2007) appointment as his opposite number at York of the evangelical John Sentamu, a brilliant communicator.

7. John Habgood: *Confessions of a Conservative Liberal* (SPCK 1988) p. 4

apt illustration of John Sentamu are appropriate. In these forms and countless many more, the never-ending task of educating an intelligent and committed laity – and clergy – in informed awareness of the more fundamental Christian principles continues to be vital.

There is a huge task of Christian apologetics needing to be undertaken if the powerful tide of militant secularism is to be turned and overcome and this (it seems to me) is a God-given opportunity for moderate, level-headed, orthodox (i.e. right thinking) Broad Church liberals. As I hope to demonstrate, with particular reference to my own Anglican Church, all of us professing Christians *ought* to be Broad Church "liberals" as well as "Low" Church evangelicals (*and* High Church Catholics and "Narrow" Church "conservatives" in the true sense of that word) into the bargain but the particular calling or expertise of the "liberal" *per se* must be in carefully, lovingly reasoned apologetic just as that of the "evangelical" *per se* must be in warm hearted evangelism, in "sharing" the Gospel, introducing our neighbours to God in Christ, by unselfconscious Christlike behaviour. But, as I have implied, all these characteristics *belong together.*

The true Christian "liberal", then, ideally is deeply concerned to establish and defend the truth, credibility and relevance to every aspect of life and thought of basic Christian belief today. To do this effectively he believes it to be essential to be completely open, with no restriction or preconception, to all *genuine* science and *true* knowledge, ancient as well as modern. He sets immense store by fearless intellectual honesty and integrity and respects it in others whatever form it takes. He is as keen as any professing evangelical to share and promote his Christian faith, but to present it in its basic *essence*, all *in*essentials ruthlessly pruned away. He sees a clear differentiation between poetry and myth, a fine distinction requiring delicate handling and sound judgment for which he constantly prays to God the Holy Spirit. And he is constantly on his guard against giving needless offence.

The foregoing is the ideal and we all fall short of it. Some Broad Church liberals are notoriously tactless and insensitive and serious offence has often been pointlessly caused. The prime case in recent years was that of David Jenkins, a guileless professional theologian appointed to the see of Durham. His rash, ill-considered remarks (such as the notorious aside about the resurrection of Christ – "conjuring tricks with bones"), eagerly seized upon and gleefully reported in the national press, caused endless embarrassment and eventually led to the publication in 1986, by the House of Bishops of the C. of E. General Synod, of a reassuring Statement and Exposition of *The Nature of*

Christian Belief, in which the wise guiding hand of John Austin Baker, the then-Bishop of Salisbury, could be detected. Yet, to do him justice, Bishop Jenkins's straightforward positive teaching away from the Press was widely appreciated by many ordinary people in his diocese.[8]

As well as sensitivity, careful use of language and a keen sense of responsibility, Broad Churchmen, especially those in prominent positions, need deliberately to seek the grace of humility and of openness, not only to reason and the findings of science, but also and particularly to awareness of transcendence, the genuinely holy and numinous. They must recognise that "with God, all things are possible" (Mark 10. 27) (even miracles!) and not be afraid to admit that within basic Christian faith there are some areas of unavoidable uncertainty. "Now we see in a mirror dimly, but then face to face. Now I know in part, then I shall understand fully." (1 Cor. 13. 12)

The Broad Churchman/liberal values St. Anselm's *credo ut intelligam* (I believe *in order that* I may understand) as well as Cowper's "Blind unbelief is sure to err and scan His works in vain". He is in the difficult business of Christian apologetics, seeking "to justify the ways of God to man", in the widest conceivable, the cosmological, perspective.

In line with Paul, John, the writer to the Hebrews and the united witness of the New Testament, the Broad Churchman finds total credibility in the divinely appointed role of the man Jesus at the very centre of time and of the created universe. Christ is seen as "the new Adam", pioneer and prototype of restored, redeemed humanity. On behalf of all mankind and in the all-conquering power of divine love, he blazed a victorious trail, "the Way", through death on the cross to Life Eternal, the Good Shepherd laying down his life for his sheep, and rising triumphant in the power and glory of his (and our) Father-Creator. In the ongoing work of the Holy Spirit, *His* Spirit, the Spirit of Truth, this same triumphant Christ breathes his vitality and energy into his living "embodiment", the universal (catholic) apostolic People of God, ideally the worldwide, outgoing, missionary "Church". (v. especially Hebrews 10.19, 1 Corinthians 15, Romans 8, Colossians and John 10). In this sense following in the wake of Erasmus and Michael Ramsey, the Broad Church Liberal is not afraid to acknowledge himself a Christian Humanist.[9]

---

8. Jenkins *The Calling of a Cuckoo: Not Quite an Autobiography* (Continuum 2002) is good reading.

9. Ramsey's Firth lectures, given in the University of Nottingham, were published under the title *The Faith of a Christian Humanist* (SCM Press 1960). v. A.M Ramsey *Introducing the Christian Faith* (SCM 1961, p. 9)

Christian Cosmology: Polkinghorne and Peacocke

A superb example of this credible, cosmological faith is John Polkinghorne's 1993/4 Gifford lectures, published in book form as *Science and Christian Belief: Theological Reflections of a bottom up thinker* (SPCK 1994). Surely this book, Polkinghorne's *chef d'œuvre*, will come to be recognised as one of the most outstanding works of Christian thought and apologetics of our time. Its author, a Fellow of the Royal Society and a Doctor of Divinity (an excellent, if rare, combination) and a former Professor of Mathematical Physics at Cambridge, writes with quietly assured authority in the cosmological sphere comparable in all respects to that of the much more widely renowned author of *A Brief History of Time*, the avowed atheist Stephen Hawking. I find this immensely reassuring, the more so when it is matched by Polkinghorne's equal expertise in theology and Biblical studies. Though probably uninterested in such "labels", I imagine he would not disclaim standing in the Broad Church tradition, with the illustrious, if a little farfetched, pedigree I have claimed for it. But that he is no wild radical is witnessed by his bold and admirable decision to frame his Giffords in the detailed, step-by-step, explicit context of the Nicene Creed (modern version). What more striking claim to orthodoxy could there be?

At this point I ought to make an abject confession. Few, if any, could be more dismally ignorant than I in the entire field of science and technology – as will become embarrassingly apparent when I attempt a description of my ecclesiometer. I have to confess, therefore, that despite having recourse to the useful scientific glossary provided in the book, I should not recognise one of Polkinghorne's beloved quarks if I met it in the street; nor have I so much as tasted quark soup (*op.cit.* p. 21). I am sure it is delicious. As for gluons . . . so I was very much at sea in his first two chapters – hard though I did try to master them. But when it came to what was more readily comprehensible by poor little me in the rest of the book, I recognised not only the truth of what was written, but also the lucidity and elegance with which it was expressed. I therefore concluded, with the Broad Churchman's trusting faith – not blind credulity or wishful thinking – that in those first two chapters the author could be trusted to know what he was talking about, as well as in the rest, even though, through my culpable ignorance, I did not.

To this I must add a kind of extended footnote. It in no way detracts from Dr. Polkinghorne's achievement that until October 2006 he was not alone on a solitary eminence. Arthur Peacocke, who died in that month, was another distinguished scientist who was later ordained in the Anglican ministry. Educated at Watford Grammar School and Oxford, he studied biochemistry under the Nobel laureate Sir Cyril Hinshelwood, and lectured at Birmingham University. He developed a strong interest in theology and after ordination was elected a Fellow of Clare College, Cambridge where he taught both science and theology and served in "the liberal apostolic succession" of Telfer, Moule, Wiles, Rowan Williams and John Robinson as Dean of Clare's austerely elegant chapel. In 1988 he returned to Oxford to run the Ian Ramsey Centre for the study of science and theology. Probably his major published work was his collected 1978 Bampton Lectures entitled *Creation and the World of Science*. He also delivered a course of Gifford Lectures. In the last week of his life he wrote, referring to the cancer from which he died: "This is a new challenge to the integrity of my past thinking. I am only enabled to meet this challenge by my root conviction that God is Love as revealed supremely in the life, death and resurrection of Jesus the Christ. I know that God is waiting for me to be enfolded in love." In this belief he founded the Society of Ordained Scientists,[10] the current chairman of which is the Suffragan Bishop of Thetford, David Atkinson.

It is surely quite something that, for all its troubles, the C. of E. should have produced two such brilliant scientist-priest-philosophers as Polkinghorne and Peacocke. Indeed, others of similarly towering stature could be named, including John Habgood and the late Bishop Hugh Montefiore, cast in the same mould, in the succession of John Ray, Stephen Hales (1677-1761) John Stevens Henslow (1796-1861) and Charles Raven (1885-1964) in earlier generations.

The task of Christian apologetics today

Having interrupted myself in full spate, I now return to the specifically Broad Church liberal standpoint today. Our overriding task (it seems to me) is that of apologetics, i.e. the defence and exposition of basic orthodox Christian belief in the face of multi-pronged attack.

Although it is essentially one unified task, in these days of advanced specialisation a threefold distinction can usefully be drawn.

1. In the widest, cosmological context, as we have just seen, this has been and still is being undertaken at the highest level, brilliantly and effectively, by the two scientist-theologians, Drs. Peacocke and Polkinghorne.

---

10. I owe this biographical information to his obituaries in *The Times* and *Church Times*.

2. In the even more rarified field of philosophical argument, in which until recently we had to encounter that formidable logical Positivist, the late Sir Alfred Ayer, the case for the very existence of God (or should we write "God"?) is conducted almost single-handedly, with equal aplomb, by another Anglican, Richard Swinburne, sometime Nolloth Professor of the Philosophy of Religion at Oxford and author of the impressive trilogy *The Coherence of Theism, The Existence of God* and *Faith and Reason*.[11]

3. In the narrower, highly specialised field of what are nowadays called "Jesus studies" and the intimately linked study of Christian Origins, which we have already considered at length in the previous chapter, but to which we return now.

The Jesus Debate:[12] Vermes versus Wright

In the previous chapter, with its focus on the distinctively *Evangelical* viewpoint, much space was devoted to Bishop Tom Wright and his monumental but still incomplete work on *Christian Origins and the Question of God*, seen there as a salutary corrective to the "popular" picture of Jesus presented in some contemporary evangelism. Here, focusing on the Broad Church/Liberal concern with the more subtle field of Christian apologetics, seen in this context as correcting radical distortions of the central figure of Jesus and his (for want of a better word) mission to his contemporaries and to posterity, I want to reconsider Wright's work from a slightly different angle. It is a major masterpiece of Christian apologetics to confute a minor masterpiece of brilliant *mis*information.

Before we can proceed any further it is essential once again to

---

11. In this connection it is relevant to refer to the outstanding BBC series *The Case against God*, so brilliantly presented in 1983/4 by Gerald Priestland, their justly renowned Religious Affairs correspondent, whose subsequent death was widely lamented. In his inimitable, even-handed way, Priestland, a Quaker, interviewed eighty one high powered representative people on both sides of the argument, among them many who have appeared in these pages. The interviews are all recorded in a fascinating book, *The Case against God* (Collins 1984). It was dedicated by Priestland, "with respect, to the doubtful".

12. *The Jesus Debate* is the title of an excellent, non-technical book by Mark Allen Powell, published in 1998 by Lion, Oxford with the subtitle *Modern historians investigate the life of Christ*. It is the story of recent work, chiefly in USA and Britain, described in the subtitle and culminating in Wright's *magnum opus*. Assuch it is strongly recommended to the non-technical reader. A more technical symposium, equally excellent, is *The Cambridge Companion to Jesus* (ed. M. Bockmuehl) CUP 2001.

underline the crucial difference between the Anglican and the continental concepts of this ambivalent word "liberal" as used to described or define a theological standpoint. From our Anglican and basically orthodox Christian angle, continental "liberalism", exemplified by Enlightenment *savants* such as Reimarus, David Strauss, Renan, Harnack, Loisy *et al.*, was radically reductionist. That is to say, it saw Jesus, not as the incarnate Son of God/Saviour, but as an unsophisticated Galilean prophet/'holy man', a teacher of timeless truths and basic morality, executed for his stubborn non-conformity to the Jewish establishment and implicit hostility to Roman imperialism. These so-called "liberals" did not themselves believe in his resurrection, which they rejected along with all miraculous elements in the gospels – but accepted that his followers had somehow convinced themselves of it. They maintained that Paul, "John" and the writer of the Epistle to the Hebrews, in contrast to Jesus all sophisticated theologians, had, between them, in effect invented New Testament Christology and applied it to Jesus. This led ultimately to the stance that Paul, not Jesus, was the founder of institutional "Churchianity". There were, naturally, infinite variations on this basic theme, most of them dressed up in an impressive display of erudition.

Such was "orthodox" continental "liberalism" as developed in the nineteenth and twentieth centuries. Its influence spread to this country and was made to seem in the highest degree plausible. In fact it is highly probable that, even among the dwindling numbers of regular churchgoers and communicants today – to say nothing of the less educated clergy and lay readers – this travesty of the truth has become common currency. Despite the plethora of much more intelligible Bible translations and the dedicated – and successful – work of J.B. Phillips and others in paraphrasing the "letters to young churches", a superficial, sporadic acquaintance with the synoptic gospels, and a lazy disinclination to get to grips with "those difficult epistles", brief extracts from which are often unintelligently or inaudibly or perfunctorily read in the Communion service, have resulted in a sentimental affection for the supposedly simple gospel of Jesus contrasted with the widely unpopular "theology"[13] of that impossibly difficult St. Paul. (Here Tom Wright's current series of short, pithy "people's commentaries" should eventually help to turn the tide.)

However this may be, this characteristic continental "liberal" travesty has recently resurfaced yet again in what, to my mind at least, is a seductively plausible form. This is a compact little book published by Penguin in 2000, by an octogenarian Jewish scholar of

13. A dirty word for most English people!

international distinction, Hungarian by birth and upbringing but now resident in Oxford. His name is Geza Vermes and the book is entitled *The Changing Faces of Jesus*. On its cover it bears a reproduction of a particularly haunting medieval Russian icon of Jesus. Above this and the title are the words in bold capitals "A Masterpiece" A.N. Wilson, Daily Mail. This blurb by our leading literary atheist, himself a discerning critic, should alert Christian readers to the nature of what they are in for. We have been warned.

This book is an extremely clever attempt to deconstruct and discredit the New Testament. As such, on a first reading it is so persuasive, so plausible, as to be extremely disturbing. Accessibly written in deceptively authoritative but non-technical language, it is constructed and arranged with consummate skill and cogently argued with cumulative force, on the basis of a detailed examination of all the relevant New Testament evidence. It has every appearance of having successfully made its point that the charismatic Galilean "Jesus of history" was deliberately overlaid by the artificial "Christ of faith" invented by Paul, "John" and the writer "to the Hebrews" (Apollos of Alexandria?). It is, in fact, only when the reader of Vermes has read and digested Tom Wright's three volumes (and what he has written elsewhere on St. Paul, pending his fourth volume devoted to that subject) that s(he) comes to the realisation that Wilson's epithet given such prominence as a blurb should in justice be applied to the work, not of Vermes, but of Wright. What the latter has achieved is, in his own words (in a personal letter to the author, 15 Feb. 2003), to offer "a comprehensive historical account of Jesus which is designed to outflank completely the sort of thing Vermes, and many others, have tried to do." I believe he has succeeded entirely and that *that*, given the strength and subtlety of Vermes's argument, is no mean achievement. But you must not take my word for it. Judge for yourself.

Before taking leave of Geza Vermes I will draw attention to his extremely interesting and well-written autobiography, published in 1998 by the SCM Press under the apt title *Providential Accidents*. With one understandable exception, it strikes the reader as commendably candid. The author's personality comes across as warm and likeable. Because I consider that these basic facts are relevant to his writings about Jesus I think it worth recording them here: they are all taken from *Providential Accidents;* I hope that this summary will not deter any potential reader – quite the reverse in fact.

An only child of assimilated Jewish parents, who for mixed reasons converted to Roman Catholic Christianity when he was young, Geza was given a Catholic education in inter-war Budapest. During the 1939-45 War both his parents were "liquidated", probably at Auschwitz. Soon after the war he was ordained a Catholic priest and as such he moved first to the Catholic University of Louvain, Belgium, where he taught and became deeply involved in the study of the then-recently discovered Dead Sea Scrolls, on which he became a widely respected authority in the world of European learning for his expertise, not only in the scrolls – which he translated authoritatively into English – but in the sphere of intertestamental studies and early Judaism, which was of course their context. Still a respected Catholic priest he eventually moved to the Sorbonne, Paris for further research. Vermes came to England in 1957, and promptly fell in love with the wife of a professor at Exeter University. Following her divorce he married her, living happily ever after, but, of course, abandoning his celibate priesthood and with it Christianity, and reverting to his Jewish roots – from time to time visiting his Jewish kinsfolk in Hungary. It is at this delicate point that his autobiography seems a little less than frank.

His work on the scrolls as well as contemporary Jewish literature and rabbinics gave Geza a new interest in the Jesus of history as distinct from the Incarnate Son of God in whom he had, as a Christian priest, for so many years professed his faith and whose sacraments he had celebrated. This interest became predominant and he wrote several influential books on *Jesus the Jew* (the title of the first, published in 1983). They emphasised, with interesting new parallels from the world of Judaism, Jesus' ministry as an itinerant healer, thus making a useful and positive contribution to the growing contemporary Jesus studies. After some years teaching at Newcastle on Tyne University, he achieved the recognition by Oxford University for which he had yearned, being appointed the first Reader in Jewish Studies and (appropriately) a Fellow of Wolfson College and of the prestigious British Academy. He still lives in Oxford in active retirement.

Such is the author of *The Changing Faces of Jesus*. It may strike some readers as (at least) idiosyncratic of me to personalise the Jesus controversy between Vermes and Wright as I have done. I am aware, of course, that Wright set out on his monumental "quest" long before Vermes published his (minor) and tendentious "masterpiece" and that Vermes may not have read and pondered *Jesus and the Victory of God* (1996) before completing *The Changing Faces.* If not, he surely should have done! (It does not feature in his otherwise ample bibliography). My defence, if one is needed, is that Vermes and Wright struck me as, in every way, worthy protagonists.

If we do agree to see "the contest" in these terms, there can surely be no question but that Wright's "outflanking" manoeuvre, even though his conclusive volume on Paul is yet to appear, is entirely successful – but at a cost. Vermes' challenge is comprised in a mere 270 highly readable pages in an attractive slim paperback. It was soon reprinted and must have been read by a great many readers of whom only a fraction would have the time, ability or staying power to read, much less absorb the 1,864 pages of Wright's text so far published. This surely lends point to the suggestion I advanced in the previous chapter that for Wright's majestic work, when complete, to obtain the fair hearing/reading it so richly deserves, it *must* eventually be both readably and authoritatively reproduced in a drastically abridged form.[14]

Wright has shown himself perfectly capable of writing intelligibly about Jesus at the *popular* level, as witness *The Original Jesus* (Lion 1996). What is surely needed is something between the two, between the popular picture book and the daunting pile of tomes, and only Wright could produce it – or so it seems. But the trouble is he simply will not have the time. The same need applies to Polkinghorne's *chef d'oeuvre*: a simplified version for the educated, intelligent but non-technical public. Failing that, the (literally) Heaven-sent labours of these two brilliant divines will be wasted where most needed. At least that is the risk as I see it. I hope I am wrong.

Conclusion

We are approaching the end of this brief survey of the positive Broad Church contribution to present day Anglican thought. It is a contribution of which the Church, for all its manifest disunity and numerical decline, can be modestly proud. Not only those writers I have singled out for mention above – Polkinghorne and Peacocke, Swinburne and Wright – but others hardly less distinguished, among them John Habgood, Rowan Williams, Stephen Sykes, Keith Ward and John Bowker, together represent an intellectual and spiritual power house in no way inferior to that of earlier generations.

---

14. The orthodox Christian case, it seems, often suffers from this unfortunate handicap. When that other damagingly tendentious book *The Myth of God Incarnate* was published in 1977, it received massive publicity. It was conclusively answered later in the same year by C.F.D. Moule's *Origin of Christology*. That book was closely argued with consummate scholarship but it was not easy reading and required close study. It was also far "above the head" of the non-technical layman.

I have deliberately used the expression Broad Church in its widest sense to embrace the intellectual vanguard of the present day Church in preference to the usual description "Liberal", which to many is like a red rag to a bull. Some of those I have categorized in this way might object to being described by such an emotive word. I have no idea what "churchmanship" labels, if any, most of those named in the preceding paragraph would give themselves. Probably they are, rightly, indifferent to such matters. But whatever they think or do not think of themselves in this way, they surely *are*, they *must be*, in the positive sense as I have described it, Broad Churchmen. From their natural habitat in the east they gaze, wistfully perhaps, but not in uncomprehending hostility, along the dead straight latitudinal axis of Truth to the Narrow (conservative/traditionalist) camp in the distant west. They need to fraternise with their seeming opposite numbers, meeting at or under the Cross halfway. For the fact is, though they may be totally unaware of it, that inside every Broad Churchman is a Narrow Churchman struggling to get out. And conversely, outside every Narrow Churchman there is a Broad Churchman longing to get in. They belong together and need each other as much as High and Low. Broad needs the natural corrective of restraint, awe and reverence only to be had of his brother Narrow, who, in turn, needs the encouragement, the bold spirit of adventure and spiritual and intellectual courage to be found with the Broad folk. They belong together.

We Broad Churchmen (it will come as no surprise that I identify myself as one) are pretty thick skinned. There is something of Potter's Lifemen in most of us and we relish rather than resent the ploys and gambits of our fraternal opponents. I close this chapter with two of the best, worthy of the Lifeman himself.

The first comes courtesy of Charles Smyth, who was fond of saying: "Always remember that an open mind is generally a vacant one".

And if Broad Churchmen have never achieved anything else, we can surely claim the credit for provoking Ronald Knox, past master of the art of parody, to write a collect for Broad Church agnostics.

> O God, forasmuch as without Thee
> We are not enabled to doubt Thee
> Grant us all by thy grace
> To convince the whole race
> It knows nothing whatever about Thee.

No. After all I cannot allow Knox to have the last word. It shall rest with the noble Collect he dared so brilliantly to parody, that, in both the *Book of Common Prayer* and *Common Worship*, for the Nineteenth Sunday after Trinity.

O God, forasmuch as without thee we are not able to please thee; Mercifully grant, that thy Holy Spirit may in all things direct and rule our hearts; through Jesus Christ our Lord. Amen

Appendix to Chapter 3

The Declaration of Assent

The Declaration of Assent is made by deacons, priests and bishops of the Church of England when they are ordained and on each occasion when they take up a new appointment (Canon C15). Readers and Lay Workers make the declaration, without the words "and administration of the sacraments", when they are admitted and when they are licensed (Canons E 5, E 6 and E 8).

Preface

The Church of England is part of the One, Holy, Catholic and Apostolic Church, worshipping the one true God, Father, Son and Holy Spirit. It professes the faith uniquely revealed in the Holy Scriptures and set forth in the catholic creeds, which faith the Church is called upon to proclaim afresh in each generation. Led by the Holy Spirit, it has borne witness to Christian truth in its historic formularies, the *Thirty-nine Articles of Religion*, *The Book of Common Prayer* and the *Ordering of Bishops, Priests and Deacons*. In the declaration you are about to make, will you affirm your loyalty to this inheritance of faith as your inspiration and guidance under God in bringing the grace and truth of Christ to this generation and making Him known to those in your care?

Declaration of Assent

I, A B, do so affirm, and accordingly declare my belief in the faith which is revealed in the Holy Scriptures and set forth in the catholic creeds and to which the historic formularies of the Church of England bear witness; and in public prayer and administration of the sacraments, I will use only the forms of service which are authorised or allowed by Canon.

Chapter 4
High Church/Anglo-Catholics

Off we go once more on our anti-clockwise circuit of my ecclesiometer dial, until we come to a temporary halt at the top, the far North, the High Church summit.

When we arrive there, what do we find? Who, today, are these "High Church" people, these so-called "Anglo-Catholics" and what, essentially, do they stand for? And why am I to be found, with some reservations, among them?

Definitions

All these labels we have been dealing with in this book are to some extent unsatisfactory. They are not rigid definitions – far from it. Although for convenience I have put "High Church" and "Anglo-Catholic" together in the heading to this chapter, that must not be taken to mean or to imply that they are synonymous, any more than "Low Church" and "Evangelical", or "Broad Church" and "Liberal" are synonymous. They are not, but in each case they have quite a lot in common. Because these people to whom these labels are affixed are individuals, there are plenty of gradations, rough edges, shadings, in each grouping – and none are monolithic. Among ordinary, non-churchy folk, "High" and "Low" church are generally used in a rough and ready way, colloquially, to include "Anglo-Catholics" and "Evangelicals" respectively.

All this can be very confusing, but if what we write or say is to make any kind of sense, we must *attempt* clear definition, while at the same time realising that some edges may be blurred. And for such definitions of what this chapter is about we could hardly do better than quote the authoritative *Oxford Dictionary of the Christian Church* (third edition, 1997) as follows:

High Church: This term was coined in the late seventeenth century to describe those members of the C. of E. who emphasised its historical continuity as a branch of the Catholic Church and upheld "high" conceptions of the divine basis of authority in Church and State, of the rights of monarchy and episcopacy, and of the nature of the sacraments. (op.cit. p. 767)

Anglo-Catholicism: . . . that section or party within the Anglican Communion which stems from the Tractarian Movement of the 1830's, indeed the term in its English form appears to date from 1838 (the Latin Anglo-Catholicus is found in the 17th cent.).[1] Anglo-Catholics hold high doctrine of the Church and Sacraments; they attach great importance to the apostolic succession, that is to an episcopal order derived from the Apostles, to the historical continuity of the existing C. of E. with the Church of the earliest centuries and to the church's ultimate independence of the state. (op.cit. p. 69)

Anglican continuity with the historic Catholic Church in England

From the above two definitions it is obvious that, wherever else they may differ, old-fashioned High Churchmen and present day Anglo-Catholics are agreed in their desire to maintain the essentially unbroken continuity of the (Reformed) Church of England of the late sixteenth and subsequent centuries with the historic pre-Reformation Catholic Church in England, tracing its roots back through the early Tudor, medieval and "dark" ages to its earliest beginnings in missions from Lindisfarne and Rome – or even to the vestigial Church of Romano-British times.

In order that there should be no possible misunderstanding, the official, or classical, Anglican position, which endorses this High Church/Anglo-Catholic claim, is as follows: the Church of England (and likewise the Church of Ireland and the Anglican Church in Wales)[2] is, more or less uniquely in Christendom,[3] both Catholic

1. Interestingly this phrase occurs in a Latin inscription on a handsome late-17th century Maynard family tomb in Little Easton Church near Great Dunmow, Essex.
2. The position in Scotland is slightly different. The Scottish Episcopal Church has not been the "established" Church in Scotland since 1689, when the presbyterians became the established Church, which they remain today.
3. The main exception is the Church of Sweden, which had a conservative reformation under the Swedish Crown, with Lutheran influence and theology

and Reformed.[4] It was not founded by Henry VIII or Elizabeth I as a new schismatic Protestant sect or "church" (as claimed by Roman Catholics). Basically what happened in the sixteenth century Reformation was that, admittedly for political reasons in the first place, the Papal Supremacy which had been acknowledged in England etc. for roughly a thousand years was abrogated (by Act of Parliament in 1534) and replaced by the Royal Supremacy, thus "nationalising" the Church and inaugurating a thorough going Reformation, including the provision of an English liturgy. The Papal supremacy was briefly restored under Queen Mary I in 1554 repealing the legislation of her father Henry VIII and step-brother, Edward VI. The Royal Supremacy was restored in 1559, following the accession of Elizabeth I the previous year. Apart from the Cromwellian interregnum, it has remained in force, although in recent years in a modified form, ever since. Thus, to the puzzlement of many, the churches of England, Wales and Ireland and with them those of the worldwide Anglican Communion are said to be simultaneously Catholic and Protestant. A necessary corollary of this is that Papal Supremacy, the claim of the Bishop of Rome to be Universal Supreme Pontiff, is not an essential element of Catholicity. This claim is, of course, strenuously denied by Rome. Indeed, the present Pope, Benedict XVI (aka Josef Ratzinger) went so far in July 2007 as to make the outrageous counter claim that the Roman Catholic Church is the "one true Church of Christ" and all non-Roman churches are only "ecclesial communities", essentially counterfeit.

The Anglican claim to Catholic continuity is, undoubtedly, a bold one. Is it true? Is it credible? Can it be justified, historically and theologically? These are crucially important questions and we, Anglicans, must surely face them honestly, in the light of both history and theology, and seek to find the right, the true, answers.

In the second paragraph of this chapter I wrote, with careful choice of words, that I am to be found in this High Church/Anglo-Catholic churchmanship grouping – "admittedly with some reservations". You naturally ask what are those reservations? One "reservation", if that is the right word for it, is that in facing this question of the truth and credibility, or otherwise, of the High Anglican claim to Catholic continuity, I insist on myself approaching it along two lines *simultaneously*. The first is as a candid and (I hope) honest student of history, in this case of the complex history of the English Reformation. The second, in my view equally important, is as a committed

preserving the episcopate.
4. This is the title of an admirable book (SPCK 1962) by the historian Florence Higham.

ecumenist, acutely and painfully aware of the continuing weakness, amounting to near paralysis, of a deeply divided Christendom, whose rifts derive ultimately from the Reformation. That awareness leads me to yearn for an all-embracing reconciliation leading to some form of visible reunion based, not on an unattainable, impracticable and undesirable monolithic uniformity of doctrine and order, but on both a visible unity in mutual recognition and authorisation of ministries, as well as a common allegiance in loving brotherhood and fellowship to the Triune God, our Creator, Redeemer and Holy Spirit. This would be genuine visible Christian unity *embracing* rich diversity and freedom of expression.

I believe that this twofold approach is perfectly possible, although likely to prove painfully difficult, and that if we really *want* genuine reunion, there is no other option. Simply to go on hurling arguments at each other from deeply entrenched positions, however well prepared and plausible those arguments may be, will continue to prove an utterly wearisome way of getting nowhere. The only alternative is to make real and costly efforts to appreciate and understand the opposing viewpoint – that is, to practice *genuine* ecumenism.

How then do we set about this dual approach? Taking the historical route first, I suggest that we should begin with the frank recognition that Reformation history is, and is bound to be, controversial. Inevitably, even where there is agreement about the actual facts, their interpretation is certain to differ; they are going to look very different according to the historian's viewpoint. In other words, *merely on the historical level,* as things are at present, churches divided from one another, let us candidly agree that we are *never* going to get agreement. What we shall get is what we have already got, viz. an Anglican view and a Roman Catholic view, both perfectly legitimate from their particular stances, but completely irreconcilable.

Now let me simultaneously take the ecumenical route. The art, or business, of ecumenism does not consist (as many people imagine it does) of a kind of ecclesiastical diplomacy, finding a form of words, a mutually agreed formula by way of a mutually acceptable compromise of which each negotiating church would have its own interpretation. Ecclesiastical diplomacy has its uses and is not to be despised, provided it is honest and genuine and based on mutual respect and goodwill. What is *crucial*, however, is that in addition to having his own clearly defined and thought out principles, not rigid but flexible within clearly defined limits, on the basis of God's will sought in constant prayer, the ecumenist must be not only a patient listener but be able *fully* to see, enter into, appreciate and understand a Christian point of view other than, or completely opposed to, his own. This is the only basis for fruitful dialogue. Provided he has this genuine gift of empathy, her/his ecumenical interlocutor will almost certainly respond and reciprocate. This kind of ecumenism requires endless patience and perseverance. It is immensely hard work but can be richly rewarding. Ultimately there is no other way than this, of endlessly persistent love and endlessly loving persistence. The result when it is applied in the case under review is that there will still be two *apparently* irreconcilable viewpoints, *but each will fully understand and sympathise with that of the other*. That will bring about an entirely new situation!

Having got this reservation, if reservation it be, off my chest, I am going, presently, to look closely at the High Anglican claim to unbroken Catholic continuity with the pre-Reformation Church, beginning with one of its earliest and most persuasive exponents, Richard Hooker.

But before I do that, I would like to offer one, I hope, relevant observation. It is very much to be desired that, both for its own sake, and because we Anglicans are all, willy nilly, heirs of the English Reformation and involved in its consequences, right or wrong, we would whether clerical or lay make it our business, if we have not already done so, to acquire a good working knowledge of Christian history in general and in particular of that of the Reformation, its causes, effects, and consequences, as well as its place in the history of Europe. A classic book on the subject which was published just under half a century ago, but has never (so far as I know) been superseded or surpassed is *The Reformation* by Owen Chadwick. Still living at the time of writing, Professor Chadwick is one of our most distinguished historians. This book is the third volume in the *Pelican History of the Church* series published by Penguin in 1964. It sets the English Reformation in its full European context with illuminating chapters on Luther and Calvin as well as their English counterparts and it also usefully covers the (Roman Catholic) Counter-Reformation and its remarkable missionary outreach. An even older standard, *History of the Church in England* by John Moorman, sometime Bishop of Ripon and a fine Anglican historian, sets the Reformation in its purely English context. It was published by A. and C. Black in 1953. I hope both these highly readable and reliable books are still available through public (county) libraries. Both authors are Anglican but Chadwick especially goes out of his way to be fair, objective and as far as possible, impartial. Both can be thoroughly recommended to the non-specialist general reader. More recent books by Paul Welsby

(Anglican) and Adrian Hastings (Roman Catholic) bring the story of English Christianity up to date. They were both first rate historians, no longer with us.

Hooker's defence of the Anglican Reformation

Richard Hooker (c.1554-1600) has been described as "perhaps the most accomplished advocate that Anglicanism has ever had" *(Oxford Dictionary of the Christian Church* 3rd. edn. 1997, p. 789). A Devon man and a protégé of our earliest Anglican apologist, John Jewel, Bishop of Salisbury, Hooker followed Jewel to Oxford where he became a don of his mentor's old college, Corpus Christi. Following ordination he served for a time as Master of the Temple, where he famously disputed with its Calvinist lecturer, Walter Travers; they contradicted each other in alternate sermons. That was the only preferment of distinction that Hooker occupied. A gentle and modest man, he was content to serve in quiet country parishes, where he thought out and wrote his justly celebrated work *Of the Laws of Ecclesiastical Polity* in seven magisterial books. Of these only the first five were published in his lifetime, 1593 and 1597. A contemporary of Shakespeare, he wrote fine English prose.

In this, his *magnum opus*, Hooker set out to justify Elizabeth I's "Reformation settlement" of the Church of England, putting it in the widest possible framework in a broadly conceived philosophical theology which had a little in common with Aquinas and the Schoolmen. In so doing he struck out a middle way (via media) between its Calvinist Puritan critics on the one hand and those of Rome on the other. In this he was following in the footsteps of his patron, Jewel, but whereas Jewel had largely based his *Apology for the Church of England* on the Fathers, Greek and Latin, of the first six Christian centuries, Hooker went to the root of the matter.

His earlier post as Master of the Temple had brought him into stimulating contact with some of the finest legal minds of his day and this is no doubt what gave him his initial starting point, in the "laws" of nature and of reason in the mind of God. The first, and longest, book is concerned with "laws and their several kinds in general". He begins with "that Law which God from the beginning hath set for himself to do all things by", "that Law which giveth life unto all the rest." "Dangerous it were for the feeble brain of man to wade far into the doings of the Most High; whom although to know be life, and joy to make mention of his name; yet our soundest knowledge is to know that we know him not as indeed he is, neither can know him; and our safest eloquence concerning him is our silence, when we confess without confession that his glory is inexplicable, his greatness above our capacity and reach. He is above, and we are upon earth; therefore it behoveth our words to be wary and few". (LEP I. 2.2.) "Our God is one, or rather very Oneness, and mere unity, having nothing but itself in itself and not consisting of many things. In which essential Unity of God, a Trinity personal nevertheless subsisteth after a manner far exceeding the possibility of man's conceit . . . For being Three, and they all subsisting in the essence of one Deity; from the Father, by the Son, through the Spirit all things are." (I. 2.2.)

In chapter 16 he sums up his argument so far. "A Conclusion, shewing how all this belongeth to the cause in question" (XVI).

> . . . we have endeavoured in part to open, of what nature and
> force laws are, according unto their several kinds; the law
> which God with himself hath eternally set down to follow in
> his own works; the law which he hath made for his creatures
> to keep; the law of natural and necessary agents; the law
> which angels in heaven obey; the law whereunto by the light
> of reason men find themselves bound in that they are men;
> the law of which they make by composition for multitudes
> and politic societies of men to be guided by; the law which
> belongeth unto each nation; the law that concerneth the
> fellowship of all; and lastly the law which God himself hath
> supernaturally revealed. It might peradventure have been
> more popular and more plausible to vulgar ears, if this first
> discourse had been spent in extolling the force of laws, in
> shewing the great necessity of them when they are good,
> and in aggravating their offence by whom public laws are
> injuriously traduced. But forasmuch as with such kind of
> matter the passions of men are rather stirred one way or
> other, than their knowledge any way set forward unto the
> trial of that whereof there is doubt made; I have therefore
> turned aside from that beaten path, and chosen though a
> less easy yet a more profitable way in regard to the end we
> propose. Lest therefore any man should marvel whereunto
> all these things tend, the drift and purpose of all is this, even
> to shew in what manner, as every good and perfect gift, so
> this very gift of good and perfect laws is derived from the
> Father of lights (James 1.17) to teach men a reason why just
> and reasonable laws are of so great force, of so great use in
> the world; and to inform their minds with some method of
> reducing the laws whereof there is present controversy unto

their first original causes, that so it may be in every particular ordinance thereby the better discerned, whether the same be reasonable, just and righteous, or no. (Book I. 16. 1)

That here we may briefly end: of Law there can be no less acknowledged, than that her seat is the bosom of God, her voice the harmony of the world: all things in heaven and earth do her homage the very least as feeling her care, and the greatest as not exempted from her power: both Angels and men and creatures of what condition soever, though each in different sort and manner, yet all with uniform consent, admiring her as the mother of their peace and joy. (I. 16. 8)

The Second Book, "concerning their first position who urge Reformation in the Church of England: namely that Scripture is the only rule of all things which in this life may be done by man," is shorter.

One extract will suffice for the whole book: "As that which in the title hath been proposed for the matter whereof we treat, is only the ecclesiastical law whereby we are governed; so neither is it my purpose to maintain any other thing than that which therein truth and reason shall approve." (II 2.1)

* * * * *

I break off to plead guilty. I fear I have sorely tried your patient forbearance and let my enthusiasm for Hooker[5] run away with me, and, with it, my anxiety to let him tell his story in his own words and context. I have kept you waiting far too long and you may be weary of my hero's Elizabethan prolixity. In which case, please accept my apologies. But now, at long last, with the opening of his Third Book, the delay is *almost* over. But not quite. Your patience will be rewarded, richly I hope, *in due course*. Let me explain.

* * * * *

The Third Book is entitled "Concerning [the Puritans'] second assertion, that in Scripture there must be . . . contained a form of Church Polity, the laws whereof may in no wise be altered." Leading up to this, the subject of Chapter 1 is "What the Church *is*, and in what respect Laws of Polity are hereunto necessarily required." We need, writes Hooker, "to consider the nature of the Church, as is requisite for men's more clear and plain understanding in what respect Laws of Polity are necessary thereunto." (III. 1. 1.) He then

---

5. An enthusiasm shared by no less than Dr. Rowan Williams, the current Archbishop of Canterbury, who has expressed it in more than one of his books.

proceeds to set out at length what modern professional theologians call his "ecclesiology" – his doctrine, or concept of the Church.

He draws a clear distinction between the Church as Christ's mystical Body, which he sometimes refers to as "the mystical Church", on the one hand, and "the visible Church" on the other.

The mystical Church is one body, inclusive of all faithful humanity from the archetypal Abraham, and all his spiritual descendants in the old Israel/people of God, as well as the new Israel inaugurated by Christ – all those "in Christ" both in heaven ("already with Christ") and on earth. It comprises the Church Triumphant as well as the Church Militant here on earth – although Hooker does not use that terminology. "Concerning this flock it is that our Lord and Saviour hath promised, "I give unto them eternal life, and they shall never perish, neither shall any pluck them out of my hands" (John 10. 28). They who are of this society have such marks and notes of distinction from all others, as are not object unto our sense; only unto God who seeth their hearts and understandeth all their secret cogitations, unto him they are clear and manifest." (III 1.2.). It is axiomatic that it is "only the Searcher of all men's hearts, who alone intuitively doth know . . . who are his." (III 2. 1.)

Over against this "mystical Church", Hooker draws a more detailed picture of *"the visible⁶ Church"*. He writes:

> As those everlasting promises of love, mercy and blessedness belong to the mystical Church, even so on the other side when we read of any duty which the Church of God is bound unto, the Church whom this doth concern is a sensibly known company. And this *visible* Church in like sort is but one, continued from the first beginning of the world to its last end. Which company being divided into two moieties, the one before, the other since the coming of Christ; that part, which since the coming of Christ partly hath embraced and partly shall hereafter embrace the Christian religion, we term as by a more proper name the Church of Christ . . . The unity of which visible body and Church of Christ consisteth in that uniformity which all several persons hereunto belonging have, by reason of that *one Lord*⁷ whose servants they all profess themselves, that *one Faith*⁸ which they all acknowledge that *one Baptism*⁹ wherewith they are all initiated (Ephesians 4, 5). (III 1, 3)

6. Unless otherwise noted, all italics are my own.
7. Hooker's italics.
8. Hooker's italics.
9. Hooker's italics.

Hooker further defines "the visible Church", as distinct from "the mystical Church" in the next section as follows:

> The visible Church of Jesus Christ is therefore one, in *outward* profession of those things, which supernaturally appertain to the very essence of Christianity and are necessarily required in every Christian man. "Let all the house of Israel know for certainty,' saith Peter, "that God hath made him both Lord and Christ, even this Jesus whom you have crucified" (Acts 2, 36). Christians therefore they are not, which call not him their Master and Lord (St. John 13, 13; Colossians 3, 24 and 4, 1). And from hence it came that first at Antioch, and afterwards throughout the whole world, all that are of *the Church visible* were called Christians even amongst the heathen. Which name unto them was precious and glorious, *but* in the estimation of the rest of the world even Christ Jesus himself was execrable (1 Corinthians 1, 23); for whose sake all men were so likewise which did acknowledge him to be their Lord. (III 1. 4.)

In the next two sections, 5 and 6, Hooker makes crystal clear the nature of "the *visible* Church". Simply to name Christ as Lord is insufficient to claim membership; we must also embrace the Christian faith, and be admitted "by the door of Baptism." Similarly in section 7, he writes of other disqualifications:

> We speak now of the *visible* Church, whose children are signed with this mark "One Church, One Faith, one Baptism". In whomsoever these things are, the Church doth acknowledge them for her children; them only she holdeth for aliens and strangers, in whom these things are not found. For want of these it is that Saracens [i.e. Muslims], Jews, and Infidels are excluded out of the bounds of the Church. Others we may not deny to be of the visible Church, as long as these things are not wanting in them. For apparent it is that all men are of necessity either Christians or not Christians.

He then goes on to make his point forcibly:

> If by external profession they be Christians then are they of the visible Church of Christ: *and Christians by external profession they are all, whose mark of recognizance hath in it those things which we have mentioned, yea, although they be impious idolaters, wicked heretics, persons excommunicable*

yea, and cast out for notorious improbity. Such withal we deny not to be the imps and limbs of Satan, even as long as they continue such. (III 1.7)

Hooker then confirms his distinction in these words:

Is it then possible that the self same men should belong both to the synagogue of Satan and to the Church of Jesus Christ? Unto that Church which is his mystical body, not possible; because that body consisteth of none but only true Israelites, true sons of Abraham, true servants and saints of God. Howbeit of the visible body and Church of Jesus Christ those may be and oftentimes are, in respect of the main parts of their outward profession, who in regard of their inward disposition of mind, yea, of external conversation, yea, even of some parts of their very profession, are most worthily both hateful In the sight of God himself, and in the eyes of the sounder part of the visible Church most execrable. Our Saviour therefore compareth the Kingdom of heaven to a net, whereunto all which cometh neither is nor seemeth fish (St. Matthew 13, 47); his Church he compareth unto a field where tares manifestly known and seen by all men to grow intermingled with good corn (St. Matthew 13, 24) and even so shall continue till the final consummation of the world. God hath had ever and ever shall have some Church visible upon earth." (III 1. 8)

* * * * *

With Book III chapter one, section 10, we *at last* reach, in its proper context, what you have been kept waiting for so long!

Hooker begins with a question put by his opponents:

They ask us where our Church did lurk, in what cave of the earth it slept for so many hundreds of years together, before the birth of Martin Luther? As if we were of opinion that Luther did erect a new Church of Christ. No, *the Church of Christ which was from the beginning is and continueth unto the end: of which Church all parts have not been always equally sincere and sound. We hope therefore that to reform ourselves if at any time we have done amiss, is not to sever ourselves from the Church we were of before. In the Church we were, and we are so still.*[10] Other differences between our

10. The reference to Judah in the following sentence is to 2 Chronicles 13,

estate before and now we know none but only such as we
have seen in Judah; which having sometime been idolatrous
became afterward more soundly religious by renouncing
idolatry and superstition.

Following a further Old Testament reference, Hooker again reverts
to his own time: *"The indisposition therefore of the Church of
Rome to reform herself must be no stay unto us from performing
our duty to God; even as desire of retaining conformity with them
could be no excuse if we did not perform that duty."* The following
sentences are also crucial:

> *Notwithstanding so far as lawfully we may, we have held
> and do hold fellowship with them. For even as the Apostle
> doth say of Israel that they are in one respect enemies but
> in another beloved by God (Romans 11,28); in like sort
> with Rome we dare not communicate concerning sundry
> her gross and grievous abominations, yet touching those
> main parts of Christian truth wherein they constantly still
> persist, we gladly acknowledge them to be of the family of
> Jesus Christ; and our hearty prayer unto God Almighty is,
> that being conjoined so far forth with them, they may at
> the length (if it be his will) so yield to frame and reform
> themselves, that no distinction remain in any thing, but
> that we "all may with one heart and one mouth glorify
> God the Father of Our Lord and Saviour" (Romans 15, 6)
> whose Church we are.*

Such[11] was "the judicious Hooker's" unequivocal opinion. *"In the
Church we were (before the Reformation) and we are so still."* For it he
had the wholehearted support of the Church's "establishment" of his day,
headed by John Whitgift, Elizabeth's third Archbishop of Canterbury.
It would no doubt have gained the equally enthusiastic applause not
only of Hooker's old mentor, John Jewel, of the celebrated *Apology*,
but also of Jewel's contemporary, Archbishop Matthew Parker, whose
intuitive sense of Anglican continuity with the old Catholic Church
was reflected in his vast and immensely precious collection of pre-
Reformation MSS. salvaged from the great monastic libraries at and
after the Dissolution (1536-39) and bequeathed to his old Cambridge
college, Corpus Christi, of which he was later Master.

4-11 (which Hooker does not seem to have compared to 1 Kings 15, 1-8
which contradicts it).

11. I hope it has been worth waiting for – in its full, rich, context!

What of Hooker's masterpiece which enshrines not only his intuitive understanding of Anglican essential continuity with England's Christian past, but also what was, in the prevailing climate of his time, a remarkably warm – if qualified – ecumenical attitude to Rome, from which Anglicanism was now separated by an ever-widening gulf of mutual prejudice? Constantly reprinted in great quartos and folios, it immediately became – and long remained – a key text for generations of High Churchmen. Not least amongst those greatly indebted to Hooker may be counted his devoted admirer and biographer Izaak Walton (the compleat angler), Lancelot Andrewes, William Laud, Gilbert Sheldon, John Evelyn, and Thomas Ken, right through to John Keble, who published a definitive edition in 1836, the early days of the Tractarian Movement. Thereafter, gathering dust and cobwebs on many a rectory bookshelf, it remained largely unread, its thesis of continuity taken for granted by newer generations of Anglo-Catholics and Central Churchmen alike. The C. of E's assumed unbroken and unchallenged possession of the entire ancient heritage of churches and cathedrals throughout the land, with lists of bishops, deans and incumbents stretching back far beyond the Reformation, seemed to put the matter beyond question. *But did it?* Does this boasted continuity, *despite* the violence, the bloodshed, the iconoclastic destruction of those thirty years in the middle of the sixteenth century which accompanied the Reformation and all its disruption really hold water? Is it *true*?

Choosing my adjective with careful precision, I wrote several pages earlier that our precious High Anglican claim to Catholic continuity is "undoubtedly a *bold* one". It is indeed. Even so, as a loyal Anglican, I stand with Hooker, and believe it, from our point of view, justifiable and true. *But, in the light of history,* I qualify it in at least two respects. I would add another carefully chosen adjective – "tenuous". It is a *tenuous continuity* to which we lay claim. And, secondly, both as an historian and as an ecumenist, I would want to add that our Anglican claim is not an exclusive one.

An Alternative Claim

So far, I have concentrated exclusively on the Anglican claim, that we are as a Church both Catholic and Reformed. There is, however, an alternate position to be argued. As the classical exposition of the via media, the middle way, our Anglican claim was open to attack both from the Left, Geneva, and Right, Rome. It remains vulnerable today as an interpretation of the English Reformation, history inextricably entwined with theology. Indeed, the position is so delicately balanced that any intelligent and tolerably unprejudiced reader of two recent books by a distinguished Cambridge historian, Eamon Duffy – *especially* if he has not read much else of weight on the Reformation – might well find it impossible to accept Hooker's judgment. The first of these books is the massive result of seven years painstaking and wide-ranging research: *The Stripping of the Altars: Traditional Religion in England c. 1400-1580* (Yale University Press 1992, 2nd edn. 2005). The second is the much shorter but deeply moving *The Voices of Morebath: Reformation and Rebellion in an English Village* (Yale 2001)

The Stripping of the Altars is in two parts. The first and longer section is devoted to an in-depth study of traditional late-medieval and early-Tudor piety and folk religion of which much more evidence has survived in record offices and libraries than one might have expected. The second part is a retelling of the history of the English Reformation with a particular emphasis on its negative aspect, notably (1) the Dissolution of the entire heritage of English monasteries large and small, and the parcelling out of the vast monastic estates to a new class of Tudor landowning profiteers (thereby creating a powerful vested interest in the Reformation); and (2) the wholesale destruction of five or more centuries' accumulation of medieval art, craftsmanship, piety and devotion carried out under royal authority by Protestant Reformers during the brief reign of Edward VI (1547-1553) and the consequent drastic reordering of all English places of worship without exception. To sum it up so is also to say nothing of the deep distress caused to so many devout worshippers by this violent iconoclasm. The author, Professor Duffy, is an honest historian. He is the first Professor of the History of Christianity in the University of Cambridge[12] and a Fellow of Magdalene College. It is also not without significance that, as his name suggests, he is an Irish Roman Catholic (born at Dundalk) and a member of the Pontifical History Commission based in Rome.

In the Preface to the second edition of *The Stripping of the Altars* of 2005 he is disarmingly frank about his very definite Roman Catholic point of view and his hope, and expectation, that his work in these two impressive volumes will ultimately be accepted as definitive, thereby replacing the established interpretation of the Reformation epitomised by the late Professor A.G. Dickens.

Duffy is the latest in a long and honourable line of revisionist historians of the Reformation. Their pioneer was John Lingard

---

12. This used to be the Dixie chair of Ecclesiastical History. This seems to have replaced it.

(1771-1851) whose work continues to be held in high regard for its accuracy, objectivity and reliance on original sources. Some of his later followers failed to live up to his high standards and integrity. One of these was Cardinal F.A. Gasquet whose shoddy scholarship was famously unmasked by the great medievalist G.G. Coulton. Others, like Hilaire Belloc, were brilliantly and excitingly readable but blatantly prejudiced and propagandist. I remember reading a book of his on the Reformation when I was an impressionable schoolboy. I was tremendously impressed, it was only later that I began to realize that his beguiling portraits of people like Cranmer were, in fact, grossly one-sided caricatures.

Duffy is not like that. He is a serious, if opinionated, historian and the evidence he has so impressively marshalled deserves to be read and pondered with full seriousness. In particular his second book, whose central character is Christopher Trychay, priest of a remote Devon country parish, Morebath, from 1520 to his death in 1574, is a moving story taken from the actual records of that parish. It details the devastating impact of the whole course of the Reformation in a part of the country where it was deeply unpopular and provoked in 1549 an armed revolt in which some of Trychay's parishioners took part. Trychay dutifully cooperated with the church and state authorities in all the successive alternations of the quarter century which covered this most eventful period in our church and national history, but the records leave us in no doubt where his conservative sympathies lay, reflecting those of most of his parishioners.

There are, very definitely, at least two sides to the interpretation of Reformation history *and it is hard to resist the conclusion that each has its own validity, that they are not so much alternatives as complementary aspects of the one event.* That at least is my considered opinion, as both a candid student of history and a dedicated ecumenist. It is reinforced by another consideration, not without its peculiar irony. I suspect that many of Duffy's readers and admirers are unaware that, while he, the leading R.C. revisionist historian of his day, is prestigiously installed as Professor of the History of Christianity at Cambridge, *another* perhaps equally distinguished Reformation specialist from a diametrically opposite standpoint is installed as Professor of the History *of the Church* at the University of Oxford. He too has a Celtic name – Professor Diarmaid MacCulloch, Fellow of St. Cross College. He is the son of an Anglican clergyman and was educated at Stowmarket Grammar School (Suffolk) and Cambridge (Churchill College). I read and enjoyed his widely acclaimed *Life of Cranmer* (1996). He has also written on *The Later Reformation in England 1547-1603*. He made his name with *Suffolk and the Tudors*, 1986. It is interesting that, whereas Duffy, an R.C. layman, is a D.D. (Cantab.) MacCulloch, an Anglican layman, is a D.D. (Oxon.). It would be intriguing to know if the two are friends and if there is any meeting of minds between them.

The Reformation: pros and cons further considered

I well remember, with lingering embarrassment, that shortly after I was instituted at the tender age of twenty eight to my first "living" at Reydon near Southwold, Suffolk, I rashly accepted an invitation from the rural dean to hold forth to my clerical brethren of the North Dunwich Deanery Chapter – all of them older and wiser men – on the pros and cons of the Reformation. They had heard that I had graduated in history as well as theology, and they wanted to try me out. It was a good-natured trap, really. The meeting was to be held in the Walberswick cottage of a retired priest, a well known and highly respected Anglo-Catholic. I made what old fashioned Suffolk people would call a "whully great" mess of it. (I wonder if I should have done better now – after more than half a century's reflection on the subject!)

If I'd had any sense, I should have begun by reminding my colleagues of the well-worn adage: *Ecclesia semper reformanda*; should it be translated "the Church is always in need of reform" or "of reformation"? We could put that question to Hooker's (and St. Paul's) "mystical Church" and to Hooker's "visible Church".

If we put it to the pre-Reformation Church, the answer can hardly be in doubt. Though, if we listen to the revisionists, to Lingard, Duffy et al., especially to Duffy, one wonders, was the Reformation, given its cost in violent disruption, in schism, *really* necessary? Surely, yes.

On the Continent, in Germany, what sparked off Luther's reformation was the scandal of indulgences, and their sale to swell the coffers of the Renaissance papacy and help in the rebuilding of St. Peter's, Rome. To defend such iniquity was impossible, as Rome has at last conceded in its (fairly) recent conversations with the Lutherans. Sadly, in sixteenth century Europe the voices of reason and moderation, Melancthon, from the Reformers, and Contarini at the Council of Trent, were not able to prevail and history took its bitter course.

In England, as we all know, the spark that ignited the Reformation was Henry VIII's matrimonial, dynastic, and political problems, a spark that was to be fanned into flame by his ambitious greed and brutality. The then-Pope, Clement VII, to all intents and purposes a prisoner of the Emperor Charles V, nephew of Catherine of Aragon, was in no position to give the King the decree of nullity he so badly wanted. Henry had no difficult in persuading his sympathetic Parliament to pass the Act of Supremacy of 1534, which abruptly abrogated the thousand-year-old Papal supremacy over the Church in England, replacing it with that of the King. His newly appointed Archbishop of Canterbury, Cranmer, promptly gave Henry his decree of nullity so that he could marry Anne Boleyn. Two of England's outstanding Christians, John Fisher, Bishop of Rochester, friend of Erasmus and co-founder of two Cambridge colleges, and Sir Thomas More, Henry's erstwhile Lord Chancellor (the "man for all seasons"), could not square this with their consciences and suffered martyrdom by beheading in 1535. They would prove to be only forerunners of the many to die as martyrs for conscience's sake. This brazen act of nationalisation of our ancient Church was followed by the plunder of our huge monastic heritage between 1536-1539, involving a few more martyrdoms (notably the Carthusians) and, by the parcelling out of the great monastic estates to a new class of Tudor landowner profiteers, the creation of a powerful vested interest in the Reformation. All this, so far, was sordidly negative. If we are registering "pros" and "cons", this was a "con".

But it was swiftly followed by one of the great "pros". Thomas Cromwell, the King's vicar general, who had successfully organised the Dissolution of the Monasteries, persuaded Henry to agree to issue the royal Injunction of 1538. This required all clergy "on this side of Easter to provide one book of the whole Bible of the largest volume in English to be set up in some convenient place in the Church that you have care of, whereby your parishioners may most commonly resort to the same and read it." The edition referred to was Coverdale's translation known as the Great Bible.[13]

This provision of an open English Bible in every church was the first positive achievement of the English Reformation. It was the ideological launching pad of the movement, both here and on the

---

13. It is not always realised that the version of "the Psalms of David" in the 1662 Prayer Book, so familiar to an earlier generation of churchgoer and chorister, is that of Coverdale. His translation was the first *complete* English Bible. He made extensive use of Tyndale's Pentateuch and New Testament and other sources including the Vulgate (St. Jerome's Latin version) and even Luther's new German translation which did so much to popularise the Reformation in Germany.

Continent, and it was the criterion by which the old, unreformed
Church was judged – and so widely found wanting. Its being
made accessible to all and sundry in this way was of incalculable
importance, not least in softening up public opinion for what was
to follow once the heavy restraining hand of the fundamentally
conservative King was no longer there. All this, despite the fact that
only a tiny handful in every parish were literate enough to read and
understand it.

But, as was to be expected given the hermeneutical limitations of
the time (and indeed for long after) those who could, and did, read and
study their Bibles interpreted them crudely, literally, and (of course)
uncritically and therefore did not hesitate to apply (for example) the
teaching of the Old Testament *directly* to the traditional "folk religion"
of their own time, as represented by medieval Catholicism at the
popular level. This tendency is described at length in the first part of
Duffy's *Stripping of the Altars*. This was especially true of the second
commandment of the Decalogue ("Thou shalt not make to thyself
any graven image – nor the likeness of anything that is in heaven
above or in the earth beneath . . . Thou shalt not bow down to them
or worship them . . ." Exodus 20, 4-6) and of its, to them, uncannily
apposite application in the Reformation undertaken by Josiah, King
of Judah, in 621 B.C. If you look up and read right through chapters
22 and 23 of the Second Book of Kings you will see exactly what I
mean. Those two chapters are a graphic description of the providential
discovery in Solomon's Temple of what appears to be the book of
Deuteronomy, and of how this discovery (or rediscovery) prompted
the godly King Josiah to carry out a sweeping "reformation" of the
Canaanite folk religion which had all but obliterated the primitive
spiritual worship of YHWH, the Lord God of Israel.

To the Reformers the parallel to the times in which they lived
seemed exact and irresistible. For "Josiah" read "Henry VIII" or
his son "Edward VI". For the re-discovery of Deuteronomy read
the rediscovery of the Scriptures. It was all too obvious – a perfect
precedent. Cranmer made it the specific theme of his sermon at the
Coronation of Edward VI, alluding to "your predecessor Josiah". It
outlined the agenda/programme for the child King's reign.

And indeed this is exactly what happened in those traumatic
six years. Every church, every cathedral, every English place of
worship without exception was the scene of violent and ruthless
iconoclasm, as described with relish by Duffy. It was nothing less
than the wholesale destruction of the centuries-old accumulation of
priceless medieval art and craftsmanship, of the piety and devotion

of generations of simple English Christian men and women. And all this violence carried out in the name of God as an extirpation of "Popish idolatry and superstition", to make way for a simple, plain reordering for Scriptural worship within walls new whitewashed over, the old Poor Man's Bible – crude if graphic (and often movingly lovely) paintings – replaced with suitable Scripture texts in black letter. It was like a tidal wave, a religious tsunami. Is it any wonder that old-fashioned Christian folk like the Martyns of Long Melford were saddened and grieved beyond measure? Were *they* the evil idolaters?

What one would dearly like to know is: was there no English Patristic scholar then living to remind his countrymen and their Church, especially the Reformers, that the Christian world had seen it all long before – and resolved the matter? I refer to the great Iconoclastic Controversies in the Eastern (Greek) Church in the eighth and ninth centuries; terrible troubles with violence and martyrdoms between c.725 and 842, exacerbated by the recent "explosion" of Islam with its strict prohibition of imagery on the lines of the second commandment. The first outbreak of controversy spearheaded by successive iconoclastic Byzantine emperors, with army support, was brought to an end by the Seventh and last General Ecumenical Council held at Nicaea in 787. This Council decreed that the *"veneration"* of icons was lawful and good, defining the limits of "veneration" as falling short of the "adoration" rightly reserved for the invisible Deity Himself. (There is more to it than that.) For a more detailed outline see the article Iconoclastic Controversy in the *Oxford Dictionary of the Christian Church.*

If that precedent had been known, considered and followed sensibly, no end of suffering and violent destruction – together with so much censorious and hurtful ill feeling – might, probably would, have been avoided.

But that was not to be. And it has to be admitted that for the Reformers only the validity of the first four of the seven General Ecumenical Councils, Nicaea I, Constantinople I, Ephesus and Chalcedon, was recognised. So for Protestants the Thirty Nine Articles of Religion had the last word. Article 22 read: "The Romish Doctrine concerning [Purgatory, Pardons, i.e. Indulgences] Worshipping and Adoration, as well of Images as of Reliques, and also Invocation of Saints, is a fond thing vainly invented, and grounded upon no warranty of Scripture, but rather repugnant to the Word of God." Furthermore, in the pre-Reformation Church, although there was much of what many would agree in excusing as harmless and devout veneration, there did exist much too, as in Southern Europe today, of indefensible, morbid, unhealthy and superstitious Mariolatry and relic (often *bogus* relic) worship.

On balance, then, the new accessibility of the vernacular Bible in Protestant Europe, despite these serious dangers and drawbacks ('cons') was an overall and undoubted "pro". The ideal of the Bible in the homes, as well as in the churches of rich and poor alike did bring untold blessing, as more and more became literate. But the Scriptures are far from self-explanatory, although God the Holy Spirit does speak clearly through the Word Incarnate, Crucified and Risen, to all who listen humbly and attentively and respond to what they read in faith and obedience. We shall return to this theme in later chapters.

The other great *positive* gain, or "pro", from our Reformation was the *Book of Common Prayer and Administration of the Sacraments and other Rites and Ceremonies of the Church according to the Use of the Church of England together with the Psalter or Psalms of David printed as they are to be sung or said in Churches and the Form and manner of making, ordaining and consecrating of Bishops, Priests and Deacons* to give it its full title at the last revision (1662).[14] How incredibly out of date that sounds today! Yet the *Prayer Book* (to abbreviate its title) still retains full statutory authority as an alternative to all that is contained in *Common Worship*. A Parochial Church Council is fully entitled to require its exclusive use in a particular church, if it so desires.

In its heyday, our Anglican forbears boasted of "our incomparable liturgy", and with good reason. Compared with the (to most people) incomprehensible mumbling of "hocus pocus" at a distant altar that was the unreformed Latin mass on the one hand, and the long-winded extempore ramblings and rantings in the Dissenting chapels on the other, the established church, so largely thanks to Cranmer's wonderful command of plain but sonorous English, offered an uncomplicated, uniform and orderly liturgy which gave full scope to

---

14. In addition to the contents, which also included Forms of Prayer to be used at Sea, listed in this full title (as printed on the title page) Prayer Books normally contained (a) the Act of Uniformity 1559 (and sometimes also that of 1661) which remained in force, and in the Statute Book (b) The Forms of Prayer with Thanks-giving to Almighty God for use on the Sovereign's Accession Day each year, (c) His Majesty's Declaration (of Charles I 1627) prefacing (d) the (Thirty Nine) Articles of Religion, and finally (e) "A Table of Kindred and Affinity wherein whosoever are related are forbidden by the Church of England to marry together." (This last began with "A Man may not marry his Grandmother"). Useful reading during dull sermons.

the reading of the Scriptures, the preaching of the word and the regular administration of the Sacraments. (At least that was the ideal.)

Cranmer's first and second Prayer Books, so radically superseding the unchanging traditional liturgy of long centuries of use, were not, and could not be expected to be, popular. But after the brief reign of Mary (1553-1558) had brought the return of the old ways of worship, with Elizabeth's accession, the very Protestant second book of 1552, tempered by small but highly significant additions from the more Catholic first book, was introduced and gradually became more widely accepted. The later books of Hooker's *Ecclesiastical Polity* were devoted to a detailed defence and rationale of this second book. The Prayer Book in use under the first two Stuart Kings, James I and Charles I, remained almost unchanged but with one most welcome addition. The Catechism, with its strong teaching of the concept of Christian duty to God and our "neighbour", was to influence generations of English folk for good in the formation of character.

The BCP, Book of Common Prayer, attained its final and present form following the Restoration of the Monarchy and the Church in 1660, and the Savoy Conference of 1661, which gave its Puritan critics the opportunity of a say in its revision. In the event they were mostly overruled, although we are indebted to one of them, Edward Reynolds, Bishop of Norwich, for one of its most enduring treasures, the General Thanksgiving. The BCP (1662) retains, even today, its privileged, protected status in law as an authorised alternative to what in the majority of parishes has replaced it, *Common Worship* (2000). This had gradually evolved through the years of authorised liturgical experiment *(Series Two* and *Series Three)* in the 1960s and 70s and the (temporary) *Alternative Services Book* 1980. Through all these developing stages, there was a lingering, but ever-fainter resemblance between these infant liturgies and their venerable Cranmerian ancestor.

It is worth remembering at this time of Anglican disruption that the Prayer Book was originally one of the chief bonds of unity in the Anglican Communion world-wide – and so it remained at least until the mid-twentieth century. By this time, each constituent Anglican Church was going its own liturgical way, with the consequent weakening of the bonds between us. And, another point often overlooked these days: when I was a boy, at the time of the abortive 1928 Revision which was thrown out by a largely non-Anglican House of Commons, and for some time thereafter, until revision began again in earnest after 1959, most C. of E. families possessed their own copies of the Prayer Book, often bound together with Hymns Ancient and Modern, and these we brought to church, Sunday by Sunday. Everything needful (even if it *was* hopelessly archaic) was bound together between two covers.

But no longer: *Common Worship* is fragmented into umpteen different coloured booklets, one of which is thrust into our hands as we enter the church. Is this progress? There is a great deal to be said in favour of having all that is needful for Sunday worship, whether the Eucharist or a Service of the Word, together with a shortened Litany and the services of Baptism and Confirmation, and a straightforward modern Catechism *all bound up together* – and available for purchase, so that they can be studied at home and the Sunday and Holy Day Collects be incorporated in private prayer.

The Book of Common Prayer, in its great days in what one might call the Classical Church of England of the seventeenth and eighteenth centuries, when its language was not yet anachronistic, was a tremendous asset. The pity is that, due to a combination of Church apathy and Parliamentary indifference, there were not periodic revisions, both conservatively to modernise its language, and, (of equal importance) in the light of a developing study of comparative liturgy, to modify its theology and liturgical structure. The result of this long delay was that when the so long overdue revision did eventually begin, the process went too far and too fast for many older and devoted Anglican worshippers, while it was not radical enough for others. Also, it is to be feared that, despite an outpouring of often admirable explanatory literature, the process of transition was not handled with sufficient sensitivity and patience in all parishes, meaning many of its most loyal and devoted worshippers were alienated from the church they had loved.

Now for another confession. Early in my ministry, I prided myself on being *one* of the most, if not *the* most punctilious, literal, rubrick-obedient users of the BCP in the C. of E. Also, I would boast that there was almost no part of it that I had not, at some time, performed. And then it gradually dawned on me that I was being absurdly pedantic and obscurantist and that drastic Prayer Book revision was long overdue. So I welcomed *Series Two* when it was authorised, and persuaded my PCC to agree to it, making us one of the first parishes in our conservative corner of East Anglia to do so. I compared the change to the welcome relief of Churchill's marvellous wartime rhetoric being followed by the total contrast of Attlee's matter of fact, flat, plain English after the war.

So that, as well as my lazy (?) unwillingness to sign up to any party pressure group, is the explanation of my declining to join the Prayer Book Society, despite approval of much of their "platform". But I am still very much of the opinion that, *for its time* – that of the mellow classical Anglicanism of the seventeenth, eighteenth, and *early*-nineteenth centuries, before the Tractarian/Romantic Revival, the Age of Wren, Hawksmoor, Gibbs and Archer, of Gibbons, Handel, Greene and Attwood – the Prayer Book was one of the prime fruits of the Anglican Reformation, of which we are right to be proud. These fruits are now overripe; their time is past. Reconciliation all round is long overdue.

Summing up

The Reformation, *at the fearful cost of the unity of Christendom*, was part tragedy, part triumph. The English Church exchanged the Papal for the Royal Supremacy. The *medieval* Papacy had brought us little advantage, much *dis*advantage. The Interdict in the reign of John, participation in ultimately disastrous Crusades preached by Popes, financial exactions – all took their toll. The royal supremacy, too, proved deeply divisive under the Stuarts. Establishment brought with it the curse of corrupting worldliness implicit in patronage from the top downwards and identification with "the powers that be". Anglicanism failed to take root, *deep* roots at any rate, among the working proletariat.

The stubborn persistence in the face of, at worst, active persecution and at best, social disadvantage and civil disenfranchisement, of a small but courageous recusant minority – serviced by a heroic fugitive priesthood trained on the Continent at Douai and Rome and reinforced by Jesuits – constituted *by its very existence* a challenge to Anglican claims of a *monopoly* of continuity from pre-Reformation times. Eventually in 1850, Catholic Emancipation having won its way, "the Papal aggression" (as we Anglicans indignantly termed the establishment (or re-establishment?) of a Roman Catholic hierarchy, of Romish archbishops and bishops in England) led eventually to the present situation of a parity in numbers of committed membership between Anglicans and Romans, or even of a Roman Catholic preponderance over the established church. In the present climate of militant secularism, of course, both communions are in decline, while in Ireland, the Reformation only really "caught on" among the Anglo-Irish ascendancy.

Questions like these must be faced, not least by we who call ourselves Anglo-Catholics – High Churchmen. As Anglicans, we are heirs of a great tradition, but one that seems to have had its day.

The need for genuine reconciliation with our Roman Catholic fellow heirs is surely overdue, and presses daily upon us.

A beginning has been made. Both traditions have "a noble army" of Reformation martyrs. Neither has a monopoly. We have begun to honour them *together* – John Fisher, Thomas More, Edmund Campion and Oliver Plunket alongside Thomas Cranmer, Hugh Latimer, Anne Askew and Rowland Taylor. That is good but we must go further. A suggestion how is made in a later chapter.

Newman's Challenge 1845/64

In 1845 John Henry Newman's defection to Rome, for reasons which he explained and defended in his *Apologia pro Vita Sua* (1864), shook the Church of England to its foundations. It was challenged, as it had not been since the Reformation, to think out and face afresh the issues that separated us from Rome in spheres doctrinal, liturgical, and moral/ethical.

This new appraisal of the divide had several consequences, one of which was aesthetic. A new interest in the middle ages began to arise, coinciding with the Romantic Movement in English literature and the Gothic Revival in art and architecture. Both of these movements themselves grew in part out of the late-eighteenth century light-hearted Strawberry Hill-type Gothick aesthetic, as well as Gothic novels such as the *Mysterious Tale of Udolpho* (later lampooned in Jane Austen's *Northanger Abbey*). This interest, as the nineteenth century advanced, matured into a more serious appreciation of medieval art, architecture and religion, and, combined with the Tractarian movement, gave rise to the Anglo Catholic cult of "Ritualism". Much of this new "cult" consisted of conscious imitation of current Roman Catholic fashions in birettas, cottas and Gothic-style Eucharistic vestments, accompanied by plainsong, incense, and bitter arguments about the interpretation of the Ornaments Rubrick.

This in turn provoked a powerful Protestant backlash epitomised by John Kensit who died a "martyr", killed by an iron bar thrown in a riot in Birkenhead, 1902. Anglo-Catholics were also far from lacking "martyrs", with the likes of dedicated slum priests such as A.H. Mackonochie and Charles Lowder at St. George's in the East and St. Alban's, Holborn, both happy to go to gaol for infringing Church law.

This renewed interest in medieval religious traditions also manifested itself in the revival of religious orders within the Church of England. The late-nineteenth century saw the rise of the

Cowley Fathers of the Order of St. John the Evangelist, pioneered by Richard Meux Benson (1824-1915), and the Community of the Resurrection founded by Charles Gore (1853-1932) in 1895. The latter came later to be established at Mirfield, near Leeds, where men were and still are very thoroughly trained for the ministry. Indeed, Mirfield expanded sufficiently to nurture an offshoot in South Africa where the late Trevor Huddleston was an outstanding representative of their missionary ideals.

Anglo-Catholic liturgists

Going right back to Hooker and the classical rationales of the Book of Common Prayer by such as Comber, Sparrowe and Wheatley[15] among the old pre-Tractarian High Churchmen, liturgy, its history and rationale was a speciality, almost a monopoly, of later Anglo-Catholicism. Outstanding names include the pioneering scholar F.E. Brightman (1856-1932) to whose definitive work, *Liturgies Eastern and Western*, liturgists will always be indebted; A.G. Herbert of the now defunct Society of the Sacred Mission; Kelham, who did so much to familiarise Anglicans with the Liturgical Movement on the Continent and whose *Liturgy and Society* was influential; and, most of all, Dom Gregory Dix of the Anglican Benedictine monastery at Nashdom, Bucks, (now moved to Elmore). His monumental *Shape of the Liturgy* (1945), based upon his researches in the third century *Apostolic Tradition* of Hippolytus and his comparative study of primitive liturgy, lay behind much of the thinking underlying the new Anglican liturgies culminating in *Common Worship.* Because this massive liturgical scholarship transcended the denominational barriers between Canterbury and Rome, it has resulted in a welcome liturgical *convergence* between the Eucharistic rites of the post-Vatican II Roman Catholic Church and our own Anglican rites. I have been immensely struck by this when attending, with an Italian friend, a beautiful and deeply moving mass at the (R.C.) Quarr Abbey in the Isle of Wight.

It is also very much to be welcomed that present day Evangelicals, notably Bishop Colin Buchanan through his *Grove Books* publications, have played a constructive part in the evolution of the rite in *Common Worship* (2000) and its acceptance across a wide swathe of churchmanship.

15. These were the subject of an admirable study by G.W.O. Addleshaw, Dean of Chester, entitled *The High Church Tradition* (Faber 1941). He summed up the Prayer Book principles under three headings (i) edification (ii) order (ii) uniformity.

Liberal Catholicism

On the purely doctrinal front a unique part was played by Bishop
Charles Gore (1853-1932) a devout, quintessential Anglo-Catholic.
In his concise and influential book *Roman Catholic Claims* (1889)
he succinctly countered R.C. pretensions. That book has not been
successfully confuted and retains value today. 1889 also saw the
publication of *Lux Mundi*, a collection of essays around the theme of
the Incarnation, written by Gore himself and a group of like-minded
friends, with Gore as editor. Seven years earlier the ultra-conservative
and greatly revered Edward Bouverie Pusey. Pusey, the leader of the
Catholic wing, was succeeded by H.P. Liddon, canon of St. Paul's,
an almost equally revered, and equally obscurantist, theologian. The
stated purpose of *Lux Mundi* was to put the (Anglo-) Catholic faith into
its right relation to modern, intellectual, doctrinal and moral problems.
Accepting in principle the critical views of the Old Testament,
pioneered by Wellhausen and others, it marked a definite break with the
conservative standpoint of the Anglo-Catholic old guard represented by
Liddon. Gore's cautious acceptance of the broad principles of Biblical
criticism ultimately found monumental, if unwieldy, expression in what
soon came to be widely known as *Gore's Commentary*. Published as *A
New Commentary on Holy Scripture* by SPCK in 1928, under the joint
editorship of the three G's: Gore, the masterful General Editor – he did
not scruple to criticise his fellow editors' and his contributors' opinions
in lengthy footnotes when he saw fit – H.L. Goudge (New Testament)[16]
and A. Guillaume (Old Testament and Apocrypha). It comprised three
parts in one *huge* volume bound in grey cloth, with a grand total of
1,593 pages, *all in double columns on each page.*

Of this mammoth undertaking, not the least remarkable feature was
that all its contributors were without exception Anglicans, including
several from overseas provinces of the Anglican Communion, and all,
with the exception of Edwyn Bevan, clerical. Not all, though, were
Anglo-Catholics. J.W. Hunkin and L.E. Elliott Binns were certainly
not. This mighty tome soon found its way onto the bookshelves of
many an English parsonage, with two inevitable results – the rapid
obsolescence of its New Testament scholarship in particular, and the
equally assured breaking of its spine. Still, we are compelled to salute
a noble achievement.

A vast majority of Anglo-Catholics (myself included), in the nature
of things less prone than evangelicals to Biblical fundamentalism,

---

16. Sometime principal of my old Theological College, Wells, and father of
the novelist Elizabeth Goudge, author of *City of Bells* etc.

still follow Gore's example in qualifying for the epithet. Liberally, I must now be one of a dwindling number who still have Gore's *Commentary* with spine broken from overuse on our shelves. Though in general hopelessly out of date, it is still occasionally useful. I must just add that an outstanding Liberal Catholic of a later generation is Alec Vidler whose books and personality I found entirely congenial. I still think his *Christian Belief* (S.C.M. 1950), as a thoughtful, reasoned exposition of basic Christianity, unrivalled.

Anglo-Catholicism since 1928: A.M. Ramsey

After Gore, Anglo-Catholics had to wait some years for the emergence of another leader of comparable calibre and influence. As a promising young theologian and Biblical scholar (though he notoriously never *looked* young), Arthur Michael Ramsey (1904-88) had made his mark with the publication, in 1936, of *The Gospel and the Catholic Church*. Reissued in 1956 when its author was already Archbishop of York, it was justly acclaimed as a brilliantly effective synthesis, Biblical, theological, and historical, of the Catholic/evangelical/Protestant divide.[17] The devoted son of a Congregationalist father and an Anglo-Catholic mother, Ramsey himself epitomised this synthesis. And when, in 1966, following his translation to Canterbury in succession to Geoffrey Fisher, he also followed his predecessor's historic pioneering call on Pope John XXIII with an *official* visit to John's successor, Paul VI, he presented the Pope with a signed copy of that epoch-making book. (It is very much to be hoped that the Pope read and pondered it. If he did, what, one wonders, did he make of it?)

ARCIC

On that notable occasion, after prayers together in the Sistine Chapel, they both signed a "solemn declaration" setting up an Anglican-Roman Catholic International Commission (ARCIC). As we all know, that Commission and its successor, ARCIC Two, set up by Pope John Paul II and Archbishop Runcie in 1982, bore fruit over the years in a series of meetings and reports which expressed what I think to *everyone* was a surprising degree of, in some cases, (e.g. on Eucharistic theology) agreement and in others (e.g. authority) convergence which raised high hopes and expectations on both sides. I myself remember the joyful excitement I then felt, only to be dashed by the cold water poured over these reports by the Roman Congregation of the Doctrine of the Faith

17. I re-read this marvellous book before writing this chapter. It has, it seems to me, stood the test of time as an unrivalled expression of the best in Anglo-Catholicism. Not one sentence needs revising.

headed by Cardinal Ratzinger. Still, that convergence and the cordiality between Anglicans and Romans which accompanied it were real enough and afford genuine grounds for hope for the future.

Abortive Anglican-Methodist reunion

In the domestic sphere, too, the long drawn-out but successful negotiations with the Methodists, on which Ramsey set great store, were once again confounded, because after the Methodist Conference had enthusiastically endorsed the resulting scheme it failed to win sufficient majorities in General Synod to enable it to go through. This was a bitter disappointment not only to the Methodists, but to the Anglican majority who supported the scheme (for which I had voted) and most of all to Archbishop Ramsey, not least because most of the Anglican opposition had come from his fellow Anglo-Catholics.

Ordination of women

The next test for those of that way of thinking came with the campaign for the ordination of women to the priesthood. This again found Anglo-Catholics divided among themselves. The theological, scriptural and rational arguments in favour were overwhelming[18] and the only grounds for opposition were the fact that it was an innovation against tradition (after nearly two millennia of male monopoly) and, what admittedly weighed heavily with me, that ever-conservative and cautious Rome would be certain to oppose it, thus putting a new obstacle in the way of what seemed at the time promising progress towards reconciliation. When it came to the vote, with a good deal of hesitation (natural in view of my cross-bench approach to most things) I came off the fence and cast mine in favour – on the Gamaliel principle (Acts 5.38f.) that if it truly was God's will, i.e. right, we should know soon enough. As a matter of fact, I believe that we *were* right to go ahead, and that, sooner or later, as with the use of the vernacular in the Liturgy, Rome will follow suit.[19] I have met Roman Catholics who admire us for having the courage to do what they too agree is right, and I believe this feeling is quite widespread.

---

18. The most powerful, cogent and succinct statement of the case in favour is from the pen of a liberal Roman Catholic priest, the late Adrian Hastings. It is published in *The Theology of a Protestant Catholic* (SCM 1990) pp. 91-99 ('Should Women be Ordained?').

19. It seems to follow naturally, that, if (as I believe) the C. of E. was right in agreeing to the ordination of women to the priesthood, there can be no valid objection to the further stage of their ordination, or consecration, as bishops.

Current debate on homosexuality

As I write, we are now beset with yet another crisis of conscience – the issue of homosexuality, especially among clergy. (I wish, incidentally, to register a protest against the hijacking of the lovely old adjective "gay". I refuse to *mis*use it.) It is not so many years since, in England, homosexuality was quite rightly decriminalised.

As I see it, the main problem is one of fact. Agreed that homosexuality, whether between men or women, is abnormal, contrary to nature, is it just a matter of "orientation" (the in-word) or choice? I am quite unqualified to express an opinion. To me, until proof is adduced to the contrary, the House of Bishops' agreed statement of 1991, *Issues of Human Sexuality*, seems to make very good sense and should continue to be regarded as binding agreed policy to be acted upon. The Archbishop of Canterbury, Dr. Williams, has undertaken to abide by it although he disagrees with it – a strange situation.

It is said that, especially among young Anglo-Catholic clergy in the Dioceses of London and Southwark, homosexual behaviour is widespread but that it does not interfere with their being deeply caring and pastorally minded. One thing seems beyond doubt. The unilateral action taken by the American Episcopal Church in approving or condoning the appointment as a diocesan bishop of a practising homosexual priest who has abandoned his wife is contrary to undertakings given, and deeply offensive to many in the Anglican Communion. I write more on this issue in a later chapter.

Tailpiece

This long chapter, you may be glad to know, is nearing its end. It has been a bit heavy going and (some of its readers may think) altogether too fixated about the Reformation, so I am going to conclude it on a lighter note by telling you (1) what kind of a High Churchman I am NOT and (2) what kind I wish I was and would like to have been.

I am *not* an Ultra Catholic, as described in some lines with that title. They were written by a very distinguished Anglo-Catholic theologian, mathematician, versifier and wit called Eric Mascall (1905-1993) and are in his book *Pi in the High* (Faith Press 1959, fairly recently reprinted). Assuming the owners of his copyright are so generous as to allow me to reproduce them here, together with the illustration by Barbara Jones, you will see what I mean. I have never felt remotely tempted to dress up or behave in that sort of way. And anyhow I suspect that Ultra Catholics are now an extinct species. They probably

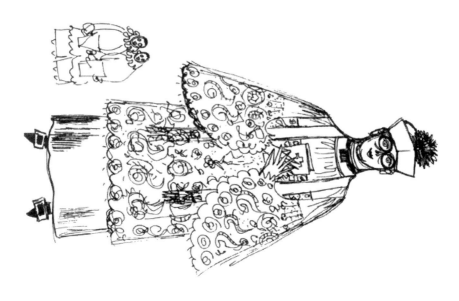

THE ULTRA-CATHOLIC

I am an Ultra-Catholic—No 'Anglo-,' I beseech you!
You'll find no trace of heresy in anything I teach you.
The clergyman across the road has whiskers and a bowler,
But I wear buckles on my shoes and sport a feriola.*

My alb is edged with deepest lace, spread over rich black
satin;
The Psalms of Dávid I recite in heaven's own native Latin,
And, though I don't quite *understand* those awkward moods
and tenses,
My *ordo recitandi's* strict *Westmonasteriensis*.

I teach the children in my school the Penny Catechism,
Explaining how the C. of E.'s in heresy and schism.
The truths of Trent and Vatican I hate not one iota.
I have not met the Rural Dean: I do not pay my quota.

The Bishop's put me under his 'profoundest disapproval'
And, though he cannot bring about my actual removal,
He will not come and visit me or take my confirmations.
Colonial prelates I employ from far-off mission-stations.

The music we perform at Mass is Verdi and Scarlatti.
Assorted females form the choir; I wish they weren't so catty.
Two flutes, a fiddle and a harp assist them in the gallery.
The organist left years ago, and so we save his salary.

We've started a 'Sodality of John of San Fagondez,'
Consisting of the five young men who serve High Mass on
Sundays;
And though they simply will not come to weekday Mass at
seven,
They turn out looking wonderful on Sundays at eleven.

The Holy Father I extol in fervid perorations,
The Cardinals in curia, the Sacred Congregations;
And, though I've not submitted yet, as all my friends
expected,
I should have gone last Tuesday week, had not my wife
objected.

* *Lector:* 'Ferraiola, surely? *Auctor:* Oh dear, not you again?'

Reproduced from E.L. Mascall and Barbara Jones'
Pi in the High (Faith Press, 1959)

all, every man Jack of them, "went over" to Rome when we decided to ordain women to the priesthood – though it is conceivable that one or two may have slunk back later, disillusioned, as some *did*.

When it comes to what kind of a High Churchman I *should* like to have been, and because example outweighs precept, this seems a good point at which to introduce three outstanding priests I have known, all of whom, exceptionally mature in Christian faith and outlook, would unquestionably have been perceived as High Churchmen, "catholics", even though their particular shade of "churchmanship" was not blatantly obvious.

First, George Tidey, for a few years vicar of three country parishes adjoining mine in East Suffolk. A fine example of a Mirfield-trained priest, before the Second World War he had served as an SPG missionary in Burma and, with his wife, had a deep, abiding love for all things Burmese. He once told me that when, during that war, he had served with the Chindits in the jungle, all his previous theological books had been turned into cigarette paper by the occupying Japanese! After the war, following a spell as Archdeacon of Rangoon, he had returned to England. As a wise and experienced priest and counsellor, he was loved and trusted by all his parishioners. Blunt and direct in speech he had a broad sense of humour. The last parish he served was St. John's Felixstowe, which has an unbroken "Catholic" tradition.

Next, Bernard Pawley, who, with John Moorman, served as official Anglican observers at the Second Vatican Council 1962-5, and, in effect, as our "ambassador" in Rome. I shall never forget hearing him speak at our diocesan retreat house, Leiston Abbey, at an ecumenical meeting chaired by our fine then bishop, Leslie Brown. Afterwards I drove him home to Reydon, where his old widowed father, Commander Pawley RN, then resided. I was *tremendously* impressed and would gladly have served and followed him anywhere. He was as straight as a gun barrel. His little book *Anglican Roman Relations* (Church Information Office 1964) was, like him, honest and straightforward. He ended up as Archdeacon of Canterbury and, as such, enthroned all Diocesan bishops in the Southern Province.

Finally, Peter May, the most unassuming of men, who, like me, had been a Scholar of Corpus, Cambridge. Under the legendary B.K. Cunningham (Principal) he served as Vice Principal of Westcott House. From there he went out to India as Principal of Bishop's College, Calcutta, the senior Anglican theological college and clergy training establishment in the sub-continent. I only came to know Peter when I was at Brandon 1970-80 and he was my rural dean, and as Rector of St. Mary's Newmarket, an exemplary parish priest. Peter was very definitely a liberal, even a *radical* catholic, whose refreshing views on Biblical or other theological matters were invariably soundly based and lucidly expressed. After his retirement c. 1978 he went to live near Newmarket, for which he retained great affection, and wrote two volumes on the history of the town and its racing industry which broke new ground and won wide and deserved acclaim. He was a very dear friend. (I succeeded him as R.D. of Mildenhall).

These three outstanding High Churchmen are no longer with us. I am proud to have known them and cherish their memory. They were all my role models. Basically I suppose I am an old-fashioned pre-Tractarian High Churchman, not interested in the pseudo-Roman, Anglo-Catholic trappings. A recent re-reading of that very remarkable, and moving, autobiography by Harry Williams, *Some Day I'll Find You* (1982) confirmed me in this stance.

Chapter 5
Narrow Church/Conservatives/Traditionalists

Off we go again, on the final lap of our circuit of the ecclesiometre dial. On the way we shall encounter a disgruntled overlap calling itself, rather grandly, catholic traditionalism or something of the sort, and loudly demanding attention. Ignoring it for now, we will press on to our destination and consider all overlaps when we get there.

The positive meaning of Narrow

The unfamiliar nomenclature of "Narrow Churchmanship" calls for explanation. It is really obvious, a simple matter of symmetry with, I insist, *no derogatory overtones*. The opposite of Broad is Narrow, as the opposite of Low is High. The dial *must* be symmetrical. But human nature, and especially ecclesiastical human nature, being what it is, the moment the Narrow Churchman calls to mind our Lord's reported words in the Sermon on the Mount (Matthew 7.13f.), the temptation to score a sound Potterian point will be almost irresistible – though the second of the two verses may give him pause. "Enter by the *narrow* gate, for wide is the gate and *broad* is the way that leads to *destruction*, and those who enter by it are many. For narrow is the gate and hard is the way that leads to life and *few* are those who find it." So remember, no derogatory overtones.

The question now arises, what exactly is this apparently new-fangled Narrow "Churchmanship"? Is it not, in fact, just a straightforward *negation* of (positive) Broad Churchmanship? And if so, has it any just claim to represent a *legitimate positive* type of "Churchmanship" – as legitimate as Low, Broad and High? My reply to all these questions is emphatic. Narrow is every bit as positive as Broad, just as slim is no less than stout.[1] Conservative traditionalism,

1. An intriguing query: Was the (presumably second) Duke of Cambridge who is credited with the sublime conservative aphorism, "Any change at any

properly understood, is as legitimate a stance as radical liberalism. Conservatism, in a political as well as a theological sense, *can* easily be distorted into a purely negative, "reactionary" (i.e. obscurantist) standpoint, which is indefensible. Still as a useful debating point it is worth noting that there is, perhaps, something positive to be said for a "reactionary" application of the brakes if you are heading, at top speed, straight for a precipice. It depends on your point of view.

This is a crucial point, too often overlooked. With the essential qualifying adverbial phrase, "properly, positively understood", Conservatism, traditionalism, the essence of "Narrow Churchmanship", is a fundamental, good and positive God-given feature of human nature. As such it finds full expression in Holy Scripture, as well as in Reason, Nature and, of course, Tradition.

Conservatism in the Bible

"Look to the rock from which you are hewn" (Isaiah 51 v.1). Those words, and they are not unique in the Bible, give perfect expression to the sound, healthy conservative instinct that is in all of us. Take an honest pride in your Christian (as in your national, local and family) heritage, in all that is of permanent value, in Christian art, architecture, liturgy, music, poetry and prose, medicine and healing, nursing and care, in the saints and martyrs, teachers and sages, throughout the ages and across the world. "We are surrounded by so great a cloud of witnesses" (Hebrews 12.1). Shall we not find immense encouragement and cause for heartfelt thanksgiving for and from them, not forgetting those of our own time?[2]

That is a totally different thing from a purely reactionary sentimental nostalgia for a non-existent "golden age" in the past. That same letter to the Hebrews tells us that "Jesus Christ is the same, yesterday, today and for ever" (Hebrews 13.8). It is spiritually unhealthy to be escapist, to "live in the past". "Forgetting what lies behind and straining forward to what lies ahead I press on towards the goal", wrote St. Paul (Philippians 3.14). But he also wrote "Test everything, *hold fast what is good"* (1 Thessalonians 5.21). That is surely sound conservative advice. We must get the balance right.

I have to admit that, although I was rash enough lightheartedly

---

time for any purpose is highly to be deprecated" being positive or negative? Answer: Positive.

2. Such as the 20th century martyrs of all Christian traditions whose stone effigies were recently placed on the West front of Westminster Abbey. They include such diverse figures as Martin Luther King Jr., Maximilian Kolbe, Janani Luwum, Oscar Romero, and Grand Duchess Elizabeth of Russia.

to describe our Lord himself as an archetypal Broad Churchman, I probably ought to have known better. *And yet* St. Luke, at least according to some MSS, attributes to Jesus the timelessly conservative remark "No-one after drinking old wine desires new [wine] but says 'The old is better'" (St. Luke 5.30).[3] Consider also Matt. 5.18, Luke 17.10 (duty is a sound conservative concept, sadly out of fashion today).

Criteria of true and false conservative traditionalism

Scripture, Tradition, Reason: this is the threefold basis of authority for us Anglicans. "Christian understanding of these three terms and of their interrelation has been deepened and broadened over the years, especially as a result of ecumenical discussion. Tradition, for example, is far more than the ever-accumulating hoard of material from the past . . . it is that within which, as Christians, we live, pray, worship and reflect, and through which we receive the gift of truth, vision, holiness and mutual love. It is the "rule" or standard of faith which, in the hands of the Holy Spirit, guides the Church in the way of Christ. Reason, too, is more than reflection on Scripture and Tradition, vital though such reflection is. It also includes the use of our God given power of thought to grow in understanding of nature, history and ourselves, and to bring that understanding into living interaction with Scripture and Tradition" (*The Nature of Christian Belief: A Statement and Exposition by the House of Bishops of the General Synod of the Church of England.* Church House Publishing 1986, pages 4f. footnote). The statement from which these words are cited was published to reassure public opinion following adverse publicity given to unwise and insensitive remarks by David Jenkins, then Bishop of Durham.

Such is the background against which we need to exercise judgement and discretion about what does and does not merit legitimate inclusion in "Narrow Churchmanship"/conservative traditionalism properly so-called. The line between them is an extremely fine one. Clearly not all those who claim the names of conservative and traditionalist deserves to have that claim acknowledged. Ostrich-like refusal to accept factual reality, as in the case of "blindness" to agreed findings of sound Biblical scholarship, is a case in point. On the other hand, as we recognised when considering the fundamentalist leanings of present day so-called conservative evangelicalism, (regrettable as they undoubtedly are) they are, to a degree, excusable. One must allow for the fact that before modern methods of literary and historical

---

3. The alternative reading is "The old is good." (Equally conservative)

criticism were brought to bear on Holy Scripture, we, or rather our ancestors, were *all* in a sense Biblical fundamentalists. Thus, we can presume that wise, constructive interpretation of the Scriptures was not in short supply, no doubt through the sure guidance of the Holy Spirit.

This, it is true, may not seem a particularly convincing "plea in mitigation" for what may look like deliberate obscurantism, but it is offered for what it is worth in defence of those who still have recourse to Matthew Henry.[4]

In this connection, I feel constrained now to bring forward a matter I had intended to reserve until my description of the ecclesiometer, which is the subject of Chapter 10.

Conflicting spiritual "forces" of attraction and repulsion

It is a fundamental principle of ecclesiometry, a fact of experience, and (or so I believe) an instance of the grace of God, that *along the radial axes of the four points of the compass which indicate the four legitimate types of "churchmanship"*, Low, Broad, High and Narrow, *there are two powerful forces or influences pulling in opposite directions*. One is centri*petal,* pulling, or driving towards the Central Point of Convergence: *this I believe to be nothing less than the Grace of God and the power of the Holy Spirit*. The other force, equally (it *seems*) *powerful, but, like the first, not irresistible*, is centri*fugal,* sucking or dragging away from the centre and outwards, away each from the other points of the compass. This, if (like John Milton, C.S. Lewis and some of the writers of the New Testament – but unlike me) you believe that Evil is personal, you would describe as the work of the Devil, otherwise as the forces of Darkness, Chaos, Confusion, Division, Anarchy and Disunity. These contrary forces are invisible, like the wind, but, also like the wind, can be exceedingly powerful (cf. John 3.8).

Thus, between Broad and Narrow, as between Low and High, there is both a mutual attraction – and a mutual repulsion. As has already been hinted, these two pairs of "opposites" are also complementary. High *needs* Low, Broad *needs* Narrow, and *vice versa*. They *belong together*. There is between them, a synthesis, as, in the case of High and Low, Michael Ramsey so triumphantly demonstrated, not only in his book (see page 131 above), but in his genes. Translating this into terms of the current jargon, Liberal *needs* Conservative – as indeed

---

4. Matthew Henry (1662-1714) Nonconformist Biblical exegete, whose *Exposition of the Old and New Testaments* (1708-10) is still highly valued by some evangelicals.

Conservative/Traditionalist *needs* Liberal, just as Catholic *needs* Evangelical and Protestant (and *vice versa*). There is, as I have said, or there needs to be, a synthesis.

I have not quite finished this mini excursus. In the "churchmanship" quarter at present under review, viz. Narrow, there is, or there ought to be, a sense of awe and reverence in face of the sheer transcendent otherness of the Holy One whom we call "GOD" – a sense too of the unique indispensability of Holy Scripture which, as the Broad Churchman so well knows, in the mysterious workings of Divine Providence is wholly and entirely human, fallible, *yet inspired* by the Holy Spirit of Truth, in whom both Broad and Narrow should unreservedly trust. On this further, see pp. 259-265.

But, if so, and if they are willingly exposed to the Grace of God, they, with their High and Low brethren, should beware of the insidious, destructive, *centrifugal* force, its powerful pull *away* from the Centre, where (and, again, I had intended to reserve this to Chapter 10) the two axes of Truth converge and make, at the very Centre, a Cross. That is no accident. And round that Cross there is an unmistakable radiance.

One further point. The centripetal "force", as I have dared to call it, of the Grace of God often takes the salutary form, from our side, of restraint, tact, sensitivity, always of a due reverence. Where that restraint, that reverence are lacking, liberal scholars and thinkers, blissfully self-absorbed in their exciting theories, blind to the sacred, the numinous, at their very elbow in the holy things they are handling with such apparent levity, are allowing themselves to be sucked inexorably to destruction in oblivion. Need I say more? This is just how things *are*. But the Holy One has left us, all of us, free agents. If, recognising Who it is with whom we have to deal, we resolve to cooperate unreservedly with Him, all will be well. If not. . . .

We should now, I hope, be in a better position to look around us in this Narrow quarter, the far West, the land of golden sunsets. Sometimes it has the look of a large refugee camp, or, if you prefer it, the asylum for which asylum seekers yearn. Though whether all those who seek it should be *granted* asylum in this quarter is an open question.

Cases for admission to and rejection from asylum in "Narrow"

First to be considered are those "catholic traditionalists" we saw clamouring for attention on our way here. They are, presumably, Anglo-Catholics – some may well be Ultra-Catholics like the subject of Mascall's brilliant satire, who call themselves "traditionalists" because they disapprove of the majority decision in 1993 to proceed

with the ordination of women as priests, on the grounds chiefly that
it was a novelty with no "catholic" precedent and would widen still
further the gulf between Canterbury and Rome. Special pastoral
provision was made for those who decided to remain Anglicans,
in the form of Provincial Episcopal Visitors ("Flying Bishops") – a
departure in Church order completely without precedent, and, some
think, tending to encourage, or even legitimise, schism. I will not add
to what I wrote about this in the preceding chapter.

About "conservative evangelicals" I have also written at length
and need to add little. Those who support Reform and the Church
Society agree with the dissident Anglo-Catholics in opposing the
ordination of women but on different grounds. They also hold strong
views on another controversial subject of which I know little viz.
homosexuality.

That leaves two more categories to be found in, or aspiring to be
admitted to, the Narrow quarter.

The first of these is members of the Prayer Book Society, including
their Patron, the Prince of Wales.

In view of what I have written under the heading of High
"Churchmanship", it might be thought that I too would be a strong
P.B.S. supporter. Not so. In my earlier years, when there was, in
fact, no lawful alternative, I used to think I was about the most
enthusiastic and law abiding user of the BCP (1662) in the country,
and I probably was. In my first parish we sang the (old) Litany
after full Mattins once a month, we dutifully "comminated" on Ash
Wednesday, I churched women, all of whom if Psalm 116 (the first
of the two alternatives)[5] were chosen, dutifully said "I said in my
haste, All men are liars". Almost the only 1662 service I have never
conducted was Burial at Sea – and I would readily have done that
had the occasion called for it. However as the years went by, and
when in 1967, *Holy Communion: Series 2* (the little blue books,
do you remember them?) was authorised for experimental use
– leading eventually via Series 3 to the *Alternative Service Book
1980* – I thought how refreshing it was, both in its much improved
order and its plain English, and, after full consultation with my
PCC (Reydon, Suffolk) and with very little dissension, (and that
good tempered), they agreed with me, we were the first parish in
the Deanery to adopt it.

In short, I came to feel that to continue to use 1662 in the latter half
of the twentieth century was anachronistic play acting, not pleasing

5. I came to prefer the second, gentler, more poetic Psalm 127

to the Almighty, and that, to be logical, if we did go on using it we should all dress up in Charles II period costume, periwigs and all. I enormously admire Sir Christopher Wren and all his works, not only St. Paul's, but such exquisite city churches as St. Stephen Walbrook, St. Mary Abchurch, St. Benet Paul's Wharf, St. James Garlickhythe and St. Martin Ludgate.[6] But if I were asked to design a church or cathedral for today, I would not design it like that! I would go for contemporary, functional.

I cannot help feeling some sympathy with the Prayer Book Society, but I also feel that they are wholly misguided. It is very sad indeed that there should be contention over such matters, unnecessary contention. There were undoubtedly faults on both sides. The Liturgical Commission, after so long a delay in the necessary modernising of our Liturgy, was in *far* too much of a hurry, and a great many faithful worshippers were deeply hurt and some lost altogether to the Church. The Church of Ireland and the Anglican Church of Canada were more cautious and properly conservative, perhaps too much so.

But in revising the ASB in the light of lessons learnt, those who created *Common Worship*, while again they created bewildering (and needless) diversity, complexity and confusion with *far* too many alternatives, incorporated the Prayer Book in the new Book, and they did give us a fine Eucharistic Rite (with alternative Eucharistic Prayers). And, as I discovered only the Sunday before writing this, when leading Morning Prayer in a remote and unspoilt Essex country church,[7] it is perfectly possible to have a traditional Mattins with good dignified up-to-date wording in the Canticles, Psalms and Creed *and* a wholly admirable crisp, *modern* Litany – also the best of those wonderful Prayer Book collects, carefully reworded where necessary, and some excellent new ones.

Those are some reasons for believing that the Prayer Book Society is seriously misguided. I pray that ere long they will have the grace to see this for themselves and lend their full and valuable support to the present day worship of the Church of England. We badly need them.

---

6. All these churches were designed, built by Wren and furnished (some of them e.g. St. Mary Abchurch) by the greatest of all woodcarvers, Grinling Gibbons, as settings for worship in the spirit as well as the words of the BCP 1662. Those named are the least altered in later times: This also applies to Hawksmoor's superb St. Mary Woolnoth and its contemporary furnishings.

7. St. Margaret's, Tilbury juxta Clare.

Finally, Some Special Pleading

The other category I have already hinted at, earlier in this chapter. Let us call it the Cause of Conservation. And here I have to declare an interest, combined with another confession – though this time not an abject one. Especially over the last thirty or more years I have invested a great deal of (and my conscience tells me far too much) time and energy, with others, in the cause of conservation of what is nowadays unromantically called the built environment – particularly of historic churches in Suffolk and Essex. In the former county where I spent the whole of my active ministry, I was instrumental, with others, in setting up the Suffolk Historic Churches Trust. This work, which I enjoyed *immensely*, brought me into contact with so many delightful people, by no means all of them active church members, but all fired with tremendous enthusiasm for our cause, and with a deep, abiding and discerning love for these wonderful churches. The same I found true of my native county Essex following our return (my wife and I) here in retirement.

There is an entirely understandable, but I believe *deeply* misguided tendency in some areas of our Anglican church life to be impatient with this aspect of our heritage; not only to undervalue it, but to regard it as just so much unnecessary lumber, so expensive to maintain, in these days of financial stringency in the Church. I would plead for a complete reversal; that we should all be immensely *proud* of our unbelievably rich inheritance and regard it as what it is, a trust and responsibility for us to hand on intact to future generations.[8] Special pleading, yes. I would very much hope that this whole field of activity be regarded as coming well within the sphere of Narrow Churchmanship. If it does not, I, and so many others, need your prayers!

---

8. The present Bishop of London, Richard Chartres, with his discerning appreciation of, and care for, the surviving City churches and others in his diocese, and his eloquent spokesmanship on Church heritage matters has set a welcome example.

Chapter 6
The Anglican Eirenicon

We have completed our laborious circuit of the hypothetical ecclesiometer dial.

We now pause, briefly, to summarise our conclusions. Taken together, they constitute our Anglican Eirenicon, a proposal tending to make peace.

I hope that in the preceding four chapters I have succeeded in convincing you, if you needed convincing, of the simple truth that others as well as I have *experienced*, viz. that (1) Low, Broad, High and Narrow Churchmen (and women) can each rightly claim a real, but strictly limited, validity for their respective standpoints; that (2) essentially there is no fundamental conflict between these four standpoints, Evangelical, Liberal, Anglo-Catholic and Conservative/ Traditional, but that (3) each of these four individual standpoints, Evangelical, Liberal, Anglo-Catholic and Conservative/Traditional is complementary to, *belongs with*, and *needs* the other three for the *fullness*, the *completeness* of Christian belief/faith/commitment, and (4) most important of all, that the Grace of God and the power and guidance of His Holy Spirit is, whether we are aware of it or not, gently impelling, drawing and urging us *all* towards this goal, this Central Point of the Victorious Cross of the Incarnate Son of God, Christ crucified, risen and triumphant, at the point where time uniquely intersects eternity. But because the same Creator-God has made us in His own image and thereby given us freedom of will and choice; while His goodness attracts and encourages us by His Grace, He never compels, but in His infinite loving kindness only seeks to persuade and encourage us to resist the contrary pressures of temptation to turn back upon ourselves and towards the abyss of ultimate chaos and annihilating destruction we call Hell.

To put it another way, if we continue to use the peculiarly Anglican language of 'churchmanship', we are all of us called to *abandon* our *individual* standpoints, High, Low, Broad and Narrow, but, taking the truths we have learnt there with us, to converge steadily upon the Centre, for that is where, *together*, we shall find Him who is the Way, the Truth and the Life, crucified yet triumphant in His unconquerable love.

That, basically, is the Anglican eirenicon, a proposal tending to make peace. Some will say it is no more or less than Central Churchmanship, others that it is just the old *sensus* or *consensus communis fidelium*. If they do, we have no quarrel with them. But, whatever we call it, the hand of Providence may be discerned and if that is the ultimate purpose for which Anglicanism came into being, Laus Deo. God be praised.

It is now time to see if we can find evidence of it at work in its own home land, the Anglican sector of worldwide Christianity. When we have done that, we will turn our attention to the wider ecumenical scene of all Christian people in deeply divided Christendom. Finally, in a scope wider still, we will focus on the three monotheistic faiths, all of which, of course, look back to Abraham as 'their' pioneer/father – i.e. Judaism, Christianity and Islam – to see what, if any, relevance it has there. We may be in for some surprises.

Part Two:
Application

Chapter 7
**Anglicans World-Wide:
Unity or Disintegration?**

This book has been written against a background of mounting tension and conflict within the Anglican world. The bone of contention is the age old phenomenon of homosexuality; differing understandings of it in the light, on the one hand, of the Bible, and on the other, of modern knowledge and culture. Because of this duality of approach to the subject in question, Biblical/theological and practical/scientific, and the difficulty (for some, the sheer impossibility) of reconciling the two, what is at stake is inevitably on two levels: (i) the unity and harmony of the Anglican Communion worldwide and (ii) the theological, moral and practical truth of the underlying matters at issue.

This current controversy followed close upon the heels of another, which at the time of writing still has not yet been finally resolved any more than its successor – that of the ordination of women. Both disputes had, and are still having, a marked effect upon the subject of this book, Anglican party alignments and the possibility of genuine consensus.

Our chief concern in this chapter is with the current controversy. But the unprecedented expedient adopted following the General Synod's decisive vote in favour of the ordination of women to the priesthood viz. the innovation of Provincial Episcopal Visitors, more colloquially known as Flying Bishops, to provide alternative pastoral oversight to clergy and parishes still opposed to women's ordination, but remaining loyal to the Church of England, cannot go unremarked here. At the time of writing this "experiment" has been in operation for some fifteen years. I am in no position to judge, but my *impression*, for what it is worth, is that it has resulted in a disastrous subversion of what old-fashioned High Churchmen (like me) always regarded as basic Catholic order – the diocesan bishop exercising undisputed authority in every parish in his diocese. What we now have instead is a number of "no go" parishes in every diocese, in which the bishop is unwelcome, and from which he is excluded. This was originally proposed (if I remember rightly) by John Habgood, a former outstanding Archbishop of York, and adopted, as a generous gesture, to those who, as a matter of conscience, had voted against women's ordination – but adopted without sufficient foresight or forethought. The unlooked-for result has been to institutionalise dissent *within* the Church, and, to judge from the tone of some of the literature displayed in these dissenting parishes, uncharitable and bitter, ill-natured dissent at that. I can see no good future for such an ill-considered experiment and hope it will never be seen as a sound precedent in the future. But once having been adopted, it is extremely difficult to see how it can be abrogated without even worse effects. A Church, like a house or a kingdom, deeply divided against itself, cannot but fall.

Apart from a salutary injection of new life into the dwindling, previously all-male ordained ministry of the Church of England (and some of this new life is of very high quality indeed), one of the principal effects of this long delayed U turn was the depletion of the Anglo-Catholic party by the defection of considerable numbers to Rome. Almost all Eric Mascall's Ultra-Catholics "went over" in a body, (including some who had wives), much to the barely concealed glee of the Roman Catholic hierarchy, led successively by Basil Hume and Cormac Murphy O'Connor, Cardinal Archbishops of Westminster. Defection was even made easier, in the circumstances, for some of these, forced to deny the reality, or validity, of their Anglican Orders, to be "re-ordained" as Roman priests – even, in some cases, those who were married! The chief defector was the former Bishop of London, Graham Leonard. But, in *fact*, in most of those cases, they were going where they really belonged, where their true spiritual home was, like Mascall's Ultra-Catholic. As a footnote, it needs to be added that a few, perhaps only a handful, of these defectors eventually drifted back, disillusioned with what they found. "The grass is always greener on the other side of the hill".

The Anglo-Catholics were depleted, but not decimated, by the ordination of women. A solid, if small, core of these, convinced in heart and mind that this was right and truly catholic remained staunch Anglicans. Of them many joined a new grouping called *Affirming Catholicism*, in the founding of which two youngish priests, friends, were concerned. Their names were Rowan Williams and Jeffrey John, both later to attain prominence in the Church.

The current controversy

We now return to the current controversy. Whatever one's viewpoint, for a clear understanding of the many complex points at issue, one book is essential reading. It is Stephen Bates: *A Church at War: Anglicans and Homosexuality* (I.B. Tauris, 2004). The author was until recently Religious Affairs correspondent of *The Guardian* newspaper. A journalist by profession and an historian by training (at New College, Oxford), he makes no attempt to conceal his emphatic viewpoint, but is scrupulously fair, if not impartial. This makes for excellent reading; Bates can be and often is brilliantly witty and his descriptions of the chief participants are keenly perceptive. This is all the more remarkable when he tells his readers that he is "by birth and upbringing a Roman Catholic", that his father was "a devoted communicant of the Church of England throughout his 89 years" and that he himself is married to "a committed Anglican Charismatic Evangelical" who is bringing up their children in the Evangelical tradition because she is "a better Christian" than he is! This means, he says, that he is "by no means as hostile to Evangelicalism as some may suppose".[1] To top it all, the book is dedicated "to my Evangelical wife, Alice, and my Evangelical children, Helena, Timothy and Philip, with much love".

This remarkable book, to which I am greatly indebted, is presented modestly therefore as "a work of journalism rather than theological and historical scholarship, written for Anglicans and others interested in the church and its fate, in an attempt to explain how and why it has come to its present pass, threatened by the most serious split in its modern history over an issue that many people within its portals and beyond regard as being of at best secondary importance to its overall mission or in the concerns of the overwhelming majority of its members".

The besetting temptation of journalists is sensationalism and Bates, honest and experienced as he is, has not altogether avoided it. His powerful sympathies with the "liberals" in this conflict, so much at variance with the official teaching of his own Church, may have led him to over-dramatise what he sees as a takeover bid by their conservative evangelical opponents. His readers need to be aware of such limitations, and of his confessed bias, which in no way detracts from the book's value as a serious, mature narrative of the origins and course of events in this unfinished controversy up to the point in early 2004 when he broke off to write his book. Much has happened since then.

---

1. Extracts from the Preface, page vii.

Origins of the dispute

Particularly valuable, in my view, is Bates's full and detailed survey of the historical background. He rightly sets it in a very wide context. Most of this is, or ought to be, uncontroversial. It is a story, very largely, of ignorance and prejudice on the part of the vast majority of the human race; of the development of tolerance in the ancient civilisations of Greece and Rome; of the sufferings of the despised and persecuted minority, lasting, even in the supposedly enlightened West, into well within living memory.

Bates devotes a lengthy chapter (pages 36-58) to a systematic review of the Biblical references on which, and on the significance and interpretation of which, so much of the argument turns. Beginning with the Old Testament and concluding with famous passages in St. Paul's Letter to the Romans (chapter 1, verses 26-27), his first Letter to the Corinthians (chapter 6, verses 9 and 10) and his First Letter to Timothy (chapter 1, verses 9 and 10), Bates quotes pertinent examples of intelligent scholarly exegesis, not attempting to "explain them away". He does not omit to record the significant fact that "Jesus did not refer explicitly to homosexuality in anything the Gospels record him as saying" and that in the New Testament the *only* references to the subject are in St. Paul's letters. These, however, are unambiguous in their abhorrence of homosexual practice as "unnatural".

Despite well-documented evidence of occasional examples of this behaviour at the highest level,[2] legislation as well as public and Church opinion in England – much as on the Continent – reflected Biblical disapproval, and in particular the Mosaic legislation in Leviticus chapters 18 verse 22 and 20 verse 13. This continued virtually unchanged for centuries and it comes as a shock to learn that the last public *execution* for homosexuality in Britain took place as comparatively recently as 1835 (Bates p. 70). The most notorious case was, of course, that of the brilliant wit and playwright Oscar Wilde, in 1895 sentenced to a term of imprisonment in Reading Gaol for his homosexual relationship with Lord Alfred Douglas.

The historical background is also usefully analysed and discussed in a valuable report by four Anglican bishops entitled *Some Issues in Human Sexuality: A Guide to the Debate* (Church House Publishing 2003).[3] Bates and the Bishops both point to the

2. King Edward II (1307-1327) and King James I (1603-1625).
3. This report was commissioned by the English House of Bishops in 2003 and

gradual but decisive change in public attitudes and sexual ethics which began in Britain after the Second World War together with significant advances in genetic, biological and psychological studies, leading to the crucial probability that homosexual orientation was less a matter of deliberate choice than of inherited tendency.

These developments, leading to a growing attitude of sometimes amused tolerance, and even sympathetic understanding, replacing the age-old taboo on the "distasteful" subject in polite society, with homosexuals driven underground in shame and fear, led also to the government of the day appointing a commission headed by the respected Anglican layman and headmaster, Sir John Wolfenden, to consider and report on the whole matter. The Wolfenden Commission reported in 1957 but its recommendations did not become law until 1967 when the Sexual Offences Act, decriminalising homosexual acts between consenting adults, received the Royal assent. It had all party support and that of the Church of England. It was an important feature of what came to be known as "the sexual revolution of the sixties", inaugurating, together with the end of official moral censorship (as the result of the *Lady Chatterley's Lover* case), the "Permissive Society" which is such a marked feature of the world in which we live today.

In the ordained ministry of the Church of England, it had for some time been a recognised fact that particularly both in London and among often highly dedicated, hardworking, Anglo-Catholic clergy, many of them with a developed aesthetic sensitivity to beauty in music and art, homosexuality was rife. It obviously cannot be known in how many cases these clergymen were celibate, but clearly some, perhaps the majority, were not. A case in point, frankly confessed in his remarkable autobiography, *Some Day I'll Find You,* is that of the brilliantly clever Anglo-Catholic, H.A. (Harry) Williams (1919-2006), in the latter part of his life a monk of the Community of the Resurrection founded by Bishop Gore. Williams in his book made no secret of having practised his homosexuality promiscuously while Fellow and Dean of Chapel of Trinity College, Cambridge, where he was famous as a preacher.[4]

---

took a full year to compile. It is intended as a discussion document on the earlier authoritative Bishops' statement of 1991 entitled *Issues in Human Sexuality* which itself was the subject of heated controversy (on which see below). The four Bishops were those of Oxford (Richard Harries, chairman), Winchester (M. Scott Joynt), Chester (P. Forster) and Chelmsford (J. Gladwin).

4. Some sermons are collected in *The True Wilderness* (Penguin 1965).

One of the many who, mindful of the unambiguous condemnation of homosexual *practice* by St. Paul in the first chapter of his Epistle to the Romans, and in the Old Testament, found such behaviour deeply scandalous and was not afraid to say so was a highly vocal conservative evangelical clergyman, Tony Higton, at that time the energetic and successful Rector of Hawkwell, Essex, and an elected member of General Synod.

The debate begins: "Issues in Human Sexuality" (1991)

The matter of homosexuality came up briefly at the Lambeth Conference of 1988 and it was this, together with Higton's intemperate attacks, especially in a notable Synod debate in 1987, which caused the then-Archbishop of Canterbury, Robert Runcie, to authorise the preparation of a balanced statement on behalf of the House of Bishops of General Synod. This was eventually issued and published in December 1991, under the title of *Issues in Human Sexuality*, with a preface by Runcie's recently appointed successor, George Carey. In this, after reminding its readers of the 1988 Lambeth Conference's call on all Anglican bishops to undertake in the next decade a "deep and dispassionate study of the question of homosexuality" (Resolution 64), he said that this statement is partly a response to that call, as well as being "our reflection on the pastoral situation we face in our own Church and Society". (*Issues* was greatly helped by the work of a small group chaired by the then sagacious Bishop of Salisbury, John Austin Baker.) Carey went on cautiously to say that its purpose was "to promote an educational process, as a result of which Christians may both become more informed about and understanding of certain human realities and enter more deeply into the wisdom of their inheritance of faith in this field". He concluded by saying: "We cannot expect all to agree with our conclusions . . . we benefited by vigorous debate in the context of mutual affection and tolerance. We encourage clergy chapters and congregations to find time for prayerful study and reflection on the issues we have addressed."

The statement, running to 48 closely argued pages, calls for "a discussion which needs to be continued throughout the Church by individuals and groups who learn humbly and prayerfully to be open to facts, to one another and to Scripture, Tradition and reasoned reflection on experience".

If only those concerned had heeded this call, *Issues in Human Sexuality* would have done nothing but good. Instead, it came to be used, for well over a decade, as a kind of football by all involved, most of whom, one suspects, had never taken the trouble to read and give it the prayerful and thoughtful consideration for which it asked and which it deserved. For it is full of mature, charitable and fair-minded wisdom *and* it made no pretence of being the last word on the subject.

To interject a purely personal view at this point, my own feeling *before* what George Carey rightly called "this fraught and sensitive issue"[5] was forced upon our (in my case, reluctant) attention was one of almost total ignorance and some prejudice, combined with smug thankfulness that I and all my family, *so far*, were free from it, in any shape or form – together with awareness that I had known, and known of, several male homosexuals, outstanding for their intelligence, integrity, charm and aesthetic sensitivity. I had never felt tempted to pass moral judgment on them, despite being aware of St. Paul's strictures in the New Testament and what is written in the Old. So in my case the "educational process" was very much needed and long overdue. How typical, or untypical, I am in this respect, I have no idea. Probably I was both lazy and inexcusably naive.

One great merit of *Issues* is that it treats of homosexuality fully within the context of human sexuality as a whole, seen in the light of God's good purposes in creation and providence as made known to us through a reasoned understanding of Scripture, Tradition and the findings of scientific enquiry. *Issues* emphasises our "common humanity". With regard to the Church, "we would draw attention to the need for congregations to be places of open acceptance and friendship for homophiles, as for people of every kind" (p. 33). There is a "clear, simple and fundamental responsibility of Christians to reject and resist all forms of homophobia" (p. 34). To extract sentences like this from their context is to risk failing to do justice to the scrupulous fairness and generosity of tone of this important document.

In its fifth chapter *Issues* discusses at length the crucial question of whether, and if so, in what way, St. Paul in Romans 1 was justified in describing homosexual practice as "unnatural or contrary to nature". "In recent years" it says, "this categorisation has been fiercely contested by those who argue that same-sex love is simply one legitimate way of being human within the wide diversity of God's created order, and should be accepted as such and affirmed as of equal validity with the heterosexual" (p. 35).

This question is very fully discussed, in the light of both male-female complementarity, and procreation, and the unnatural "mismatch" which, in the very nature of the case, puts the homosexual

5. George Carey: *Know the Truth. A Memoir* (Harper Collins 2004) p. 293.

at an unbridgeable disadvantage vis à vis the purposes of God. (This I know is a thoroughly unsatisfactory attempt to abridge the argument in *Issues* pp. 35-39, which needs to be read and pondered, in full.)

The fifth and final chapter of *Issues* is the section which proved most controversial. Its title is "The Homophile [= Homosexual] in the Life and Fellowship of the Church". It is described as "what guidance for pastoral practice can be offered to the Church in the present state of Christian understanding of this issue", and adds, "The aim of us all must be to allow the Holy Spirit to lead us into the mind of Christ for all his members in a world where homosexual orientation is the experience of some" (p. 40). It begins by setting out two fundamental principles "of equal validity and significance".

The first is,

> that homophile orientation and its expression in sexual activity do NOT constitute a parallel and alternative form of human sexuality as complete within the terms of the created order as the heterosexual. The convergence of Scripture, Tradition and reasoned reflection on experience, even including the newly sympathetic and perceptive thinking of our own day, make it impossible for the Church to come with integrity to any other conclusion. Heterosexuality and homosexuality are *not equally* congruous with the observed order of creation or with the insights of revelation as the Church engages with these in the light of her pastoral ministry.

Issues is at pains to stress that this traditional teaching does NOT devalue or degrade homosexuals. We are *all* made in the image of God and have "equal worth and dignity as human beings". The second fundamental principle, "laid upon us by the truths at the very heart of the faith", is that

> homosexual people are in every way as valuable to and as valued by God as heterosexual people. God loves us all alike, and has for each one of us a range of possibilities within his design for the universe. This includes those who, for whatever reason, find themselves with a homophile orientation which, so far as anyone at present can tell, cannot in their case be changed, and within which therefore they have the responsibility of living human life creatively and well. Every human being has a unique potential for Christlikeness, and an individual contribution to make through that likeness to the final consummation of all things. (pp. 40f.)

In the following two paragraphs (5.5. and 5.6. p. 41) *Issues* says (i) that some Christian homophiles feel called "to witness to God's general will for human sexuality by a life of abstinence" [i.e. from active sexual activity – in a word, chastity]. "In the power of the Holy Spirit and for the love of Christ, they embrace the self-denial involved, gladly and willingly. It is a path of great faithfulness, travelled often under the weight of a very heavy cross, deserving of all praise and of the support of Church members through prayer, understanding and active friendship". It goes on to say (ii) that "others are conscientiously convinced that this way of abstinence is not the best for them and that they have more hope of growing in love for God and neighbour with the help of a loving and faithful homophile partnership in intention life long". *Issues* concludes: "We do not reject those who sincerely believe that that is God's call to them. We stand alongside them in the fellowship of the Church." It adds that the Bishops "do not countenance promiscuous, casual or exploitative sex" for either homophile or heterophile and they state categorically that "the ideal of chastity holds good for all Christians" (p. 42).

Issues then turns to "the question of the homophile clergy" (pp. 43f.). Noting that, in the population as a whole, a small percentage is predominantly homophile,

> it may be that in the ordained ministry, as in the arts and the caring professions, the percentage is higher. We believe that the great majority of such clergy are not in sexually active partnerships. What we know for a fact is that the ministries of many homophile clergy are highly dedicated and have been greatly blessed. God has endowed them with spiritual gifts, as he has his other ministers, and we give thanks for all alike. There are, however, questions to be faced concerning the ministry of homophile clergy who believe that the right way of life for them is that of an exclusive and permanent but also sexually active partnership. These questions are additional to those which arise in the case of Christian people in general, and they relate to the representative and pastoral responsibilities of the clergy. (p. 44)

Up to this point, *Issues* could be said to be uncontroversial. It is here, where a clear distinction is drawn between the moral obligations of homosexual laity and homosexual clergy, that *Issues* ran into bitter opposition from the latter.

"From the time of the New Testament onwards", continues *Issues* (5.13 p. 44), it has been expected of those appointed to the ministry of authority in the Church that they shall not only preach but also *live* the Gospel. These expectations are as real today as ever they were. People not only inside the Church but outside it believe rightly that in the way of life of an ordained minister they ought to be able to see a pattern which the Church commends. Inevitably, therefore, the world will assume that all ways of living which an ordained person is allowed to adopt are in Christian eyes equally valid. With regard to homophile relationships, however, this is, as we have already explained, a position which for theological reasons, the Church does not hold. Justice does indeed demand that the Church should be free in its pastoral discretion to accommodate a God-given ideal to human need, so that individuals are not turned away from God and their neighbour but helped to grow in love toward both from within their own situation. But the Church is also bound to take care that the ideal itself is not misrepresented or obscured and to this end the example of its ordained ministers is of crucial importance. This means that certain possibilities are not open to the clergy by comparison with the laity. . . . Restrictions on what the clergy may do also stem from their pastoral function. If they are to be accessible and acceptable to the greatest number of people, both within the Church and outside it, then so far as possible their lives must be free of anything which will make it difficult for others to have confidence in them as messengers, watchmen and stewards of the Lord. There can be no doubt that an ordained person living in an *active* homophile relationship does for a significant number of people at this time present such a difficulty.

On this, *Issues* concludes:

We have therefore, to say that in our considered judgement the clergy cannot claim the liberty to enter into sexually active homophile relationships. Because of the distinctive nature of their calling, status and consecration, to allow such a claim on their part would be seen as placing that way of life in all respects on a par with heterosexual marriage as a reflection of God's purposes in creation. The Church cannot accept such a parity and remain faithful to the insights which God has given it through Scripture, tradition and reasoned reflection on experience. (p. 45)

The Bishops go on to say:

> In the light of this judgment, some may propose that bishops should be more rigorous in searching out and exposing clergy who may be in sexually active homophile relationships. We reject this approach for two reasons. (1) There is a growing tendency today to regard any two persons of the same sex who choose to make their home together as being in some form of erotic relationship. This is grossly unfair . . . and the Church should do nothing to promote it. (2) It has always been the practice of the Church of England to trust its members, and not to carry out intrusive interrogations in order to make sure they are behaving themselves . . . Although we must take steps to avoid public scandal and to protect the Church's teaching we shall continue, as . . . hitherto, to treat all clergy who give no occasion for scandal with trust and respect, and we expect all our fellow Christians to do the same. (p. 46)

In the penultimate paragraphs of *Issues* the Bishops address the question of those, clergy or laity, who voluntarily choose publicly to "come out" i.e. to identify themselves as homosexual by orientation. These are in two categories, first those who embrace chastity, abstinence from sexual activity. "Their desire is to be free to live among their neighbours with dignity and without concealment, unembarrassed by speculation or suggestions of marriage. A community which cannot accept such an honourable candour is not worthy of the name of Christian. We greatly regret the way in which candidates for appointments who are open in this way are often rejected by parishes solely on those grounds". As for those in the second category, clergy in active homosexual partnerships who "come out" as a matter of personal integrity, while the Bishops "respect that integrity", they feel "it is their duty to affirm and uphold those requirements for conduct" that will best witness to "the whole pattern of Christian teaching on sexuality set out in these pages." "Ordinarily it should be left to candidates' own consciences to act responsibly in this matter." (p. 47)

Summing up the guidance they seek to give in this final chapter, the Bishops ask for

> an open and welcoming place in the Christian community both for those homophiles who follow the way of abstinence, giving themselves to friendship for many rather than to intimacy with one, and also for those who are conscientiously convinced that a faithful, sexually active relationship with

one other person, aimed at helping both partners to grow in
discipleship, is the way of life God wills for them. (p. 47)

Issues concludes:

> The story of the Church's attitude to homosexuals has too
> often been one of prejudice, ignorance and oppression. All
> of us need to acknowledge that, and to repent for any part
> we have had in it . . . If we are faithful to Our Lord, then
> disagreement over the proper expression of homosexual love
> will never become rejection of the homosexual person.

Such, then, in outline, is this celebrated document. I have deliberately
afforded it what some may regard as excessive space, in order to
allow it to speak clearly for itself, without distortion. It set out not
only to give clear guidance on the Bishops' agreed policy for the
Church of England, but also to be a basis for discussion. Lord Carey,
(as he is now) devoting a whole chapter in his memoir *Know the
Truth* (Harper Collins 2004) to the challenge of homosexuality, gives
it as his "private opinion" that "it would be difficult to find a stronger
document that commanded such agreement among the Bishops"
(op. cit. p. 293) and he claims that "it was well received by the vast
majority of the Church of England and those beyond it", (op. cit.
p. 294) and adds, "I was delighted with it", and that its publication
"forced me to clarify my own thinking and approach on the matter, as
it was increasingly obvious that homosexuality would be one of the
most urgent and vexed issues in the Anglican Communion during my
leadership." One thing he was quite clear about was that "in the case of
same-sex relationships, it would be grievous error to offer some sort
of blessing that is a pretended substitute for a marriage, which such
union can never comprise" (op. cit. p. 298). "To do this is to harm the
people involved by offering them a pretence and a deception . . . To
perform such an act is also to mislead society at large. Offering such
ceremonies seems to suggest that something resembling a marriage
can exist where it does not. It is also a trivialisation of gender. This
is not in any sense to suggest that love, profound friendship or even
commitment are not good, but it is to say that marriage is not simply
a product of some combination of these things between assenting
parties of any orientation or gender." (op. cit. p. 299) He was equally
clear that "it cannot be right to make a Bishop of someone who
expressly proclaims that he lives in violation of what the Church
teaches." (p. 299)
These were the two main sticking points later on, when these

problems of homosexuality threatened to split the Anglican Communion in the first decade of the twenty-first Christian century. In the meantime, however, Carey and the entire House of Bishops felt "that the discussion had to be kept open" (p. 299).

Cross Currents 1991-1998

In the years between the publication of *Issues* (1991) and the Lambeth Conference of 1998, this is exactly what happened. *Issues* represented the centre ground and it was under mounting attack from both sides. It became apparent that a minority of bishops, most of them in the London and Southwark areas, had for some time past been ordaining *practising* homosexuals, and there was on their part an understandable reluctance to enquire closely into the private lives of ordinands. A homosexual organisation called the Lesbian and Gay Christian Movement (L.G.C.M.), centred round the Reverend Richard Kirker, an Anglican deacon, was extremely active in propaganda, with its base then in the London City church of St. Botolph, Aldgate. Another homosexual group called Outrage was similarly centred upon one man, Peter Tatchell. His aggressive behaviour stopped at nothing in its tactics of gaining publicity by accusing his victims, some of them leading Anglican bishops, of being covert homosexuals, and threatening to "out" them.

On the opposite side were "conservative evangelicals", notably, in England, Reform and the Church Society. On a basis of a fundamentalist interpretation of the principal Biblical passages in Genesis (the story of the men of Sodom) and Leviticus and the Pauline passages referred to above, they maintained that homosexual genital activity is definitely "sinful" and that, consequently, the proper approach should be to seek repentance. The "Reform" leaders approached Archbishop Carey with a request for separate pastoral supervision by chosen evangelical bishops as Provincial Episcopal Visitors, Flying Bishops, as in the case of clergy and parishes conscientiously opposed to women priests. This, Carey, himself from an evangelical background, very properly refused.

These groups were, so far, confined to the Church in England. But as preparations for Lambeth 1998 drew near, it became apparent that similar movements were building up in the worldwide Anglican Communion.

In the United States there was a powerful "liberal" lobby which found expression in the person of Jack Spong, the ultra-radical Bishop of Newark, New Jersey. It numbered among its supporters Frank Griswold, shortly to become Presiding Bishop of ECUSA,

the Episcopal Church of the U.S.A. Spong's extreme radicalism
was to put him outside Christian orthodoxy altogether, but a
powerful body favoured the blessing of same-sex union, and the
ordination of practising homosexuals, without any pretence to the
contrary. Naturally this rampant "liberalism" aroused "conservative"
opposition in several American dioceses, centred then and later, in
Pittsburgh, Pennsylvania.

At the same time it became evident that there was an equally
strong body of opinion in the global South, or Third World, area
of the Anglican Communion, manifesting itself in a huge swathe
from Latin America and the Caribbean to Africa and South East
Asia. It should be remembered, in this respect, that Anglican
missionary outreach, principally in the nineteenth century, had
taken with it Anglican Church partisanship, Evangelical (through
the largest society, CMS) and various shades of High Church Anglo-
Catholicism (in the case of SPG and the Universities' Mission
to Central Africa (UMCA) later to merge as the United Society
for the Propagation of the Gospel (USPG)). These party beliefs
had coloured the new churches, provinces and dioceses they had
pioneered. Also the complexities of Biblical criticism had hardly
penetrated, to modify the simplistic, uncritical, literal interpretation
of scripture.[6]

Lambeth 1998

As it was over the cross currents of opinion and the actions of pressure
groups in the run-up to Lambeth 1998 which George Carey presided,
his "memoir" *Know the Truth* is a reliable and fair minded source,
so too the chapter entitled Lambeth '98, pp. 314-333, is required
reading. To be fair, there is no doubt that it should be balanced by a
perusal of *Doubts and Loves: What is left of Christianity*[7] by Richard
Holloway, who, as Bishop of Edinburgh, was a leading protagonist
at the Conference – which left him bitterly angry and critical of
Carey's chairmanship. Since 1998 and resigning his bishopric and
primacy of the Scottish Episcopal Church, Holloway has abandoned
any pretence of orthodox Christian belief. Bates' *A Church at War*
supports Holloway's criticism.

Carey makes no attempt to disguise the ugly scenes that disgraced

6. George Carey in *Know the Truth: a Memoir* describes these currents
of opinion 1991-1998 with fairness and humour, including his own rough
treatment by Tatchell, op. cit. pp. 300-313.

7. *Doubts and Loves* was first published by Canongate Books, Edinburgh
in 2001.

the Conference's proceedings on the issue of homosexuality, but he sets them in the context of the Conference as a whole, of which they constituted an important, though largely disproportionate, part. As he points out more than once, "the issue of homosexuality could not compare in importance with the fact that two-thirds of the human family lived on less than $2 a day", (p. 330). Among the other purposes for which the Conference needed to be called for mutual consultation were problems concerning "poverty, and exclusion from the global economic order, international debt, war and civil unrest, problems concerning the individual, women and children, problems concerning mission; relations with Islam and other faiths, and problems to do with other Churches and the search for unity", (p. 316f.). Homosexuality was only one topic among many, and seems to have been the only one to have caused major dissension and scenes unworthy of a Christian assembly.

Carey rightly emphasises that Lambeth '98 will "be remembered for finally demonstrating that power had swung decisively from the North to the South." (p. 331). Altogether there were over 800 Anglican bishops worldwide, and of these over 750 attended the Conference (including a handful of women bishops), together with 650 bishops' spouses. Of this number, those from the British Isles, North America, and the white Commonwealth (Australia and New Zealand) were in a minority, and this had an obvious effect when it came to voting on divisive issues. "How ultimately," asks Carey,

> will Lambeth '98 be remembered? Those who attended will have their own personal memories and will have made their own judgements. The Bishops themselves rated it a great success. As President, and the one finally responsible for its success or failure, I considered it a great success, for many reasons. (p. 331).

But, he admits, "for many Lambeth '98 will be remembered for Resolution 1.10 on homosexuality". Here, he says, "the underlying issue that was exposed was an embarrassing ambiguity concerning the interpretation of Scripture." (p. 331). Here Carey put his finger on the fundamental cleavage revealed by the debate. In the next sentence he refers to "the proud claim of Anglicans since the Reformation…that truth emerges from a strenuous process of prayerful reflection on the threefold authority of Scripture, tradition and reason, with primacy given to Scripture". (Carey, op. cit. p. 331)

What Carey described as "embarrassing ambiguity", or what I (rather more boldly) call "the fundamental cleavage", bypasses this "threefold authority" altogether. Holloway in his radical *Loves and Doubts*, published four years after Lambeth, wrote

> Since I believe that the Christian account of meaning has to be separated from its historical packaging if it is to work for us today, I spend time in this book deconstructing important aspects of the Christian doctrinal tradition, such as original sin, incarnation and resurrection, but my ultimate intention is resoundingly positive . . . I try to distinguish between the transient and the enduring elements of both the Hebrew and the Christian scriptures, and suggest that it is better to see them as good poetry than as bad science if they are to have meaning for us today. My aim is to craft from the Christian past a usable ethic for our own time. (op. cit. p. 17)

Whether Holloway went as far at Lambeth in 1998 as he did in 2002 I do not know, but he was evidently thinking along lines of extreme theological radicalism even then in his passionate advocacy of practising homosexuality in the Church. Between his view and that of classical Anglican hermeneutic as described by Carey, there was rather more than "embarrassing ambiguity"! Even wider was the gap between the literalist fundamentalism of the "Global South" fanatics and the ultra-radicalism of the Spong/Hollowayites. No wonder they nearly came to blows!

Carey, with commendable candour, describes (op. cit. p. 326) how, as the Conference (which had so far gone so smoothly) "entered its third and final week, the tension mounted regarding the resolution on homosexuality to be laid before the Bishops. Unfortunately campaigning groups had infiltrated the Conference and were deepening the sense of Armageddon facing the Communion". He described Richard Holloway as "one of the principal leaders seeking a change in Anglican attitudes to homosexuals", and says that there was an exchange of gibes between him and some leading African bishops, and that "the opposite side" was equally guilty of heightening the sense of conflict.

There were various motions put forward in an attempt to strengthen the homosexuality resolution, some of them, in Carey's view "extremely objectionable. Tension was visibly mounting and many Bishops were distressed at the likelihood of an extremely happy Conference being wrecked by a matter which imperilled the unity of the Communion. I was conscious of the burden of my office, and the need to give a lead." (op. cit. p. 327)

"On the morning of the debate on the resolution a number of

African and Asian Archbishops came to see" Carey to tell him that they could not and would not vote for the resolution as it stood because it was too weak and would send the wrong message to the Anglican Communion, but they were equally worried about others which were too strong in condemnation of homosexuals. They felt caught between two extremes. (op. cit. p. 327f.)

Carey sought to resolve their difficulty by proposing to add eight crucial words: "While rejecting homosexual practice as incompatible with Scripture" to a sub-section of the Resolution (1.10) to be debated and voted upon. This was agreed.

The meeting on 5th August was chaired by Robin Eames, Archbishop of Armagh, with his customary geniality and firmness. "The tension was high with speeches ranging from the measured to the wild and intemperate. Some very hurtful things were said, which lowered the tone of the debate (p. 328). In the event 526 bishops voted for the Resolution and 78 against, with 45 abstentions. The huge majority surprised us all, and was a clear statement of the mind of the Conference across the Communion. Later comments that this was a victory for the African Bishops and that it expressed a rigid cultural divide were nonsense. The high figure indicated that a majority of Western Bishops voted in favour."

The actual terms of Resolution 1.10 (which *Some Issues in Human Sexuality* accepted as being "more conservative" than those produced in 1978 or 1988), recognised

> that there are among us those who experience themselves as having a homosexual orientation. Many of these are members of the Church and are seeking the pastoral care, moral direction of the Church, and God's transforming power for the living of their lives and the ordering of their relationships.

It also stated that the bishops committed themselves "to listen to the experience of homosexual persons" and wished to assure them that "they are loved by God and that all baptised, believing and faithful persons, regardless of sexual orientation, are all full members of the Body of Christ". It continued to call on all Anglicans to "minister pastorally and sensitively to all irrespective of sexual orientation and to condemn irrational fear of homosexuals, violence within marriage and any trivialisation and commercialisation of sex". However, it rejected homosexual practice as "incompatible with scripture", declared that "abstinence is right for those not called to marriage" and refused to advise "the legitimising of same-sex unions" or "ordaining those involved in same gender unions".

This summary of Resolution 1.10 is quoted directly from *Some Issues of Human Sexuality* (2003) p. 31. It adds these words

> there are Anglicans who have refused to accept it on the grounds that it does not adequately reflect the development of contemporary scientific and theological understandings of homosexuality. Nevertheless, it remains the nearest thing there is to an official statement by the Anglican Communion on the subject, though it needs to be remembered that resolutions of the Lambeth Conference have not been seen as binding upon the Anglican Communion. (Ibid. p. 31)

Immediately after the result of the vote was announced, Archbishop Carey intervened once more, to say: "I am aware that not everyone is comfortable with the revised motion and it seems to me that we need to pledge ourselves to carry on listening to one another, especially to those who disagree with our point of view. "As I sat there [he writes] I became conscious that we could not at this point allow disagreement to become division".

"Alas, despite my hopeful words, division had truly set in and the wide differences were clearly exposed for all to see." (*Know the Truth* p. 329). Carey's final comment in what is inevitably a somewhat defensive chapter is:

> The call that came from Lambeth for a deeper engagement with scripture in the light of human knowledge was well made, and is a challenge to all. To the conservative and traditional Christian the challenge must be to relate human experience and new knowledge to the teaching of the Bible. To the liberal Christian it will be a challenge not to empty scripture of all meaning, when its testimony conflicts with cultural assumptions. (op. cit. p. 332)

We will return to this "challenge", this "fundamental cleavage" later.

Post-Lambeth 1998

In the years immediately following the Conference, which coincided with the final years of George Carey's archiepiscopate, there were (as far as I recall) no striking *new* developments, merely a resumption, or continuance, of hostilities over *Issues*, with a dawning awareness that the Anglican Communion was facing the most severe crisis in the whole of its history.

Towards the end of 2003 the Church of England published two books, both designed to help Church people, and others interested, to clear their minds on the complex and difficult subjects under discussion.

The first of these, entitled *Some Issues in Human Sexuality: A guide to the Debate*, has already been referred to in these pages more than once. It was in fact directly commissioned by the House of Bishops with this specific object in view, ten years or more after the original *Issues in Human Sexuality* which had proved so controversial.

A senior bishop, Richard Harries, of Oxford, with three of his colleagues, chosen for the known diversity of their viewpoints – viz. Scott-Joynt of Winchester, Forster of Chester and Gladwin of Chelmsford, newly translated from Guildford – were invited to undertake a fresh in-depth study of all the issues involved. They were free to enlist the expertise of competent moral theologians, psychologists and biologists, as necessary. They discharged their demanding and difficult task with commendable thoroughness. The work took them a whole year and the result was published in November 2003. It was a ponderous tome of 326 densely packed pages, compared with the modest 48 of the original *Issues*.

In a foreword Bishop Harries wrote:

> It is a guide to the theological debate on questions that have arisen in response to the 1991 House of Bishops report *Issues in Human Sexuality*. It works within the parameters of this earlier statement and does not seek to change the position of the House of Bishops from the one expressed there . . . The document is intended to help people to enter into that debate, especially with issues connected with scripture and its interpretation . . . enabling us to enter more deeply into the outlook and theology of those with whom we agree *and* those with whom we disagree.

Some Issues treats its readers to an extremely detailed step-by-step exploration on "the use of the Bible in sexual ethics", "the theology of sexuality" and "Homosexuality and Biblical teaching". I dutifully waded through all this, finding it hard work. Much I found helpful and full of insight, but, looking at my copy, I find that I rudely wrote the word "gobbledegook" across several of the more obscure paragraphs and that I have forgotten most of the rest!

For a serious, informed study of the relevant Biblical passages it is nothing less than the barest essential. It shows, in fact, how much we are in the hands of the trained, dedicated expert. In the absence of such trustworthy expertise, it is fatally easy, by looking superficially at a few, scattered texts in both Testaments, in translation of course, and taken out of context, to jump to entirely wrong conclusions, prefaced by those dangerous words, "the Bible (i.e. the word of God, i.e. God) says . . ."

And this, tragically, is what so often happens. *Some Issues* is a valuable resource, to help us form a sound judgment, but it requires hard work, hard thinking and a readiness to learn, and perhaps, to change one's mind.

The second book published late in 2003 is called *Being human* with the explanatory subtitle *"A Christian understanding of personhood illustrated with reference to power, money, sex and time"*. (Church House Publishing). It is a report by the Doctrine Commission of the General Synod of the Church of England, whose Chairman at that time was Stephen Sykes, former Bishop of Ely and Regius Professor of Divinity of Cambridge University. It is in size a much slighter book than *Some Issues*, totalling 148 pages, and is packed tight with richly mature wisdom on those four basic characteristics of human life. This, the compiling of reports by panels of experts on a variety of subjects relevant to the Christian pilgrimage, is one of the things the Church of England does superbly well. But, and it is a real "but", they are presented with an academic readership in mind, and the language in which they are written is not popular or journalistic. (It is enormously desirable that a report like *Being Human*, which is about everyday life and its decisions and responsibilities, and therefore of direct concern to everybody, should be "translated" and presented in a popular, accessible language and format. It is what the Church ought to be saying to all of us and what we need to hear – in our everyday language which we really understand). *Being human* is, of course, not only about sex, and, again, is in its existing form, quite heavy going – but the fact remains that it is totally *positive*. To the ordinary layman it is much more accessible on the subject to which this chapter is devoted, than the more detailed *Some Issues*. They are both admirable but both could do with a simple, clear *translation*. That said, I recommend them both.

One final word on *Some Issues*. Some of its best sections are "Voices from the Debate" prefaced to the chapters on "Homosexuality and Biblical teaching" (pp. 117ff.) and "Trans-sexualism" (pp. 251ff.) – moving evidence of the grievous hurt experienced by Christian homosexuals from exclusion (or perceived exclusion) from Christian fellowship, communion and worship. "Homophobia" in the form of discrimination against homosexuals or any expression of hatred or contempt for them may possibly be made a criminal offence in the fairly near future.

A New Archbishop of Canterbury (ABC[8])

Late in 2002, while *Some Issues in Human Sexuality* was still in the course of preparation, George Carey's retirement was due to take effect. Naturally given all the circumstances, there was immense public interest in and speculation on the choice of his successor. Various names were canvassed in the Press but the two front runners were Michael Nazir Ali, the Pakistani-born Bishop of Rochester, and Rowan Williams, Bishop of Monmouth and Archbishop of Wales. Both were men of obvious integrity and outstanding intellect.

Nazir Ali will feature later in this book, but, as we all know, the lot fell upon Williams. A Welshman of the Welsh, and, like most of his fellow countryman, of Non-Conformist background, he had early become attracted by the historic Church in Wales, and, himself a bard, had become a crony of the outstanding but craggy parson poet, R.S. Thomas. But he had made his name in England as an Oxbridge academic theologian and prolific author. A graduate of Christ's College, Cambridge, he migrated to Oxford, where he was elected Lady Margaret Professor of Divinity and had a large and admiring following. He had not been forgotten in Wales and was eventually enthusiastically elected Bishop of Monmouth in 1992 and in 1999, Archbishop of Wales. He had been present at Lambeth 1998 and made quite an impression there. Williams was happily married to Jane (née Paul), daughter of a bishop and herself a competent evangelically inclined theologian and Biblical scholar in her own right – they had a young family and together made a strong team.

In the interval between the announcement of an impending vacancy in the Primacy and the new Archbishop's enthronement at Canterbury, there was a vicious and sustained campaign against his appointment on the part of the "conservative" evangelicals of Reform and the Church Society. The two charges against Williams were that he was a heretic (for which there were no grounds whatever) and a notorious "liberal", sympathetic to homosexuals. For this second allegation there was some evidence.

Stephen Bates, an investigative journalist with the developed instincts of a first rate sleuth, in his confessedly biassed but indispensable book *A Church at War: Anglicans and Homosexuality* (I.B. Tauris 2004) draws a vivid and convincing picture of the brief years of Williams's Monmouth episcopate. His next door neighbour and friend, Martin Reynolds features prominently in

---

8. From now on in this book the Archbishop of Canterbury will usually be described by the acronym ABC. This abbreviation is purely for convenience.

this picture (op. cit. pp. 59-64). Reynolds was then an energetic young Anglican priest and a practising homosexual, a friend of the aforementioned Richard Kirker, the embodiment of the Lesbian and Gay Christian Movement. Years earlier when Williams was still an Oxford professor, Kirker had invited him to deliver the 10th Michael Harding Memorial Address – Harding was another homosexual curate, ordained by Runcie at St. Albans, but killed in a motor bike accident in 1977 aged 25.

Williams's lecture was delivered and originally published, entitled *The Body's Grace*, in 1989. As soon as Kirker got the news of Williams's appointment to Canterbury – no doubt with the latter's permission and approval – he lost no time in reprinting it, updated and in a smart format complete with a striking photograph of the lecturer in cope and mitre as Archbishop of Wales *but*, jumping the gun, captioned as Archbishop of Canterbury. Widely advertised, this did nothing to dowse the flames of controversy!

Curious to read something written by our new Primate, I bought a copy and duly read it. When I had done so, I was frankly not much the wiser. I was out of my depth. As has become well known, Rowan Williams, guileless though he undoubtedly is, has or had an extraordinary knack of veiling his generally impressive wisdom in an almost impenetrable fog of obscurity – at least to my thick head that is how it seemed. As the years have passed since his return to prosaic England the fog has cleared, or given way to a slight mist.

Fortunately Bates, with his accustomed percipience, came to my rescue. *The Body's Grace* was *not* lost on *him*, and, because it is vital to understand the mind of our future archbishop on these controversial matters, with his kind permission,[9] I am going to avail myself of his (Bates's) paraphrase and quotation (to be found in *A Church at War* pp. 144f.)

Bates comments: "Wrapped up behind the lecture's generally sunny tone and some characteristic densely expressed ideas, is a deeply subversive and unwelcome message for those who insist that sex can [legitimately] take place only within heterosexual marriage."

The Lady Margaret professor began by expatiating at some length on the "irredeemably comic" nature of sexual intimacy with "so many opportunities for making a fool of yourself". But he claimed that this was a necessary part of human relationships, a willingness to surrender oneself to one's partner. Insistence on domination, in a relationship which could just as easily occur between heterosexuals, could be considered a perversion just as much as rape or paedophilia. Williams was blunt.

9. Proleptic!

> An absolute declaration that every sexual partnership must conform to the pattern of commitment or else have the nature of sin …is unreal and silly… Much more damage is done…by the insistence on a fantasy version of heterosexual marriage as the solitary ideal, when the facts are that an enormous number of "sanctioned" marriages are a framework for violence and human destructiveness on a disturbing scale.

His address argued that celibacy was not the only accessible (or acceptable?) lifestyle for the homosexual.

> Anyone who knows the complexities of the true celibate vocation would be the last to have any sympathy with the extraordinary idea that sexual orientation is an axiomatic pointer to the celibate life; almost as if celibacy before God is less costly, even less risky, for the homosexual than the heterosexual.

He argued that in the Bible Jesus and St. Paul both discussed the idea of marriage without arguing that it should be for procreation.

> If we are looking for a sexual ethic that can be seriously informed by our Bible, there is a good deal to steer us away from assuming that reproductive sex is a norm, however important and theologically significant it may be . . . If we are afraid of facing the reality of same-sex love because it compels us to think through the processes of bodily desire and delight in their own right, perhaps we ought to be more cautious about appealing to Scripture as legitimating only procreative heterosexuality.
>
> In a Church which accepts the legitimacy of contraception, the absolute condemnation of same-sex relations of intimacy must rely either on an abstract fundamentalist deployment of a number of very ambiguous texts or on a problematic and non-scriptural theory about natural complementarity, applied narrowly and crudely to physical differentiation without regard to psychological structures.

Such, thanks to Stephen Bates and no thanks to my thick headedness, is the gist of Rowan Williams's *The Body's Grace*. Despite occasional calls for recantation and repentance it's author has never repudiated it. Bates's comment is apt: "Perhaps it was as well that at the time he made it he was not exactly a prominent public figure and that *Issues in Human Sexuality* had yet to be published in all its mighty totemic significance to the conservative faction." To this I would merely add the rider (on top of my sincere gratitude to Bates) that the slightly mischievous re-issue of *The Body's Grace* at such a sensitive time explains George Carey's misgivings over the choice of his successor. The two men were so different – Carey had much practical common sense but was no intellectual giant. *The Body's Grace*, slight as it is, alongside Williams's other writings and utterances, reveals a mind and outlook of rare breadth and Christian maturity. But whether to these great gifts of human warmth and moral, intellectual and spiritual stature were to be added those of decisive and principled leadership and diplomatic finesse remained to be seen. The first omens were not promising. But what is certain is that, with the change of archbishop, the conflict entered a new and probably decisive stage.

ABC put to the test by three events of 2003

A crucial test was not long delayed. The first of three major events in 2003 might almost have escaped public notice. It was the decision by the Canadian diocese of New Westminster in British Columbia to go ahead with an officially sanctioned rite for the blessing of same-sex partnerships. This directly contravened Resolution 1.10 of the 1998 Lambeth Conference. It could not be ignored. The ABC issued a statement regretting "the inevitable tension and division" that would result. It certainly did but was as nothing compared with the outcry, both at home and in the Anglican Communion worldwide, caused by an act of defiance by the American Church later in the year.

The second event was on the domestic front. It constituted a serious, but understandable, blunder on the part of Williams, which played into the hands of his opponents and, at least temporarily, dented his prestige. In May 2003 there was an official announcement from Downing Street that the Queen's approval had been given to the appointment of Dr. Jeffrey John, a canon and chancellor of Southwark Cathedral, as Suffragan Bishop of Reading in the Diocese of Oxford. The Bishop of Oxford, Richard Harries, had chosen John with the tacit approval of the new ABC. John, a capable and experienced Anglo-Catholic, had made no secret that he was a homosexual with a male partner of many years, but no longer active – in other words he was celibate. He was a friend of Williams.

Following this announcement, it soon became apparent that the Oxford diocese was deeply split. There was a well organised and vocal opposition to John's appointment from a powerful Evangelical group, led by a widely respected lay member of General Synod, Dr. Philip Giddings. It made a big splash in the national Press. The opposition was reinforced from far afield by Peter Akinola, Primate of Nigeria, who went on record as saying that God's Church was now under Satanic attack, adding "I cannot think of how a man in his right senses would be having a sexual relationship with another man". Bates tells us that he and another evangelical, Peter Jensen, Archbishop of Sydney, threatened to split the Anglican Communion if John's appointment were not rescinded (Bates op. cit. p. 170). On top of this, nine English diocesan bishops and seven suffragans signed a letter opposing the appointment. Not all the signatories were evangelicals. They included Scott-Joynt of Winchester, Nazir Ali of Rochester and Dow of Carlisle.

All this unprecedented pressure and the accompanying press publicity combined to make the positions of Williams, John and Harries untenable. Because the appointment had been announced, and the likelihood of serious opposition discounted, there was no way out of the impasse but for the ABC to bring pressure on his deeply distressed friend to withdraw his acceptance. This he did. John, who was ambitious, was eventually found another job, as Dean of St. Albans. (Another bishopric was obviously out of the question.) Williams's authority was damaged and he lost face.

But it was the third event of that tumultuous year for the Anglican Communion which cumulatively did the greatest damage. The scene shifts to the Episcopal Church of the United States of America, known for short as ECUSA, a prominent constituent of the Anglican Communion, with a mind and ethos very much of its own.

Originating soon after the War of Independence with the consecration in Aberdeen in 1783 of Samuel Seabury as its first presiding Bishop, ECUSA has traditionally held an influential position in the States, both socially and intellectually, out of proportion to its relatively small membership. In my lifetime at least three U.S. Presidents, F.D. Roosevelt, Gerald Ford and George Bush senior, have all been staunch Episcopalians. In recent years ECUSA has acquired a reputation for avant garde liberalism, for example, pioneering not only women priests, but also women bishops. The year 2007 saw the election of the first woman Presiding Bishop. (Unlike their Canadian neighbours, they have never gone in for archbishops.) Most recently this liberal tradition, not universally shared in ECUSA, has shown itself in advanced thinking on homosexuality. Thus ECUSA in the Anglican world is at the opposite extreme to the quasi-fundamentalists of Nigeria, Sydney and "the Southern Cone", with the C. of E. somewhere in the middle.

Such, in brief, was the historical background to (i) the election, (ii) the endorsement of the election by General Convention and (iii) the consecration as Bishop of New Hampshire of Gene Robinson. The story, *his* story, is an extraordinary one by any standards, and everyone interested in the current controversy, whatever his/her standpoint, should make themselves acquainted with it, *for its own sake*, if for no other reason. I know of no better way of doing this than by reading what Stephen Bates writes about him in *A Church at War* pp. 64-69 and 180-210. Bates made it his business to get to know ECUSA at first hand and to meet and interview its leading personnel and record their words – as well as his shrewd and often racy impressions of them as people. His comments seem to me to have the ring of truth. In what follows I had to do a drastic abbreviation job, but can only refer my readers to my principal source with (once again) grateful commendation.

Gene Robinson, the first openly "gay" bishop in the modern history of Christianity, was born in 1947, apparently paralysed and not expected to live. A bright boy, he went to college in Tennessee, graduating in history. Later ordained, he moved to New Hampshire in 1975 and continued his ministry there, winning golden opinions. A small genial extrovert, he seemed the archetypal vicar. He met his future wife at college. They were happily married for 15 years, with two daughters. In 1985 they separated and were later divorced, asking mutual forgiveness for the failure of their marriage and promising to continue to bring up their daughters together. Later, Robinson, discovering his homosexuality, met Mark Andrew, with whom he lived openly as his partner, and does so still. His former wife, Isabel, and his daughters as well as his partner strongly supported his candidature for the bishopric and were all enthusiastically present at his consecration. Astonishingly, there were no less than 150 candidates for the vacant see of New Hampshire and it therefore took sixteen months to choose the new bishop of this small diocese in a small conservative(!) state. Robinson had long been closely associated with the previous bishop in the diocesan administration. The New Hampshire Episcopalians knew when they elected him that he was "gay" and living with his partner. They "did not like being told by outsiders" that in the interests of the wider world "they should not have elected him", so they defied the world and did so in June 2003.

By American Church law a bishop's democratic election by the registered Episcopalians of the vacant diocese requires formal endorsement or ratification by the next General Convention, ECUSA's equivalent to our General Synod. Convention meets only every three years. It so happened that its next session was due in Minneapolis in August. Robinson's campaign was organised to the nth degree, in the full knowledge of the furore in the Anglican Communion provoked by his election. The Anglican Primates emergency meeting hastily called by the ABC, had warned that his consecration would "tear the fabric of the Church".

Following passionate debates in the three separate "houses", bishops, priests and laity, voting took place. The laity were in favour of confirming Robinson's election by 63 to 32; the clergy by 65 to 12. The bishops voted last, the result being 62 for 43 against with the then-Presiding Bishop, Frank Griswold voting in favour.

ECUSA was clearly deeply divided. Robinson's opponents coalesced round the Bishop of Pittsburgh, Robert Duncan, and their organisation round the American Anglican Council (A.A.C.). This conservative-liberal split in ECUSA was complicated by legal considerations concerning Church property, leading to litigation in the courts. The situation was certainly not improved by uncalled for interference by African sympathisers with the minority. Back in 2001, Emmanuel Kolini, Archbishop of Rwanda in Central Africa, himself one of Akinola's most vociferous supporters, together with another Anglican archbishop from South East Asia travelled to Denver, Colorado to consecrate four "conservative" American priests as Bishops for breakaway congregations from ECUSA.

Robinson's consecration in November 2003 was not the least bizarre feature of this whole event. Because of the congregation of 3,000, it took place, not in a cathedral, but in the largest auditorium in New Hampshire, the ice hockey stadium of the university. Because of the possibility of violence, Robinson himself, his "gay" partner, Mark Andrew and Presiding Bishop Griswold wore bullet proof vests under their outer garments (vestments in the case of Robinson and Griswold). These did not prove necessary. There was a strong police presence and some ugly scenes, both before and during the service. The congregation sang the Victorian hymn "The Church's One Foundation" including the verse, often suppressed, "Though with a scornful wonder, men see her sore oppressed, by schisms rent asunder by heresies distressed . . .". Fifty bishops were present to demonstrate solidarity. The new bishop publicly embraced his male partner as the service ended.

The Fall-out of Robinson's Consecration

Full coverage in the world's press ensured shock waves throughout the Anglican Communion, with predictable outbursts of indignation from the Global South. But it was not all one sided. In England a new group (yet another!) was founded, calling itself *Inclusive Church*, to emphasise that the Church is, or is meant to be, welcoming to all and sundry – the exact opposite of an exclusive *sect*. One of its promoters was the Rector of Putney, London SW15; another the

Dean of Southwark, a friend of Jeffrey John. Also, Desmond Tutu's successor as Archbishop of Cape Town and Primate of Southern Africa, Njongonkulu Ndungane, had the courage to come over loud and clear in defence of ECUSA's right to take the action it had, as an autonomous province of the Anglican Communion. Its integrity deserved respect, if not approval, he said.

But his was a lone voice. The ABC, whose *private* view expressed in *The Body's Grace* differed little from that of the American and Canadian liberals, had called all the Anglican Primates to an emergency meeting at Lambeth to take urgent stock of the new situation and decide what action was appropriate.

Basically, the situation facing the Anglican Communion was unprecedented. As our old friend, Tom Wright, Bishop of Durham, was to put it in a speech in General Synod in 2005, "Never before has there been a moment when, after each of the four so-called Instruments of Unity have advised against a particular action, a province or diocese has gone ahead with it unilaterally." In this instance, of course, *two* such actions had been so taken; same-sex blessings by New Westminster Diocese and the election and consecration of a "gay" bishop by ECUSA. They also had to take account of the African interference in Denver and similar moves later. These were bound to cause bitter resentment.

The Primates decided to set up a Lambeth Commission headed by the veteran and experienced Primate of All Ireland, Robin Eames, Archbishop of Armagh, to advise and report on how best to tackle the present crisis and any other "grave difficulties" if and when they arose. An important member of this Commission was the Bishop of Durham. The Commission was originally to report back to the Primates in September 2004 but this was later deferred to February 2005, when they were to meet again, in deference to Eames, in Armagh.

This afforded a useful breathing space. It was already half way between two Lambeth Conferences and with the turbulent disagreements of 1998 still vivid in the memories of those who had participated, there was a nervous sense of foreboding. Heavy were the responsibilities of the Lambeth Commission.

The Windsor Report 2004/5

The Lambeth Commission's report, called the Windsor Report because its first and some subsequent meetings were held there, was published in October 2004, and initially well received.

Its authors devote much thought to the implications of being, not a federation of independent churches, but a "communion" of autonomous but *interdependent* provinces. Asking "what has gone wrong in recent years?" they find that the four existing "instruments of unity" viz. (1) the Lambeth Conference, (2) the meetings of Primates, (3) the Anglican Consultative Council, and (4) the Archbishop of Canterbury, have proved insufficient to cope with new questions. They urge a further "tuning up" of the four instruments, expanded to include (1) a Council of Advice to support and assist the Archbishop of Canterbury and (2) "crucially" an Anglican *Covenant* "to produce a framework in which its future life can flourish". À propos the Anglican ideal of unity in diversity they are at pains to distinguish degrees of diversity, local differences "we can all happily live with", and others which raise deeper theological issues which cannot be decided locally – the "subsidiarity principle". In section D they set out suggestions for dealing with the current crisis, viz. that the persons concerned with the events in New Westminster and New Hampshire be "invited to express regret that the proper constraints of the bonds of affection were breached in the actions that were taken". In other words: "We recognise that there were proper constraints belonging to the bonds of affection at the heart of our common life and we went ahead and breached them". There was also a similar request to the bishops who intervened in the jurisdictions of others. Finally they said, "We were clear that we must work harder than before at the rich unity in diversity that declares to the world that Jesus is Lord."

It is important to note that there were no threats of expulsion or suspension of the delinquent North Americans.

The *Church Times* leader on the Report concluded its observations:

> This excellent report gives Anglicans the prompting they need to become a functional international family. In the process, they should not be tempted to forget that their family is but one branch of a larger one. Agreement among Anglicans is worthless unless they recognise its provisionality in relation to the restoration of the visible unity of the Church of God.

Reaction of the Primates' Meeting to the Report

The Windsor Report was considered in detail at a special residential meeting of the Anglican Primates who had commissioned it. They met over five days in February 2005 at Newry, Northern Ireland. Of the total of thirty-eight Primates only three, including those of Canada and U.S.A., were absent.

Welcoming "the general thrust" of the Report "and the proposals for developing the Instruments of Unity, they "recognised serious questions about the content of the proposal for an Anglican Covenant and the practicalities of its implementation" and left it in the hands of the ABC. They were cool about the proposed Council of Advice which "could ride over our proper provincial autonomy" – and it was quietly dropped.

They continued to view the situation in North America "with the utmost seriousness". Time needed to be given to the Anglican provinces in Canada and U.S.A. for consideration of the Windsor recommendations "according to their constitutional processes". Between then and the next Lambeth Conference "we request that both provinces respond . . . to the questions addressed to them in the Windsor Report". They encouraged the Anglican Consultative Council (ACC) to organise a hearing at its June 2005 meeting, to give the North American churches "an opportunity to set out the thinking behind their recent actions". They reaffirmed Lambeth '98 Resolution 1.10 as "the present position of the Anglican Communion", and "request the ACC. to initiate the listening and study process which was the subject of resolutions in 1998".

"In the meantime, we ask our fellow Primates to use their influence to persuade their brothers to exercise a moratorium on public rites of blessing for same-sex unions, and on the consecration of any bishop living in a sexual relationship outside Christian marriage". "These strategies," they conclude, "are intended to restore the full trust of our bonds of affection across the Communion".

ECUSA accepted the Primates' invitation to attend the A.C.C.'s triennial meeting in June 2005 and sent a strong representative delegation to the Anglican Consultative Council in Nottingham, England, headed by Presiding Bishop Griswold. Copies of ECUSA's 130 page response to the Windsor Report were circulated. There were six speakers, one of whom, the Bishop of Louisiana, Charles Jenkins, had opposed Robinson's election and consecration. The entire presentation seems to have been notable for its candour, fairness and good humour. The Canadian Primate, Andrew Hutchinson, was also in attendance to make a presentation about same sex blessings. The Canadians had agreed to observe a moratorium for the time being. Hutchinson had commended the Windsor Report. Such a hearing can only have done good.

The Events of 2006

1. In the U.S.A.

The next main developments in this long running dispute did not occur until June 2006. In the meantime, the voices of the disputants became progressively more and more shrill, the rhetoric more and more vituperative, the word "schism" appeared more and more frequently in the headlines of the British press, and the reality that word signified looked increasingly unavoidable. Then in June 2006 two major events occurred almost simultaneously on opposite sides of the Atlantic.

The first was a session of the General Convention of ECUSA, held in Ohio. It was at the previous session in 2003 that the election of Gene Robinson as Bishop of New Hampshire was ratified by a majority vote, causing a major split in ECUSA and repercussions worldwide.

This time General Convention had to deal not only with the divisive results of that ill-advised decision in its own ranks, but also the crisis caused thereby in its relations with its sister provinces of the Anglican Communion, and the consequent demands upon it in the Windsor Report. There were long and anxious debates on what action to take to repair the damage, from which it was clear that membership of the Communion was valued highly by most of the delegates. From the reports in the *Church Times* it is not altogether clear what finally occurred, but it was not sufficient to satisfy the ABC. What *was* clear was that ECUSA's own divisions were not healed. One result of this was that one of the dissenting bishops, Jack Iker of Fort Worth, formally disowned the pastoral oversight of the Presiding Bishop and sent a request to the ABC to provide alternative oversight.

One other event at the General Convention had far reaching implications. This was the election, not unanimous, but by a majority vote, of Dr. Katharine Jefferts Schori, Bishop of Nevada, as the new Presiding Bishop in place of Frank Griswold. She is the first woman to be so elected. She is a very personable, former scientist and a liberal. The ABC sent her a formal greeting and congratulations. Her election marked the continued liberal ascendency in ECUSA.

2. In England: ABC's Reflection

Only a day or two after the conclusion of the General Convention, the spotlight moved from Ohio to Lambeth. The ABC had written a marathon 3,000 word *"Reflection"* on the whole course of events, and despatched copies of it to all the Primates and (apparently) to most, if not all, the bishops of the Anglican Communion. It was printed in full in the *Church Times* of 30th June. Two days earlier Ruth Gledhill, the Religious Correspondent of the *Times*, attempting the impossible, wrote a wildly misleading, garbled version of the ABC's rambling rigmarole on the front page of that newspaper under the still more

misleading headline: "Gay clergy ultimatum set to split Anglicans".
The sub heading was "Archbishop of Canterbury orders liberals to
sign a 'biblical covenant'." The ABC, who only eight days earlier had
been severely taken to task in a *Times* first leader headed: "A house
divided. The Archbishop of Canterbury must be bolder or schism is
inevitable", was rewarded (?) with a third leader the same day as Ruth
got her scoop (?). It was headed "The Lambeth Walk. The Archbishop
of Canterbury shows true leadership". The implication presumably
was: The ABC has promptly heeded *our* warning. One up (as usual) to
us, the wonderful *Times*. It was, of course, nothing of the sort.

After over 2,000 words of seemingly endless archiepiscopal
ruminations,[10] the ABC had finally come to the point. This is some of
what he wrote when struggling to define "the Anglican identity",

> The reason Anglicanism is worth bothering with is because it
> has tried to find a way of being a Church that is neither tightly
> centralised nor just a loose federation of essentially independent
> bodies – a Church that is seeking to be a coherent family of
> communities meeting to hear the Bible read, to break bread
> and share wine as guests of Jesus Christ, and to celebrate a
> unity in worldwide ministry and mission. That is what the word
> "Communion" means for Anglicans, and it is a vision that has
> taken clearer shape in many of our ecumenical dialogues. Of
> course it is possible to produce a self-deceiving, self-important
> account of our worldwide identity, to pretend that we were
> a completely international and universal institution like the
> Roman Catholic Church. We're not. But we have tried to be
> a family of Churches willing to learn from each other across
> cultural divides, not assuming that European (or American or
> African) wisdom is what settles everything, opening up the
> lives of Christians here to the realities of Christian experience
> elsewhere. And we have seen these links not primarily in a
> bureaucratic way but in relation to the common patterns
> of ministry and worship – the community gathered around
> scripture and sacraments; a ministry of bishops, priests and
> deacons, a biblically-centred form of common prayer, a focus
> on holy communion. These are the signs that we are not just
> a human organisation but a community trying to respond to
> the action and the invitation of God that is made real for us in
> ministry and Bible and sacraments.

So far, so (very) good. I seem to hear the echoes of what the 100th

10. Which I have actually read, word for word.

ABC, Michael Ramsey, wrote so crisply and succinctly in his masterpiece, *The Gospel and the Catholic Church*.

From this sketch of our Anglican identity the 104th ABC goes on to indicate what he believes are some of our current weaknesses, and then to suggest a possible solution.

> What our Communion lacks is a set of adequately developed structures which is able to cope with the diversity of views that will inevitably arise in a world of rapid global communication and huge cultural variety. The tacit conventions between us need spelling out – not for the sake of some central mechanism of control but so that we have ways of being sure we're still talking the same language, aware of belonging to the one, holy, catholic and apostolic Church of Christ. It is becoming urgent to work at what adequate structures for decision making might look like. We need ways of translating this underlying sacramental communion into a more effective reality, so that we . . . learn how to share responsibility.

If all that sounds a bit nebulous, when His Grace comes to his concrete proposal, it is not in the least nebulous but sounds a bit like an anticlimax – a small mouse! Here it is:

ABC's Proposals

> The idea of a covenant between local Churches . . . is one method that has been suggested and it seems to me the best way forward. It is necessarily an "opt-in" matter. Those Churches that were prepared to take this on as an expression of their responsibility to each other would limit their local freedoms for the sake of a wider witness; and some might not be willing to do this. We could arrive at a situation where there were "constituent" Churches in covenant in the Anglican Communion, and other "Churches in association" which were still bound by historic and perhaps personal links, fed from many of the same sources, but not bound in a single and unrestricted sacramental communion, and not sharing the same constitutional structures. The relation would be not unlike that between the Church of England and the Methodist Church, for example. The "associated" Churches would have no direct part in the decision making of the "constituent" Churches, though they might well be observers whose views were sought or whose expertise was shared from time to time, and with whom significant areas of co-operation might be possible.

The ABC added that "this leaves many unanswered questions".

> It could mean the need for local churches to work at ordered
> and mutually respectful separation between "constituent"
> and "associated" elements; but it could also mean a positive
> challenge for Churches to work out what they believed to be
> involved in belonging in a global sacramental fellowship,
> a chance to rediscover a positive common obedience to the
> mystery of God's gift that was not a coercion from above but
> of that "waiting for each other" that St. Paul commends to the
> Corinthians.

He concluded that

> There is no way in which the Anglican Communion can
> remain unchanged by what is happening at the moment.
> Neither the liberal nor the conservative can simply appeal
> to a historic identity that doesn't correspond with where
> we now are. We do have distinctive historic traditions – a
> Reformed commitment to the absolute priority of the Bible
> for deciding doctrine, a Catholic loyalty to the sacraments
> and the threefold ministry of bishops, priests and deacons
> and a habit of cultural sensitivity and intellectual flexibility
> that does not seek to close down unexpected questions too
> quickly. But for this to survive with all its aspects intact, we
> need closer and more visible formal commitments to each
> other.
>
> And it is not going to look exactly like anything we
> have known so far. Some may find this unfamiliar future
> conscientiously unacceptable, and that view deserves respect.
> But if we are to continue to be any sort of "catholic" church,
> if we believe that we are answerable to something more than
> our immediate environment and its priorities, and are held
> in unity by something more than just the consensus of the
> moment, we have some very hard work to do to embody this
> more clearly. The next Lambeth Conference ought to address
> this matter directly and fully as part of its agenda.

The ABC's *Reflection* did not end even there. There was much more
that was deeply and valuably thoughtful and thought provoking.
Near the end occurred two challenging paragraphs which cry out to
be reproduced because, together, they give us insight into the way in
which he conceives (and surely rightly conceives) his present role:

> The only reason for being an Anglican is that this balance
> [i.e. between the Reformed, the Catholic and the cultural/
> intellectual concerns as he outlines them] seems to you to
> be healthy for the Church Catholic overall, and that it helps
> people grow in discernment and holiness. Being an Anglican
> in the way I have sketched involves certain concessions
> and unclarities, but provides at least for ways of sharing
> responsibility and making decisions that will hold and that
> will be mutually intelligible.
>
> No one can impose the canonical and structural changes
> that will be necessary. All that I have said above should make
> it clear that the idea of an Archbishop of Canterbury resolving
> any of this by decree is misplaced, however tempting for
> many. The Archbishop of Canterbury presides and convenes
> in the Communion, and may do what this document attempts
> to do, which is to outline the theological framework in which
> a problem should be addressed; but he must always act
> collegially, with the bishops of his own local church and with
> the Primates and other instruments of Communion.

In the penultimate paragraph of this crucially important "document"
(to borrow the ABC's own word) occurs this sentence: "It is . . .
possible for the Churches of the Communion to decide that this is,
indeed, the identity, the long tradition – and by God's grace, the gift
– we want to share with the rest of the Christian world in the coming
generation; more importantly still, that this is a valid and vital way of
presenting the Good News of Jesus Christ to the world".

This concludes these extracts from the ABC's wise and
statesmanlike *Reflection* on this protracted controversy. In making
this selection I have been at pains to present the gist of his argument,
especially his concrete proposals, in their fullest context, short of
reproducing the 3,000 words of the entire document, in order to avoid
any possible distortion (as in Gledhill's *Times* synopsis).

The Covenant

My understanding of the plain meaning, in practical terms, of the
ABC's carefully phrased proposals is as follows: Taking up the
Windsor Report's suggestion of a Covenant, he proposes that, when
its wording is finally agreed by all concerned, and presumably
ratified by Lambeth 2008, it will be offered to *all* the thirty eight
Churches or provinces of the existing Anglican Communion. Those,
hopefully all thirty eight, agreeing to accept and sign it, will thereby,
ipso facto, attain the formal status of constituent Churches/provinces

of the Anglican Communion, binding themselves, in the terms of the Covenant, closely and explicitly to the responsibilities, obligations and privileges of all that is implied by *inter*dependent membership. Should there be any churches or provinces not prepared to accept and sign this Covenant, they would automatically be granted "associate' status". This two-tier constitution (supposing *any* opt for associate status) would more closely reflect present reality.

The ABC's eirenicon, for such it was, was variously received, raising the question how far it had been read, pondered, absorbed and understood by its recipients. The response from Nigeria was immediate, predictable and impudent, betraying a complete failure even to begin to understand the true nature of Anglicanism. As reported in the *Church Times* leading article a week after that newspaper's publication of the ABC's *Reflection*, Archbishop Akinola and his multitudinous bishops impertinently dismissed his proposals as "brilliant as the heartbeat of a leader who wants to preserve the unity of the Church by accommodating every shred of opinion, no matter how unbiblical, all because we want to make everyone feel at home". They likened ECUSA to "a cancerous lump that should be excised". Another statement from the Nigerian Episcopal Synod, claiming the guidance of the Holy Spirit, talked about "defending the faith against the present onslaught from ECUSA, Canada, England and their allies" and the need to redefine and/or redetermine "those who are truly Anglican", proposing an alternative Lambeth Conference organised by the "Global South", should all efforts to get the apostles of a revisionist agenda to repent and retrace their steps fail.

The *Church Times'* lead writer said that expressions of that kind illustrated the difficulty – some might say the impossibility – of trying to hold the Anglican Communion together in any recognisable form. The title of his article: "Is the Communion too much bother?"

Assuming the answer to his rhetorical question to be an emphatic "No", side by side with that depressing leader was a constructive article by Canon Vincent Strudwick, described as "a member of the recent A.C.C. sub-group working on the covenant". He made the valid point that the covenant "does not require those who engage in the process to accept all doctrinal opinion, sacramental devotion or ministerial practice characteristic of other provinces, but works on the basis that each believes the other to hold the essentials of the Christian faith and that all commit themselves to respect the integrity and good faith of those whose search has led them to different understanding in matters of importance". He adds "it is the proper role of the Communion, as part of its common life, to attempt to shed new light on these differences, attempting to discern both the truth that is our goal, as well as the grace in our search". (*Church Times* 7 July 2006) (Well said!)

Speaking at General Synod that summer, the ABC said that a working party was being established in consultation with the Anglican Communion Office and others to look more fully at what sort of covenant could be constructed on the Windsor Report's recommendation.

This working party, after consulting widely, eventually produced what became known as the St. Andrew's Draft. It was brought before the 670 bishops who attended the Lambeth Conference in July/August 2008. According to the detailed *Reflections* published immediately after its conclusion as a semi-official record of its proceedings, the first half of the draft was received with general satisfaction but there were many serious concerns over the rest and these were set out in detail in *Reflections* Section J. Conference decided that these criticisms should be referred to the Covenant Design Group for discussion and action and ultimately to the Anglican Consultative Council, on which clergy and laity as well as bishops from each Province are represented, at its meeting in Jamaica in May 2009. It is hoped by then to reach some kind of finality.

In the meantime, in the run up to Lambeth, the Windsor Report's Covenant proposal, so emphatically endorsed by the ABC, had been given the widest possible airing in the Anglican Communion as a whole, with every conceivable point of view, for and against, being given free utterance. Inevitably, deep differences became apparent.

In the present writer's view, it is very much to be desired that the Anglican Covenant will come to fruition as soon as possible, providing a much needed element of self-discipline and internal cohesion in the Anglican world.

The run up to Lambeth 2008

As the prospect of Lambeth 2008 drew ever closer, nervous forebodings of schism increased. There was a perceptible hardening of attitudes on both sides of the Atlantic. Shrill rhetoric from the Nigerian Primate, Peter Akinola, demanding nothing less than the wholesale expulsion of the "sinful, unrepentant" ECUSA from the Anglican Communion did not help. The conservative evangelicals were angry and impatient.

1. Primates' Meeting, Dar es Salaam, February 2007

Such was the crisis background of the next Anglican Primates' Meeting in Dar es Salaam, Tanzania, in February 2007. It was make or break. The agenda was to devise a realistic but decisive showdown with ECUSA in the light of its General Convention's endorsement of Robinson's consecration as Bishop of New Hampshire. The following September the ABC would be leading a delegation representing the rest of the Anglican Communion to confront the House of Bishops of ECUSA.[11] in New Orleans in the attempt to negotiate a mutually acceptable settlement of the dispute, embracing also that with the Canadian diocese of New Westminster over blessings of same sex unions. The more extreme among the Primates envisaged something like an ultimatum, the moderates an olive branch.

For the details of the strategy decided upon at Dar es Salaam we are dependent upon the wordy, official communiqué drawn up at the close of the meeting. ECUSA and New Westminster were to be confronted with a demand for an unequivocal assurance that there would in future be no further consecrations as bishops of non-celibate homosexuals or blessings of same sex unions.

Much time was spent discussing the prickly subject of unauthorised interventions by African prelates in ECUSA dioceses dissociating themselves from the radical policies of ECUSA and seeking alternative jurisdiction. (These had, understandably, caused anger in ECUSA.) But as the communiqué put it, these dissident dioceses, of which there were several, "remained in faithful fellowship with the Anglican Communion and were committed to the proposals of the Windsor Report and the standard of teaching presupposed in it and for these reasons are unable to accept the primacy of the Presiding Bishop". The primates, while recognising that these interventions had "exacerbated the situation caused by the internal split in ECUSA," report that "those who have intervened believe it would be inappropriate to being an end to interventions until there is change in ECUSA".

Such, in outline, was the package cobbled together at Dar es Salaam. Its authors clearly supposed it an impressive piece of work which had given the ABC and his entourage a strong hand to play. But they reckoned without the North Americans!

* * * * *

Besides the *official* work at Dar es Salaam, by all accounts, newspaper reports, etc., this important meeting was remarkable for a good deal of rather unsavoury politicking and backstairs intrigue, particularly among the Global South Primates led and organised by Peter Akinola.

---

11. About this time ECUSA had taken the decision to abbreviate its name simply to "The Episcopal Church", using the acronym TEC. To avoid confusion, however, in this book it will continue to be called ECUSA.

There was talk of a conspiracy to boycott the forthcoming Lambeth Conference and to hold an alternative one, perhaps concurrently. Ominously, in the latter half of 2007 a steady stream of bishops from the vibrant church of Nigeria and the area of Central and East Africa originally evangelised by CMS viz. Rwanda, Kenya, Uganda and Tanzania, were rejecting invitations to Lambeth 2008.

2. New Orleans, September 2007

Against this disconcerting background we turn to what was surely the last, and most hopeful chance, under God, of achieving a reconciling breakthrough – the autumn confrontation with ECUSA's House of Bishops in New Orleans. The Dar es Salaam communiqué, for all its shortcomings, had demonstrated what an effort had been put into what was termed "the pastoral strategy" – in more homely terms, the package deal. The ABC had succeeded in persuading his fellow Primates to "go the extra mile". It was not a peremptory ultimatum, as some had hoped, but a genuine olive branch. The Primates, while rightly maintaining their position, had left room for manoeuvre and shown tact about American sensitivities over incursions by uninvited bishops.

The official statement at the end of the discussions in New Orleans was diplomatic and courteous but at the same time firm and uncompromising from ECUSA's point of view. It began by expressing gratitude for the gift of the Anglican Communion as a sign of the Holy Spirit's ongoing work of reconciliation throughout the world. ECUSA's response was offered in the hope of "mending the tear in the fabric of our common life in Christ". Sincere and heartfelt thanks went to the ABC and his companions for accepting their invitation to join them. "Their presence was a living reminder of the unity that is Christ's promised gift in the power of the Holy Spirit." "We engaged in careful listening and straightforward dialogue with our guests. We expressed our passionate desire to remain in communion. It is our conviction that the Episcopal Church needs the Anglican Communion and we heard from our guests that the Anglican Communion needs the Episcopal Church." "The House of Bishops offers the following response to our Anglican Communion partners."

Following this impressive preamble, they summarise their response under eight heads: (1) They confirm the General Convention (2006) resolution calling bishops "to exercise restraint by not consenting to the consecration of candidates for the episcopate whose manner of life presents a challenge to the wider Church and will lead to further strains on communion. (2) They pledge as a body not to authorise public rites for the blessing of same sex unions. (3) They commend their Presiding

Bishop's plan for episcopal visitors. (4) "We deplore incursions into our jurisdictions by uninvited bishops and call for them to end." (5) "We support the Presiding Bishop in seeking communion-wide consultation in a manner in accord with our Constitution and Canons." (6) "We call for increasing implementation of the listening process across the Communion and for a report on its progress to Lambeth 2008." (7) "We support the ABC in his expressed desire to explore ways for the Bishop of New Hampshire to participate in the Lambeth Conference." (8) "We call for unequivocal and active commitment to the civil rights, safety and dignity of gay and lesbian persons."

As so often, "the devil was in the detail". The ECUSA bishops went on explicitly to draw out some of the implications in the foregoing. The most significant of these were:

(1) that "non-celibate gay and lesbian persons" are included in General Convention's resolution referred to in (1) above.

(2) The pledge of a moratorium on blessings on same sex unions was *only* "until a broader consensus emerges in the (Anglican) Communion or until General Convention takes further action".

(3) There must be "an immediate end" to incursions by uninvited bishops, in view of the Presiding Bishop's plan to appoint "episcopal visitors" for dioceses requesting alternative oversight.

(4) "The Pastoral Scheme" proposed by Dar es Salaam was rejected as "it would compromise the authority of our own primate and place ECUSA's autonomy at risk". They nevertheless recognised a useful role for Communion-wide consultation on pastoral needs, of those seeking alternative oversight . . .

(5) *Regarding Lambeth 2008*, "we who have been invited look forward to it with hope and expectation. We are mindful that the Bishop of New Hampshire has not yet received an invitation and the ABC has expressed a desire to explore a way for him to participate. . . . It is our fervent hope that a way can be found for his full participation".

(6) Finally, the Bishops stressed "the fundamental importance" that "as we continue to seek consensus in matters of human sexuality", the civil rights and dignity of gay and lesbian persons must be respected and any action doing or encouraging violence to them be opposed.

3. New Orleans: a mixed reception

Understandably, the proceedings at this crucial confrontation met with a mixed reception.

First, the Joint Standing Committee of the Anglican Primates' Meeting and of the Anglican Consultative Committee signalled its approval of the statement released by ECUSA's House of Bishops as summarised above. In a 19 page assessment the Committee concluded that the American Bishops "have met the requirements of the Windsor Report . . . and the request of the Primates at Dar es Salaam for a moratorium on public rites for the blessing of same sex unions, and has given the necessary assurances on the subject of consecrating gay bishops."

On the third request by the Primates – to set up an external scheme of oversight for disaffected parishes and dioceses – the JSC acknowledged that the proposal infringed the polity of ECUSA Nevertheless, the Bishops had begun "initiatives which offer a viable basis on which to proceed". They castigated Primates who had encroached on U.S. territory. "We do not see how certain Primates can in good conscience call upon the Episcopal Church to meet the recommendations of the Windsor Report while they find reasons to exempt themselves from paying regard to them."

Clearly not all Anglican Primates were of one mind! To Nigerians New Orleans looked totally different. Peter Akinola: "Our pleas have once again been ignored. The unequivocal assurances we sought have not been given. What we have is a carefully calculated attempt to win support to ensure attendance at the Lambeth Conference and continued involvement in the life of the Communion. Instead of the change of heart – repentance – that we sought, what we have been offered is merely a temporary adjustment in an unrelenting determination to 'bring the Communion along'. Clerics across ECUSA have continued with same sex blessings with the full knowledge and support of the diocesan bishops, even if not technically authorised." From his point of view this was fair comment.

Similarly Nzimbi, Primate of Kenya , said: "the word 'halt' with regard to the consecration of gay bishops was not enough. What we expected from them is to repent that this is a sin in the eyes of the Lord."

To these African voices was added a third – quieter, more deeply persuasive, on a more profound spiritual and intellectual level. It was that of another Peter, another Primate, Jensen of Sydney, Australia. Historically the Sydney archbishopric is something of an anomaly in the Australian Church. It is always held by a leading conservative evangelical out of step with his fellow Australian archbishops. Peter Jensen is no exception.

In a powerful article in the *Church Times* of 12 October 2007 he developed his views on what he saw as the New Orleans débacle. There is only room here for one typical extract:

> The U.S. House of Bishops has now responded to the Primates. Many have seen in their pronouncements a sufficient conformity to the requests of the Primates to enable the Communion to continue on its way. I do not read their statements like that. I think they have failed to meet the hopes of the Primates. The Americans are firmly committed to the view that the practice of homosexual sex on a long-term relationship is morally acceptable. Not only is it acceptable, it is demanded by the Gospel itself that we endorse this lifestyle as Christian. They are prepared to wait for a short time while the rest of the Communion catches up. But they do not intend to reverse their decision about this and they intend to proclaim this message wherever possible. They want to persuade us that they are right, and that the rest of us should embrace this development. Here is a missionary faith. The biblical conservatives in Africa and Asia know this. They took irreversible steps to secure the future of some of the biblical Anglicans in North America [here Jensen is alluding to the pastoral interventions of Kolini and others in U.S.A.]. This sort of question shows why a new vision and further action will be needed. [He then goes on about episcopal oversight: "From now on there will inevitably be boundary crossing, overlapping jurisdictions" etc.] If the sexual revolution becomes more broadly accepted elsewhere, so other bishops will be appointed, as they have been in the U.S.A.

5. Events leading to GAFCON 2008

Not only that extract but all the other evidence points to the New Orleans confrontation as the decisive turning point for "conservative" evangelicals in this long drawn out controversy. What had first been mooted conspiratorially at Dar es Salaam – the boycotting of Lambeth 2008 and vague hints of an alternative assembly elsewhere – now began rapidly to take definite shape. As an ever increasing number of Global South bishops turned down their invitations to Lambeth, there soon emerged general agreement that, from every point of view, no better location for such a rival conference could possibly be found than the Holy Land, in spite of the continuing tensions there and the (understandable) reluctance of the local Arab Anglican Bishop, Suheil Dawani, to act as host. (He was not even consulted.)

The leadership of what can only be described as this large dissident group seems to have been shared between the voluble Nigerian Primate, Akinola, the Primate of Uganda, Henry Orombi, and Peter Jensen himself, with strongly sympathetic encouragement from Michael Nazir Ali, Bishop of Rochester. He and Jensen were the brains of the movement. Nazir Ali had been canvassing support among the English episcopate, with Forster of Chester his chief henchman.

Not only the financing, but the sheer physical logistics of such a vast undertaking must have been formidable indeed, in such a short time, but in the event it was brought triumphantly to pass, to the undoubted dismay of the organisers of Lambeth. Nazir Ali was the only English diocesan bishop not to attend Lambeth.

6. GAFCON: Jerusalem, 20-29 June 2008

As we all know by now, the acronym GAFCON stands for Global Anglican Future Conference. In the words of its official statement, its purpose was to launch "a spiritual movement to preserve and promote the truth and power of the gospel of salvation in Jesus Christ as we Anglicans have received it." "We cherish our Anglican heritage and the Anglican Communion," the statement goes on, "and have no intention of departing from it. And we believe that, in God's providence, Anglicanism has a bright future in obedience to our Lord's Great Commission." In other words, the Conference was, professedly, *not just* a protest movement or indignation meeting, as some Anglicans expected – though it certainly *was* that – but it was more, a serious, sober, *positive*, essentially conservative demonstration of genuine Christians who have been badly hurt by the behaviour of some of their brethren.

When the Conference ended, two very carefully prepared statements were read out to the departing participants (altogether 1,148 clergy and laity, *including* no less than 291 bishops, attended). When the reading concluded, they all loudly signified their unanimous and enthusiastic approval of the wording. These two documents were the Conference Statement and Jerusalem Declaration. Both were printed verbatim in the *Church Times* of 4 July 2008, along with detailed coverage of the Conference,[12] editorial comment headed "Treat Gafcon with respect", and perhaps most significant, a calm, considered response by the ABC, whose concluding words, echoing St. Paul's "Wait for one another," (1

---

12. GAFCON made full use of its location with inspirational organised visits to, and worship in, the holy places in Bethlehem and Jerusalem, the Sea of Galilee, etc.

Cor. 11, 33) were a plea for patience and forbearance on all sides.

There is a marked contrast between the studiously moderate tone of the Jerusalem Declaration – cynics might say "clever window dressing" – and the polemics of the statement. The Declaration stresses the orthodox stance of its promoters with disarming professions of loyalty to the historic Creeds, the sacraments, the four ecumenical Councils of the early Church, even the Book of Common Prayer and the Thirty Nine Articles, but the emphasis all along is on "the Holy Scriptures as the Word of God written as containing all things necessary for salvation". All is admirably positive *until* "we reject the authority of those churches and leaders who have denied the orthodox faith in word or deed. We pray for them, and call on them to repent and return to the Lord."

As the ABC commented, this Declaration "will be acceptable to and shared by the vast majority of Anglicans" everywhere.

The official Statement says, correctly, "The Anglican Communion is currently divided and distracted" and "GAFCON emerged in response to a crisis". It pinpoints three "undeniable facts". The first of these, it says, is the acceptance and promotion of a "different" and "false gospel which undermines the authority of God's Word written and the uniqueness of Jesus Christ . . . it promotes a variety of sexual preferences and immoral behaviour as a universal human right. It claims God's blessing for same sex unions over against the Biblical teaching on holy matrimony. In 2003 this false gospel led to the consecration of a bishop living in a homosexual relationship". The second alleged "fact" concerns conflicting church loyalties arising from local opposition to these events. The third was "the manifest failure" of the Communion's existing machinery to exercise discipline in the face of overt heterodoxy", notably in ECUSA and the Anglican Church in Canada "in proclaiming this false gospel". No effective action has been taken and the bishops of these unrepentant churches are welcomed to Lambeth 2008. After further strictures, "we can only come to the devastating conclusion that "we are a global Communion with a colonial structure". "This crisis has torn the fabric of the Communion in such a way that it cannot simply be patched together" but "it has brought together Anglicans across the globe into a fellowship which is faithful to biblical teaching . . . and stronger as an instrument of effective mission". This fellowship, in short, is GAFCON, "united in the communion of one Spirit and committed to work and pray together in the common mission of Christ".

GAFCON's members "confess the faith of Christ crucified, stand firm for the gospel . . . and affirm a contemporary rule, the Jerusalem

Declaration to guide the movement for the future. We are a fellowship of Anglicans including provinces, dioceses etc. "whose goal is to reform, heal and revitalise the Anglican Communion and expand its mission to the world". Though they do not say this in so many words, they see themselves as a kind of "faithful remnant of Israel" ready, in effect, to take over the running of the Anglican Communion!

It is interesting that they say: "While acknowledging the nature of Canterbury as an historic see, we do not accept that Anglican identity is determined necessarily through recognition by the Archbishop of Canterbury".

GAFCON "encourages" its participating Primates to form the initial Council of the GAFCON movement and "urges" them to authenticate and recognise "confessing Anglican jurisdictions and to encourage all Anglicans to promote the gospel and defend the faith".

I have endeavoured at some length to present a fair summary of these two important documents, and will now attempt to assess them.

8. GAFCON assessed

As the *Church Times* suggested, they must be treated with the respect and attention due to the anxious thoughts and feelings of a large section of the Anglican world. Their repeated assurances of Anglican loyalty are warmly welcome. But that does not imply that they should not be examined critically.

The statement contains radical criticism of the existing constitution and machinery of the Anglican Communion, and there is a thinly veiled attack on the Archbishop of Canterbury, although he is not mentioned by name. It is not difficult to see in its clever wording the somewhat jaundiced handwriting of Jensen and Nazir Ali, two of its most intelligent promoters, or to escape the reluctant impression that, for once, the cynics may not have been entirely mistaken in their estimate of the "Holier than thou" window dressing of the Jerusalem Declaration. At their best, conservative evangelicals are sincere and devoted, if naive, disciples of Our Lord and there were undoubtedly many such – probably a vast majority – in GAFCON. But at their worst, conservative evangelicals – perhaps only a tiny minority – are sanctimonious humbugs, convinced by their own propaganda. GAFCON, for all its impressive façade, may not be wholly free from such people.

This analysis does not make GAFCON any easier to deal with. GAFCON can be seen as a prime example of ecclesiastical oneupmanship. What, in those terms, is the counter ploy?

The ABC's response to the Final Statement published in that issue of the *Church Times* was in its gentle truthfulness devastating. "I believe," he wrote, "that it is wrong to assume that we are now so far apart that all those outside the GAFCON network are simply proclaiming another gospel. This is not the case; it is not the experience of millions of faithful and biblically focussed Anglicans in every province."

The ABC's response in its entirety is directly relevant and no point made in the GAFCON Statement was left unanswered. He described GAFCON's proposals for the way ahead as "problematic in all sorts of ways" and explained why. Unfortunately there is no space here for his whole *Response*, which deserves careful study. But it seems appropriate to round off this analysis by citing his challenge to GAFCON:

> If those who speak for GAFCON are willing to share in a genuine renewal of all our patterns of reflection and decision-making in the Communion, they are welcome, especially in the shaping of an effective Covenant for our future together.

An effective counter ploy.

The Lambeth Conference 2008

Hot on the heels of GAFCON, at the end of July and beginning of August came the Lambeth Conference, sadly boycotted by nearly, but not quite all the 291 bishops who had gathered in Jerusalem. Just over 650 bishops were at Lambeth (and Canterbury where the actual conference took place) out of a possible 880 eligible who were invited. A few, with the necessary stamina, attended both conferences. One solitary and redoubtable Nigerian bishop, from Owerri, bravely defied his Primate Akinola's strict order to stay away, and two came from Kenya. Gene Robinson of New Hampshire, whose consecration in 2003 was at the heart of the crisis, was not invited, despite pressure from his ECUSA colleagues. He was, nonetheless, present in England throughout the duration of the conference, thanks to a mischievous invitation from the Modern Church People's Union to address their AGM. True to his ebullient personality he did his best, supported by his English sympathisers, to promote his "cause". Inevitably, too, the Lesbian and Gay Christian Movement, through its Chief Executive, Richard Kirker, capitalised on his presence and emitted a stream of cleverly worded propaganda through the post. Robinson did not attempt to gatecrash the Conference but he couldn't resist challenging Akinola to a public debate on the issues at the centre of the dispute. Had his challenge been taken up, with a suitably tough referee, it would have been the event of the year.

As to what the Conference actually achieved and did over the fortnight during which it was in session, within days of its conclusion, a very detailed factual narrative of its proceedings, rather than formal minutes, was made available to the public and the press. It was entitled *Reflections* and in a condensed summary was published in the current issue of the *Church Times* (8 Aug. 2008). In that form it occupied four pages of small print in five columns per page – not an inducement to the ordinary reader to plough through it – and it is impossible to summarise more succinctly. This was a communications disaster, contrasting unfavourably with GAFCON, and giving the utterly false impression that little was achieved.

In these circumstances, it is vitally important to understand that the Conference organisers, led of course by the ABC, worried lest there should be a repetition of the scenes that marred its 1998 predecessor, were at pains to avoid divisive debates and votes on formal, controversial resolutions and substituted for them a "new form of converse" called indaba. This was "based on an African ideal of purposeful discussion on the common concerns of our shared life. It is a process and a method of engagement as we listen to one another. An indaba acknowledges that there are issues that need to be addressed effectively to foster ongoing communal living." I have quoted the foregoing from the Introductory Section of Reflections. It goes on from there to acknowledge that "this person to person encounter has been one of the most encouraging, engaging – if at times frustrating – aspects of the Conference."

That this was the case is no small tribute to the ABC. His unmistakably God-in-Christ centred personality pervaded the Conference for good. All the most contentious issues, such as sexuality and cross provincial "interventions" over which the GAFCON "conservative" evangelicals had lost patience came under full and uninhibited discussion in this spirit – which must have been none other than the Holy Spirit – and in some areas there was a quiet and gentle agreement to differ.

Surely this was Lambeth 2008's distinctive contribution to the controversy which has occupied us for so long in this chapter. It was little short of tragic that so many good bishops and archbishops should have decided, in their impatience, to absent themselves and confer in separation. They did not realise what they were missing. The loss was mutual. Had they been present at Lambeth/Canterbury with their brothers in Christ, their contributions in the indabas would have been listened to with respect, and would have carried due weight. They might have been surprised that Bible study took so prominent a place, and learned that self-styled evangelicals do not have a monopoly of the Scriptures. Closed minds might have been prized open a little by the grace of God.

It is very much to be hoped that the GAFCONite bishops will take the time and trouble to read, and ponder, and take to God in prayer the *Lambeth Reflections* of which they will have received a copy. In this way good may yet come out of evil.

The ABC was right. Courteous listening and patience are both essential. This is true in all human relationships and it will be the same message in the two chapters that follow. Both of which will be shorter than this one!

Conclusion

This chapter is far too long I know. I have tried to curtail it. But if the story of this controversy, so relevant to the theme of this book, is to be told fairly and in full, as I have tried to tell it, it was bound to prove a sizeable undertaking.

The subject was not a pleasant one, but it had to be faced. The result: a vigorous, long drawn out and at times bitter dispute about something which, when I was young, was taboo in polite society. Rapidly changing public attitudes together with greater scientific knowledge in the last hundred years forced it upon the Church's attention and made many who call themselves Christians change their minds. It is right that we should all face facts, however uncomfortable this may be. These facts include, for Christians, the authority and interpretation of the Bible in the light of reason, common sense, wisdom and genuine scientific discovery – all of them gifts of God who is Absolute Goodness and Truth. Even so, it is hardly surprising if Christians come to different conclusions among themselves.

This dispute, like others which preceded it, has made us the laughing stock of the unbelieving world. "Those Anglicans," they say, "can't agree about anything." To them we look (and sometimes behave) more like an unruly debating society than God's apostolic mission to proclaim and bring (and even embody) Good News to a weary world.

But there is another way of looking at it. At least we can claim to be honest; to have brought this difficult and necessary argument out in the open, as we have also done with the issue of the ordination of women. Many of our Roman Catholic friends admire us for so doing, rather than, as their official Church does, pretend that there is no problem.

The bearing of all this upon ecclesiometry and good old fashioned Central Churchmanship will have to wait until the final chapter, when

I plan to tackle the complex but crucial question of the place of Holy Scripture in a twenty-first century Christian's faith.

STOP PRESS. When I wrote this chapter I had not read Rupert Shortt's magisterial *Rowan's Rule: the biography of the Archbishop*, only published in late Autumn, 2008. Had I been able to have done so, I would undoubtedly have revised it in some respects, but not, I think substantially. Shortt is essential reading for a fuller understanding of where we are now.

Chapter 8
Christians World-Wide:
The Ecumenical Scene

There is, or there ought to be, the closest possible link between the last chapter and this one. The point was well made in an article in the leading Anglican weekly, the *Church Times*, on 22 October 2004 quoted in the last chapter as follows: "Agreement among Anglicans is worthless unless they recognise its provisionality in relation to the restoration of the visible unity of the Church of God."

The purpose of Christian Unity: "That the World may Believe"

The article in question was headed: "That the world may believe". This was a quotation from John's Gospel, chapter 17, John's alternative version of the Synoptic accounts of our Lord's agony of prayer in Gethsemane before his arrest. The words John puts upon Jesus' lips to represent his innermost thoughts at this, the supreme crisis of his life on earth are:

> I ask not only on behalf of these [the eleven Apostles] but also on behalf of those who will believe in me through them. As you, Father, are in me and I am in you, may they also be in us, so *that the world may believe* that you have sent me. The glory that you have given me I have given them, so that they may be one, as we are one, I in them and you in me, that they may be completely one, *so that the world may know* that you have sent me and have loved them even as you have loved me. (John 17 verses 20-23. *New Revised Standard Version*)

John, with his uncanny God-given insight believed that Jesus in this prayer was deliberately consecrating himself as a willing sacrifice of filial obedience to the Eternal Father, whose very nature is unbounded self giving Love, *and* that, *with* this infinitely costly, yet freely given offering of himself, Jesus is deliberately associating those followers, disciples, given him by his heavenly Father. They are united to him, "one with him", as he is united in love and obedience with his heavenly Father. Fervently does he pray that they, with those in later generations who believe in him *through* them, may be one in unity *"that the world may believe"* that he, Jesus, was truly sent by God – was indeed God's living "Word made flesh". It was John's belief that *that*, and nothing short of that, is what gives credibility to the Gospel.

We should do well to remember this whenever we practice ecumenism. That, and not just ecclesiastical tidying up, is what it is all about, and why it is so important.

Ecumenism in the New Testament and the early Church

In Chapter 1, I laid particular stress on the frantic labours for the unity of his Christian converts, notably those in Corinth, of that great foundational apostle, St. Paul. As we have now seen, that other, equally great foundational apostle, the mysterious St. John was no whit less insistent on Christian unity than St. Paul – *unity with a purpose beyond itself.* This is not to imply that the other foundational apostles of Christianity, Peter, Barnabas, James *et al.* were any less keen to preserve the unity of the movement, the Church, "the Way", they pioneered; there simply happens to be less dramatic evidence of it in their writings preserved in the New Testament.[1]

The theme of this book is unity among Christians, yet it seems full of the opposite – controversy, conflict, schism and the threat of schism. To some extent, this is also true of the New Testament and of so much Christian history. Christians seem particularly prone to disunity, to internal strife within the Church. We tend to forget that unity, peace and concord within the Church, and within smaller Christian communities and families, do not make exciting history and consequently are often overlooked! That other faiths, Judaism, Islam, Buddhism etc. also have their "little local difficulties" is no consolation.

We often forget, too, what colossal problems the earliest Christians had to face, and, by the grace of God, succeeded in overcoming once the Church's doors were seen to be open to the non-Jewish, Gentile and pagan world. The agonisingly difficult and complex problem which had so urgently to be faced and resolved by these primitive Christians, all of whom, like their Messiah, were practising Jews,

---

1. Exhortations to brotherly love and Christian unity of spirit, specific in 1 Peter 1 v. 22 and 3 v. 8, are implicit throughout the epistle.

was what to do about the age old, hallowed culture of Mosaic moral
and ceremonial law in which they had all been strictly brought up,
symbolised as it was by the distinctively Jewish rite of circumcision
for every male on the eighth day after birth. Was all, or most, or
none of this to be retained, alongside the new Christian sacraments
of baptism and the eucharist? Was the great influx of pagans,
Gentiles, to be circumcised according to the Law of Moses, or was
circumcision with all it stood for to be abolished, to signalise the total
freedom of the Gospel and the breaking down of all barriers, racial
and religious, by the all-availing sacrifice of Christ completed on the
cross and ratified by his resurrection? The options must have seemed
to range from total retention to total abolition. It was recalled that
Jesus had said that he came not to destroy but to "fulfil" the Law and
the Prophets. What exactly did that imply?

For those who had to make such crucial decisions, they must have
seemed every bit as perplexing as those dividing us today. Yet the
grace of God and reliance upon the sure guidance of the Holy Spirit,
working through their God-given common sense enabled those early
Christians to make the right decisions. As a result a small Jewish
sect was transformed into a truly catholic, inclusive, cosmopolitan
Church, its membership open to all through belief, conversion and
commitment symbolised by baptism and eucharist.

This early Church was repeatedly troubled by protracted disputes
about doctrine, particularly the precise nature of the Incarnation.
From Nicaea (325) onwards, these controversies were resolved by
ecumenical Councils establishing orthodox formulae, sometimes in
the form of a Creed, sometimes, as at Chalcedon (451), by an agreed
definition with anathemas attached against those who for one reason
or another continued to teach opinions now authoritatively defined as
heretical – and indeed, some dioceses, provinces or "Churches" did
continue to teach heresy in defiance of conciliar authority. Such was
the case with Arian and semi-Arian Churches after 325, with those
thought to be Nestorian after 431 (Ephesus) and with Monophysite
Churches after Chalcedon (451). These schisms still exist. They were
a major contributory cause of the rapid expansion of Islam in the
Middle East following the advent of "the Prophet" Muhammad in
the seventh century.

The Great Schism

It was the same with "the Great Schism" between the (Latin) Church
of the West and the (Greek and Slavonic) Church of the East which
began in 1054 when Pope Leo IX and Michael Cerularius, patriarch

of Constantinople, excommunicated each other over the Roman claim to be "caput et mater ecclesiarum" (head and mother of the Churches) and the long standing argument about the "Procession of the Holy Spirit", i.e. whether the Holy Spirit "proceeds" from the Father and the Son (the Western view) or only from the Father. There were temporarily successful attempts to heal this breach in the Middle Ages, notably at the Council of Florence (1439), but it remained in being at the Fall of Constantinople to the Turks in 1453 and, at the time of writing, despite substantial progress in reconciliation between recent Popes – including notably John Paul II and the present Pope Benedict XVI – and Œcumenical Patriarchs, it has not yet been formally resolved. Like this long-standing dispute and the protracted arguments in the early Church about the proper method of calculating the date of Easter, some of these deeply divisive controversies seem to us trivial, though they certainly did not at the time.

Thus one aspect of the long centuries of medieval Church history before the concurrent splendours of the Renaissance and the disruption of the sixteenth century Reformation is discord, strife, violence. "By schisms rent asunder, by heresies distressed". To draw an idealised romantic picture of medieval Christendom is as false and misleading as to paint it all black. The thirteenth century which saw the glorious burgeoning of Gothic art and architecture, the lives of Francis of Assisi, Giotto, Dominic and Thomas Aquinas, the coming of the friars and the birth of the great universities, witnessed also two terrible events, to the lasting discredit and shame of Christianity – both in the guise of Crusades.

The first in time was the Fourth Crusade, when "Latin" crusaders sacked Orthodox Constantinople with barbarous cruelty (1204). The other was the so called Albigensian Crusade in the South of France against the Bogomil or Catharist heresy, resulting in the setting up of the Inquisition by Pope Gregory IX in 1233, making use of the (then) newly formed Dominicans and Franciscans as Inquisitors. Impenitent heretics were handed over to the secular authorities to be punished in accordance with the laws of the land. This normally meant burning at the stake.

The Reformation and its consequences

The sixteenth-century Reformation lies at the root of most of the divisions in Christendom today. It is strange that history records so few ecumenists from that troubled time who tried to repair the damage. There were two on the Continent, one on each side, who made great, but unavailing efforts to reunite the divided Church. On the Protestant side was Melancthon, great theologian and moderating influence on his friend Luther. On the Catholic side Contarini tried, but failed, to steer the early Council of Trent towards moderation "before the influence of the Counter-Reformation finally closed the possibility of reconciliation". (O.D.C.C. art. Contarini)

In England the sole voice of anything we might recognise as ecumenism was that of Richard Hooker who, in the last decade of the sixteenth century, over thirty years after the final break with Rome, wrote in Book Three of *The Laws of Ecclesiastical Polity* (1.14) "for preservation of Christianity there is not anything more needful than that such as are of the visible Church have mutual fellowship and society one with another. In which consideration, as the main body of the sea being one, yet within divers precincts hath divers names; so the Catholic Church is in like sort divided into a number of distinct Societies, every of which is termed a Church within itself . . .".

But this "ecclesiology" of Hooker's, his notion of the nature of the Church, would not have met with approval in Rome. Besides, it was too late. Each side had inflicted such lasting hurt and damage on the other that the degree of detachment essential in an ecumenist was nowhere to be found (and still less was it in Scotland, where the Reformation had taken an even more violent form).

Hooker probably came as near it as anyone at the time. In the next generation or two, such a mind was to be found in Sir Thomas Browne, to judge by the opening passages of his *Religio Medici* (1642), but the times were no more propitious and, anyway, ecumenism was not his métier.

With one interesting but insignificant exception,[2] two and a half centuries rolled by before there were any appreciable signs of a thaw in the ice age which effectively froze all Catholic-Protestant intercourse following the Council of Trent, the event which inaugurated the Catholic Counter Reformation. In the nineteenth century, triumphant Ultramontanism in two of the longest Papal reigns, those successively of Pius IX (1846-1878) and Leo XIII (1878-1903), hardened the Catholic position by defining two new dogmas, the Immaculate Conception in 1854 and Papal Infallibility in 1870, and by the condemnation of the Anglican Orders in 1896 as null and void. Despite this discouragement there was an ecumenical initiative by that devout Anglican layman, the second Viscount Halifax, Charles

2. The exception was the abortive project for a union between the Gallican (i.e. French Catholic) Church and the C. of E. mooted in correspondence between Louis Ellies du Pin and William Wake, Archbishop of Canterbury, in 1718.

Wood, and his Anglo-Catholic friends, through his contacts with the Abbé Portal in the 1890s. After the Great War, he embarked on a second, similar effort with Cardinal Mercier, Archbishop of Malines and Belgian Primate. Both efforts, well-intentioned though they were, came to nothing, thwarted by the English R.C. hierarchy under Cardinal Vaughan.

An important Anglican initiative during this period was the so-called Lambeth Quadrilateral of 1888. Originating in the Anglican Episcopal Church of the U.S.A., but approved by the Lambeth Conference of 1888 as stating the essentials of a reunited Christian Church from the Anglican point of view, it comprised (i) the Holy Scriptures as "containing all things necessary to salvation" and as the rule and standard of faith; (ii) the Apostles' and Nicene Creeds; (iii) the two Dominical Sacraments: Baptism and Eucharist; and (iv) the Historic Episcopate.

The Ecumenical Movement of the 20th century

1. Protestants only: 1910-1958

The Ecumenical Movement has been described as "a general movement among Christian people of all denominations towards the recovery of the unity of all believers in Christ transcending differences of creed, ritual and polity" (*Oxford Dictionary of the Christian Church*. Third edition [1997] p. 528).

Taking a broad perspective in the history of Christendom as a whole, one may hazard the generalisation that, within *Western* Christendom, from the sixteenth century Reformation onwards throughout the seventeenth, eighteenth and nineteenth centuries, corresponding to worldwide missionary expansion both Catholic and Protestant, the general trend was towards ever increasing fragmentation and *away from* unity – in a word, centri*fugal*. By contrast the twentieth century witnessed a reversal of this trend, a movement *back towards* unity, i.e. centri*petal*.

The beginning of this "ecumenical movement" is usually, and rightly, dated to the meeting in Edinburgh in 1910 of a World Missionary Conference under the leadership of the American John Mott and the Englishman J.H. Oldham. What gave it its impetus was the realisation among all the various missionary agencies there represented that their mission would be infinitely more effective if, instead of working independently and in competition, they and the sending Churches they represented, were unified and united. In 1920 the Appeal to all Christian People from that year's Lambeth Conference reinforced this

aim. Between the two world wars the Life and Work and the Faith
and Order Movements led ultimately in 1948 at Amsterdam to the
formation of the World Council of Churches in which, too, some of the
Eastern Orthodox Churches showed interest.

These years saw some encouraging positive developments in
the Protestant world. In 1932 the three separate strands into which
English Methodism had split (Wesleyan, Primitive and United)
coalesced in the Methodist Church in Great Britain as it now exists.
Even this process took time.

Far more significant was the inauguration of the Church of South
India in 1947, incorporating (i) four Anglican dioceses, (ii) the
South India Province of the Methodist Church, and (iii) the South
India United Church, itself the result of a merger of Presbyterian,
Congregationalist and Dutch Reformed bodies back in 1908. The
total population of the new Church was a million and a half. The
negotiations leading up to it had begun at Tranquebar in 1919 and
were based as far as the Anglicans were concerned on the Lambeth
Quadrilateral of 1888. It claims to be a united and visible Church
in which the Congregational, Presbyterian and Episcopal elements
are happily combined and preserved. "The union was achieved by
the acceptance of ministers ordained in each of these traditions into
a united ministry (without requiring re-ordination), combined with
the introduction of an episcopate in the historic succession (from
Anglicanism) and its maintenance for the future, with the assurance
that all future ordinations would be episcopal. It was expected that
at the end of 30 years all presbyters would have been episcopally
ordained." (ODCC 3rd edn. ad loc. p. 1522.). On these grounds it
was initially criticised by some Anglo-Catholics and received only
a cautious welcome from the Lambeth Conference, but it has by
now come to be generally accepted and its bishops attend Lambeth
Conferences. It became the model for the inauguration of the Church
of North India on much the same lines, but including Baptists, in
1970. One of its most distinguished exponents, the late Bishop Lesslie
Newbiggin, was widely influential as an ecumenist and theologian.

A third development of this period was, in its way, even more
promising, although it ended in deep disappointment.

It began with a University Sermon at Cambridge in 1946 by
Geoffrey Fisher, Archbishop of Canterbury.[3] In this he suggested that,
without surrendering their identity, the Evangelical Free Churches, as

---

3. This was published in *Church Relations in England* (1950) together with
a report of conversations between Fisher's representatives and those of the
Evangelical Free Churches in England.

the Nonconformists had become known, might "take episcopacy into their systems" and thus prepare the way for intercommunion. The only Nonconformists to respond to this invitation were the Methodists. Their response led to formally authorised conversations between the two Churches, which eventually resulted in a two stage scheme for constitutional reunion, stage 1 to be inaugurated by a Service of Reconciliation including a pledge to seek organic union and a rite of unification of the two ministries. Stage 2 would be followed by the consecration of the first Methodist bishops, after which all Methodist ordinations would be by bishops. In 1968 the final report on a revised scheme was published in two parts: Part I the Ordinal, Part II the Scheme. The Ordinal contained a Preface reflecting Roman Catholic and Orthodox participation and representing wide agreement. The scheme met considerable opposition – Fisher, long since retired, had intervened unhelpfully, and when put to the vote in 1969 on the basis that a 75 per cent majority in both the Methodist Conference and the Anglican Convocations should be the minimum for the scheme to go forward, Conference voted 77% in favour but Convocation only 66% and the whole scheme on which such hopes had rested necessarily lapsed. Again it was Anglo-Catholic opposition which ensured failure. I vividly recall the sense of disappointment, especially that of Archbishop Ramsey, in which I shared, having consistently voted for what promised to be an ecumenical breakthrough.

The failure of this scheme, due to an insufficiently strong majority in favour on the Anglican side, led to some feelings of scepticism about constitutional approaches to reunion, and after a period of recriminations, a new approach by way of Covenanting for Unity was tried but it, too, failed, amid a general loss of momentum.

Throughout this period 1910 to 1958, the world's largest Christian denomination, the Roman Catholic Church, stood rigidly aloof, declining even to send observers to the World Council of Churches, lest this should appear to recognise the very existence of churches other than itself.

2. Ecumenism since 1958; Rome involved

In 1958, with the death of Pope Pius XII, all this changed. His reign of nineteen years had encompassed the Second World War, the Holocaust, the beginning of "the Cold War", and the addition in 1950 of a new Catholic dogma unsupported by Scripture or reason. In all doctrinal matters, as well as in most others, Pius, like *almost*[4]

---

4. The partial exception was Leo XIII (Pope 1878-1903) whose social teaching at all events was radical

all his predecessors for a century or more, was uncompromisingly conservative. By their own Infallibility dogma, the Popes, and with them the R.C. Church, had locked themselves into a corner, from which there seemed no escape. If you are infallible, you cannot admit to error, even if you are *proved* wrong!

But at the conclave of Cardinals to elect Pius' successor an extraordinary thing happened. They elected the Patriarch of Venice, Cardinal Roncalli, a cheerful, genial old boy of 77, who was immensely popular with the Venetians and with all who knew him, because he was so unmistakably human, and disarmingly honest and outspoken. He is recorded, on the authority of one who knew him well, as having once said, with a smile "I am not infallible; I *am* infallible only when I speak *ex cathedra* [literally, from the chair, or throne, i.e. in an official capacity] But I shall never speak *ex cathedra*".[5] And he never did. Everyone thought the election of this apparently harmless old man was a stop gap appointment, to "hold the fort" until a younger candidate, then insufficiently experienced, had matured. Roncalli, who came from a large, poor farming family, then sprang his first surprise by choosing the name John and the number twenty three. The previous Pope John XXIII who was somewhat disreputable and of doubtful legitimacy, had been deposed in 1415 and died in 1419.

The accession of the new Pope, John XXIII, was as if the Holy Spirit (i.e. the wind or breath of God, the wind of change and disturbance) had blown open the doors and windows of the Vatican. The stuffy atmosphere of centuries had gone and been replaced with the invigorating spirit of renewal and reform. John, knowing he had only a few years at most before him, decided to make history while he had the opportunity. He went out of the Vatican City and visited the prisons of Rome and their inmates. (Imagine the effect!) The first Archbishop of Canterbury to do so since before the Reformation, Geoffrey Fisher, paid an historic but unofficial courtesy call after visiting Jerusalem and Constantinople and was, of course, made welcome – though there were no photographs to mark the occasion. It was to bear fruit in the next reign.

Remembering the good old adage *ecclesia semper reformanda* (the Church is always in need of reform) John electrified the Curia, and the worried "conservatives" led by Cardinal Ottaviani (who was beginning to wonder what that Conclave had done) by announcing his intention to convene an œcumenical council, with an agenda which was to include the modernisation of the old Latin Mass and

5. H. Küng: *Infallible? An Enquiry*. Eng. trans. Collins 1971 p. 71.

much else. The Pope defined the task of the Council as renewing the life of the Church and bringing up to date (*aggiornamento* – his key slogan) its teaching, discipline and organisation, *with the unity of all Christians as the ultimate goal*. The work of preparation for Vatican 2 took nearly four years.

It is now time to reintroduce another character, happily still going strong. Hans Küng, an energetic young German Swiss priest, was 30 in the year of John's election. He already had a reputation as a scholar, and had presented his doctoral thesis, on justification, the previous year. He had been educated at Paris and Rome, but his base was to be in the Catholic faculty of Theology in the famous German university of Tübingen, where he was elected Professor of Fundamental Theology at the early age of 32. A contemporary was a Bavarian priest of totally different views, called Josef Ratzinger. We shall meet him again.

Küng, who was the rising star of a galaxy of older West European Catholic theologians of distinction, older men such as the veteran Yves Congar, Henri de Lubac, and Karl Rahner of an earlier generation, as well as the Belgian Edward Schillebeekx, soon came to the notice of Pope John, who appointed him and the much senior Congar and Rahner as *periti* – a *peritus* is a theological expert. They were charged, with others, to assist in the preparation of the agenda and were actively involved in the actual work of the Council. Küng had conceived warm admiration for the Pope and this was evidently reciprocated by the older man.

The Council opened in 1962 and continued its sessions for three years. A novel feature of Vatican 2 was that historic non-Roman Churches were invited to send observers to be present and made welcome at all the sessions of the Council. They were officially referred to as "our separated brethren". Our Anglican observers were Bernard Pawley (who established the permanent Anglican Centre in Rome), and John Moorman, the distinguished church historian, (specialising in the Franciscan Order) and later Bishop of Ripon.

John XXIII did not live to see the end of the Council. He died in 1963, mourned not only by Catholics the world over but by many Protestants as well. In his place the conclave elected Cardinal Montini, Archbishop of Milan, but previously closely associated with the old régime of Pius XII. As Paul VI the new Pope promised to see the Council through to its conclusion and to continue his predecessor's policies.

This he did, but there was a noticeable slowing down, both within the remaining sessions of the Council and in the process of reform, very much to the disappointment and rising frustration of Hans Küng, some of whose earliest books told the story of the Council, which ended in 1965, and of the behind the scenes conflicts between conservatives and liberals. Paul on his own initiative modified the Conciliar Decree on Ecumenism.

In 1966, as we have seen, Paul welcomed Archbishop Ramsey to the Vatican where, in the Sistine Chapel, they signed the Common Declaration setting up ARCIC, with the results which have already been noticed. The prospects for a reconciliation between the Roman and Anglican Communions had never looked brighter – I vividly remember the growing sense of excitement – until the Congregation for the Doctrine of the Faith, with which in 1965 Paul had replaced the old Holy Office (of the Inquisition), began to pour cold water on the ARCIC reports. In setting up the new Congregation Paul assigned it the function of "promoting as well as safeguarding sound doctrine on faith and morals" (O.D.C.C. p. 782), words which came to have sinister implications.

In his courageous book *Infallibility?* (1970), the importance of which can hardly be exaggerated, Küng, despite severe criticism of Paul VI for not living up to the ideals and promise of his predecessor, pays tribute to him as "a man of integrity, who suffers under his load of responsibility and perhaps feels overburdened by it" and "is motivated by a selfless desire to do only the best for the Church and for humanity and who sincerely believes he must act accordingly" (op. cit. p. 12). This became apparent in his tortuous dealings over the subject of contraception/birth control leading up to the publication of his highly controversial encyclical *Humanae Vitae* in 1968. Having earlier sensibly appointed a strong commission of experts to advise him on the technical complexities involved, he arbitrarily rejected their wise advice on conscientious grounds.

Küng's powerful and systematic arguments in *Infallibility?* go right to the heart of the problem – the self-inflicted quandary in which Rome has found herself ever since that foolish dogma was promulgated in 1870, a century before Küng systematically demolished it. His arguments are unassailable. Inevitably they were directed, too, against the fundamentally unchristian apparatus of the so-called *magisterium*, or "teaching office of the Church", with its antiquated machinery of intellectual coercion inherited ultimately from the Inquisition. Unsurprisingly they were wheeled out and directed at Küng, whose *missio canonica*, formal authority to teach as a Catholic theologian, was withdrawn. Küng, from his stronghold at Tübingen, has always stoutly maintained his loyalty to the Roman Catholic

Church. In the light of his later output, especially his magisterial *On Being a Christian* (1974. Eng. trans. by Edward Quinn. Collins 1978) he is widely acclaimed as the leading Catholic theologian and Biblical scholar of our time. For his *Infallible?* he declined to obtain the customary *imprimatur*. This did not prevent its widespread dissemination in Catholic Europe as well as throughout the Christian world. The words of Visser t'Hooft, the widely influential Secretary of the World Council of Churches, on reading it have already been quoted (v. section on Protestantism p. 68). The only serious criticism of it is of Küng's suggestion to replace the concept of infallibility with that of "indefectibility" which in English carries an *almost identical* meaning. His point, of course, was to safeguard the *assurance* of the guidance of the Holy Spirit "into all truth". *Assurance* conveys a very different meaning to infallibility: there is no suggestion of automatic, inflexible "infallibility", rather one of *reliability*. Therefore it is much to be preferred. I offer this suggestion *gratis* to Vatican Three in all seriousness.

Paul VI died in 1978, the year of three Popes. Once again, as twenty years earlier, the conclave made a bold choice, and once again a much loved Patriarch of Venice, Cardinal Luciani, was elected. Tactfully he chose for his papal name a combination of those of his two predecessors, John Paul I. Like John XXIII he was of humble origin, and like him, too, a cheerful extrovert of warm humanity – in sharp contrast to Paul's cautious, withdrawn conservatism. It was widely thought that he would rescind, or modify, Paul's unpopular (and, from a practical point of view, unworkable – and anyhow widely ignored) *Humanae Vitae*. A month after his election, apparently in robust health, he was dead. The news coverage from the Vatican seemed unconvincing – it was widely seen as a cover up. A British journalist, David Yallop, published a detailed investigation, or exposé, entitled *In God's Name* (Cape 1984), described by the Vatican as "infamous rubbish", but which some would say has never been satisfactorily refuted. Certainly the election of John Paul I caused widespread alarm in reactionary circles – i.e. the Vatican – while hopes ran high among those who thought like Küng, on both sides of the Catholic/Protestant divide. These hopes were again due for disappointment.

The outcome is, of course, well known. The second conclave elected a man of immense energy both physical and intellectual, Karol Wojtyla, Archbishop of Cracow, the first Slav to be elected Pope, taking as name John Paul II. Twenty five years later, aged 83 and suffering from Parkinsons, he was still Pope. He died in 2005.

Historians of the future will undoubtedly be deeply divided when they come to assess his reign and achievements, but on at least two points they are likely to agree.

He was elected at a time when the Cold War between democratic capitalist West and atheistic Communist East still had about ten years to run, and his beloved Poland, with the rest of Eastern Europe, still endured ruthless Marxist oppression. There was, as yet, little or no light at the end of the tunnel: the Solidarity movement had yet to be born, and the name of Lech Walesa, its future leader, was still unknown outside the Lenin Shipyard in Gdansk where he worked. Historians are likely to agree that the overthrow of Communism, the recovery of freedom and independence in the nations it had so long oppressed, most of all Poland, and the victory of the West in the Cold War – the tremendous events of 1989 and 1990, which when he was elected seemed unthinkable – owe more to him than to any other single individual. Nothing can take that enormous achievement away from him. The second point on which there can be no dispute is the fact that John Paul II is far and away the most widely travelled pope in history – one could say the most restless. As a young man he showed great interest in the stage and this mastery of showmanship and sense of theatre never left him. His monument in that respect will be the famous Popemobile and his custom of kissing the ground of every land he visits will long be remembered.

Also, as with Paul VI, and indeed John Paul I, his personal integrity and sheer strength of character and will are not in doubt. One cannot but admire him for it. But, having said all that, (and it is true), what a tragedy it is, for the cause of Christian Unity, and of Truth, that the version of Christianity which he so tenaciously held dear, and worked to promote, was such a sad distortion of the real thing.

Even so, John Paul II must still be given credit for his unquestionably sincere work for Christian unity *on his own uncompromising, ultramontane terms*. In that sense he sought to be faithful to the legacy of John XXIII, as did Paul VI. Three events are outstanding. The first of these, of course, for Anglicans, was his historic visit to the United Kingdom, including the memorable occasion when, with Archbishop Robert Runcie, he joined in prayer in Canterbury Cathedral, the mother church of the Anglican Communion, and together they agreed to set up a second ARCIC – Anglican-Roman Catholic International Commission for further dialogue on Christian doctrine.

That was in 1982. The other two events were in their ways not less notable. In 1984 the Pope addressed the World Council of

Churches and welcomed the Ecumenical Movement which, he said, was "irreversible" although he rejected intercommunion as a means of attaining unity. And in 1986 he, with other Christian leaders and representatives of non-Christian world faiths joined together in prayer in St. Francis's Assisi – on his invitation, thus recognising the value of inter-faith dialogue. Finally, on a visit to the Œcumenical Patriarch at Constantinople/Istanbul, each attended the other's liturgy. All this must be entered on the credit side.

On the debit side of the account is his rigid and uncompromising doctrinal and ethical conservatism, his unbalanced devotion to the Blessed Virgin, so much in evidence on his visits to Fatima and Lourdes, and his habit of packing an already swollen college of cardinals with men of his own way of thinking. For all that, he will be remembered as a great and, in many ways, a good Pope, especially in the vigorous earlier years of his long reign.

It is hard to escape the impression that in his declining years, he allowed himself to come under the baneful influence of the even more reactionary Cardinal Ratzinger, whom he seems to have been grooming to succeed him.

So when John Paul finally breathed his last, in April 2005, Ratzinger, created a Cardinal over a quarter of a century earlier, was Dean of the College of Cardinals, and in that capacity presided over one of the shortest of conclaves, in which it seemed a foregone conclusion that he himself was elected Pope, choosing the name Benedict XVI. It cannot be pretended that there was great rejoicing in the non-Roman Catholic world, whatever the feelings may have been in Rome. Benedict, said to be a charming and cultivated man, and a Mozart lover, was reaction personified. It was as though Rome was back in the days of Pius XII. A chill darkness had long been descended on the ecumenical scene. With Benedict's election, the curtain seemed finally to have fallen upon Rome's involvement in the Ecumenical Movement.

All the civilities continued to be observed, of course, but, for the time being at any rate, all hope of further progress towards reunion with Rome had died. One could not forbear to speculate how different it would have been if Ratzinger's old sparring partner and one time colleague and friend at Tübingen had been elected Pope. There was a curious report that shortly after Benedict's election Hans Küng called at the Vatican to congratulate his old rival – and that he was seen leaving with a smile. That was the last heard of one of Europe's finest Christian, and Catholic, theologians.

But all was by no means lost on the Roman-Anglican front – far from it. Two points stand out. The ARCIC conversations had not been a waste of time, even though Ratzinger's Congregation of the Doctrine of the Faith had done its best to rubbish them. What to many was a surprising degree of convergence had emerged, particularly in the field of eucharistic theology, and the very fact that real difficulties had been frankly faced in an atmosphere of openness and honesty was itself an enormous gain and a happy augury for a Ratzinger-free future. Equally important, genuine lasting friendships and (it is said) comradely feelings *across* the increasingly artificial divide would be likely to endure and on both sides, a new understanding had grown up of each other's viewpoint.

This all ties in with the second point. Since the Big Thaw brought about by Popes John and Paul and Michael Ramsey and Bernard Pawley, an altogether new relationship had grown up in academic circles especially between scholars of *all* Christian denominations, so that joint, co-operative undertakings such as *The Oxford Dictionary of the Christian Church* became the rule rather than the exception. In the ancient universities such as Oxbridge, and others where Divinity Faculties were established, Roman Catholic scholars were admitted on an equal footing and Professorships, Chairs of Divinity, which not so very long ago were the sole preserves of Anglican theologians were now open to R.C. and Free Church scholars. On the diocesan and parochial fronts too, exchanges of pulpits, especially in cathedrals, and R.C. participation in all kinds of events, even in shared schools, became increasingly common. All this was immensely healthy. In a brief section at the end of this chapter, I have told the story of my own ecumenical involvement, which is typical, I suspect, of many others who have been able to go further.

In recent years with the marked decline in the number of vocations to the priesthood and in the size of most congregations affecting Roman Catholics as well as Protestants of most denominations, this must have given rise to a sharply increased awareness of the sinful absurdity of our continuing disunity and the overwhelming need to close ranks and to sing the Lord's songs *together* and in harmony. Unfortunately, ecclesiastical human nature being what it is, an element of *schadenfreude* still occurs, as when "conversions" such as Tony Blair's defection to Rome, or the incidence of paedophilia among compulsorily celibate Roman clergy are news.

One particularly welcome development during the long reign of Pope John Paul II was his willingness to admit and apologise for historic Roman errors and blunders in the field of science. The case in question was the notorious Papal condemnation of the Copernican revolution, the heliocentric cosmology proclaimed by Copernicus in the sixteenth century and endorsed by Galileo in the seventeenth. It was the foundation of Newtonian physics and astronomy. In 1981 John Paul appointed a high powered scientific commission to study the matter, and in 1992 endorsed its inevitable findings, admitting the "subjective" error of Galileo's judges. It was only a few centuries late, but at least a step in the right direction.

If only this could be taken as a precedent! The absurd infallibility dogma has had the disastrous effect of painting the Popes into a corner from which there is no escape other than a retreat so humiliating that it is almost inconceivable that any Pontiff would have the courage and candour to undertake – almost but not completely.

Imagine the effect of some future Pontiff having the guts, the sheer moral and intellectual courage and honesty to publish a Bull or Encyclical in which he would systematically make a wholesale admission of errors past and present. They would include (i) the encouragement of Catholic anti-Semitism over the course of many centuries and, in particular, the failure of Pius XII to condemn the Holocaust; (ii) complicity in barbarous cruelty to Muslims and Eastern Christians in the Crusades, particularly the Fourth Crusade; (iii) complicity in the brutal expulsion of Jews and Muslims from Spain in 1492 (iv) and in the appalling cruelties of the Inquisition; (v) the promotion of the unchristian and unwholesome extravagances of Mariolatry, especially the unscriptural dogmas of the Immaculate Conception (1854) and the Assumption (1950); (vi) the unjust condemnation of Anglican Orders (1896); topping it all with a (vii) formal renunciation of the Dogma of Papal Infallibility (1870) and (viii) an acceptance of the *established* findings of Biblical scholarship.

What a salutary clearing of the decks that would be: the removal of centuries' accumulation of intolerance, prejudice and insensitivity. It would stimulate us all to follow suit. All Christian denominations have faults past and present for which an apology is due – in most cases, overdue. We Anglicans may be called to account for intellectual and spiritual snobbishness, for a sense of superiority, even arrogance that goes with the status of the established Church. I will not particularise further but it is a fact of experience that social grievances, underlying distinctions of Church v. Chapel have played a large part in "our unhappy divisions" – often as much as, or more than, disagreements over doctrine or liturgy.

Intercommunion as a shortcut to reunion?

When, as at present, we seem to have reached an ecumenical impasse in spite of the genuine, if limited, gains recorded in the last few pages, there is likely to be raised the question whether in seeking doctrinal accord between churches, we have been in pursuit of an impossibility, an unattainable ideal, and should have been better employed in seeking unity by a different and simpler route – through Intercommunion.

At a certain level, by some deemed naïve and superficial, this seems to have a great deal to commend it. What could be more appropriate, more obviously *right* and straightforward – it is said by its proponents – than for Christians separated from one another by centuries of hostility, to receive the Bread of Life and the Cup of Salvation, the very Body and Blood of Christ, from the hands of each other's accredited ministers? To throw off historic doctrinal, litugical or organisational differences to meet together at the Lord's table, the Altar, and by doing so regularly and devoutly, does not the opportunity arise to grow together in a unity transcending their separate polities? Expressed like that, it sounds compellingly simple, deceptively attractive.

It was seriously put, very much in that form, by Archbishop Donald Coggan on his visit to Rome in 1977, but firmly brushed aside by Paul VI and has not been suggested again since then. The argument against it is basically two-fold. For one thing, it mistakes the end for the means of unity, and secondly it makes a pretence of a unity which does not exist. In short, it is hopelessly simplistic and less than honest.

Before dismissing intercommunion, however, it is worth noting that it was discussed as an alternative possibility by an outstanding ecumenist, church historian and theologian, the late Adrian Hastings (1929-2001) in a lecture in York Minster in May 1987 entitled "Where does the Ecumenical Movement stand now?"[6] "In so far as anyone, including the hierarchical authority of any church," he said,

---

6. This was printed in a collection of essays and sermons with the title *The Theology of a Protestant Catholic* (SCM 1997). Hastings, a son of a mixed marriage – his mother a devout Roman Catholic, his father an equally devout Anglican – was brought up an R.C. and after education at Oxford and Rome, was ordained and served as a priest in Africa. He later wrote a definitive history of African Christianity. He had an extraordinary empathy with Christians of all denominations, particularly Africans. A liberal Catholic, his best known work was his outstanding *History of English Christianity 1920-2000* (SCM 2001). He married but continued to exercise his vocation.

endeavours to prevent intercommunion, its instructions should be disregarded, charitably but firmly, as un-Christian, wrong, un-Catholic and *ultra vires*. The only sound reason not to do so is a pastoral, not a theological one – that we are as yet insufficiently conscious of being one church to be able to share communion with one another charitably and sincerely. To some extent this remains the case today. One must not force one's own conscience nor that of others. One must not offend people by making the sacrament of unity an apparent act of defiance or aggression. For many of us our sense of unity, even if much greater than it used to be, may not be sufficient as yet for eucharistic sharing . . . (op.cit. p. 88)

This characteristically quizzical utterance should not be dismissed as that of a maverick, although Hastings was regarded in that light by the reactionaries of Rome. As I see it, Hastings' points about conscience are crucial and, indeed, determinative. Whatever our feelings we should not take the law into our own hands. Intercommunion involving the Roman Catholic Church, unlike the intercommunion authorised by fairly recent Anglican Canon Law with Christians of other denominations, who are in good (i.e. communicant) standing with their own denominations, is, as I understand it, only authorised in very rare and exceptional circumstances. A case in point in my experience was my son's wedding in 1985. His bride is half French, half German. Her parents' home was in the parish of Gallardon in the diocese of Chartres. Presumably with the knowledge and approval of the Bishop of Chartres, I was invited by the French parish priest, the Abbé Jeanne, to participate fully, robed, in the wedding and in the Nuptial Mass which formed part of it. I gladly did so, giving an address in English and taking part in the marriage vows and also administering the chalice to a mixed French, English and German Lutheran congregation, which I esteemed a great privilege.

I have honestly to confess that I cannot claim complete consistency in this matter. On the one hand, when taking part on more than one occasion in an official link between my diocese of St. Edmundsbury and Ipswich and the Belgian diocese of Bruges in the 1970's and 1980's, I, with other Anglican clergy, was a guest of Pastor Dean Joris Fénaux, a most warm hearted Belgian priest. He expected me to receive the sacrament in his parish of Blankenberge and, reciprocally, when staying as my guest in Suffolk he received the sacrament (in both kinds of course) at Monks Eleigh Church.

On the other hand I have twice attended Sunday Mass at (Roman

Catholic) Quarr Abbey Church in the Isle of Wight, where it is celebrated with the most beautiful and moving simplicity. I would not have dreamed of receiving the Sacrament there, *very much* though I would have *liked* to have done so. I refrained however, because I knew full well that if I had done so I should have broken the rules of the Roman Catholic Church, which I ought in conscience to respect.

There is the further very sound rationale underlying that rule, viz. that our two Churches remain (sadly) entirely separate and had I presented myself at Quarr Abbey altar I should have been acting a lie. It is surely good that we should feel the very real pain of our mutual separation while this remains, and it cannot but be painful to be excluded from participation in the Blessed Sacrament of Christ's Body and Blood, and union with his "one perfect, and sufficient sacrifice, oblation and satisfaction for the sins of the whole world". It follows that our Anglican hospitality of the Altar runs the grievous risk of falsely blessing our painful divisions, so that the pain is deadened. Total consistency is a luxury denied to most of us!

What part has Churchmanship in Ecumenism?

By this time the reader may be wondering if I have forgotten the promise implied in the title of this book. Has my vaunted claim for *(principled)* Central Churchmanship any conceivable relevance for ecumenism, the elusive quest for the Unity of Christendom, for the healing reconciliation of all those apparently insoluble problems that persist in dividing one "Church" from another. I have not forgotten; how could I?

But before attempting to answer the question, let us be clear about one thing. The Unity we seek is surely NOT a total monochrome and monolithic *uniformity*, such as was implied in the Soviet or Chinese Communist Party or the German National Socialist (Nazi) Party. To pretend to seek such a thing would be not only totally unrealistic, but also completely wrong in itself. God has made us diverse and given us freedom in diversity. The unity we seek is surely a True Unity in Diversity in Brotherly love. We should *cherish true* diversity and seek a genuine framework of unity which will encompass its reasonable manifestations. We may in fact be much closer to the real thing than most of us realise. It was Blaise Pascal who wisely put on the lips of God: "You would not be seeking Me if you had not already found Me."

If that is true, and it surely must be, the answer to this question forming the above sub-heading may not be so elusive after all.

Near the beginning of this book I claimed "churchmanship" and the whole theory of ecclesiometry that goes with it as a purely Anglican monopoly, and in doing so I think I can claim the support of history. You might well say it has proved a mixed blessing if not a curse, and claim the support of history for that, too, pointing to the troubles from which Anglicanism is currently suffering as described at length in the previous chapter. Fair enough. We Anglicans are notorious for washing all our dirty linen in public. We are a kind of Ecclesiastical Launderette.

But washing dirty linen is something all Churches, not only the Anglican, have to do. What I am now suggesting is that, in actual fact, all Churches from the Roman Catholic to the Quaker Society of Friends that claim a basis of distinctive Christian beliefs, commitment and regard for the Holy Scripture as in some sense their indispensable Title Deeds, hold their beliefs and practices, willy nilly, within a four square framework. This embraces the corporate (High); the individual (Low); openness to God given reason, science and wisdom (Broad) and true and necessary restraint (Narrow) to balance latitude. These four elements are, in fact, part of the Divine Economy. St. Paul *had* to be "all things to all people" if he was to save some (1 Cor. 9.22).

We Anglicans are, alas, still painfully learning the lessons of ecclesiometry. So far, some of us have hardly begun. If we, who claim to be its inventors, are taking so long to discover the central core of our churchmanship, we can hardly complain if our brothers and sisters in other branches of Christendom to whom this is a new and strange "game" are slow in acquiring proficiency in it. They are finding it a rough and ready means of gauging what that wise evangelical report of 1950 called the *Fullness of Christ*, the necessary process of "growing into catholicity" in which, without fully realising it, we are all engaged. *This is true ecumenism.*

This chapter really ends here, but if only for some optional light relief, I append a section on my own ecumenical experiences, such as they were, in Suffolk where I spent the whole of my active ministry (1947-87). Don't hesitate to skip it if you've already had enough.

Ecumenism with the author

In my one and only curacy, All Saints' Newmarket, I don't recall anything worthy of the name. The Roman Catholic parish priest, Father Burrows, whose unpretentious little church close to my lodgings was later replaced by a larger more conspicuous one on a different site, was a cheerful, friendly little man, always much in evidence at the racecourse in race weeks. He is the only non-Anglican minister I remember.

In my first parish (Reydon near Southwold 1951-70), keen though I was to be ecumenical, I suffered from the fact that, with the sole exception of a little green painted wooden chapel largely run by one family (and that closed down sometime before I left) there was no one to be ecumenical with! (I was on cordial enough terms with the Forwards, the chapel family, Methodists.)

It was different in my second cure (Brandon with Santon Downham 1970-80). Baptists, Roman Catholics and Methodists all had their places of worship in or near the town. Before my time there no one had heard of ecumenism and all had kept themselves to themselves. We changed all that. They were all very friendly so we formed a Brandon Council of Churches which always met at the Rectory, and we had joint services in each others' places of worship. In my earlier years the RC priest was an elderly Irish Benedictine, Father Ildefonso Flannery, OSB He had a rich Irish brogue and drove like the wind.[7] I remember a joint Eucharist in Brandon Church at which he read the Epistle and it was his first experience of anything of the kind. On our return visit to his long narrow wooden church near the railway station (replaced in my time with a fine modern one, of which I attended the dedication) he greeted us all with the announcement: "Our Anglican friends will be pleased to hear that in this Mass there will be no collection and no sermon". It didn't take long. The Methodists were quite strong in Brandon and they, too, sold their two old chapels and built a new one. I invited them to join us at the Parish Church for the Midnight Eucharist every Christmas and they readily responded and their minister, Carl Howarth, assisted me at the altar. This became a regular feature in my time but I don't know if it still obtains.

Father Flannery eventually retired – he was greatly loved by his congregation, several of whom were Irish. His successor was a much younger American Franciscan, Father Emmanuel Sullivan. He has written a book on ecumenism entitled *Baptized into Hope*, oddly enough published by SPCK in 1980, of which he gave me a signed copy before I left Brandon. We were good friends. There was quite a strong Polish and Ukrainian community in Brandon, unable to return to their then-Marxist homeland. They had their Polish Mass every Sunday as well as the English one. All those I got to know I liked. We were still in Brandon when Cardinal Wojtyla was elected Pope in 1978 and they all went wild with excitement. Shortly after I retired in 1987 my wife and I went on a fortnight's Saga trip to Poland, then still under Communist rule, although Solidarity was much in evidence

---

7.. Or like Jehu, the son of Nimshi (2 Kings 9.20)

and the churches were very much alive as centres of patriotism. Our journeys took us to Krakow where the Pope had been Archbishop and to Wadowice where he was born. We went into the house and even the bedroom where he was born, kept as a shrine. His father had been an officer in the old Austro-Hungarian Army before Poland regained its independence after the 1914-18 War.

While I was at Brandon and later after the move to my third benefice (Monks Eleigh etc. 1980-87) I was actively involved in an official link between our Diocese of St. Edmundsbury and Ipswich and the Belgian Roman Catholic Diocese of Bruges. This was a stimulating and most enjoyable reciprocal experience, facilitated by the excellent communications of the then-Townsend Thoresen Felixstowe-Zeebrugge ferries, on which I travelled several times. There were several clergy involved on both sides and they were all most hospitable and warmly friendly. The visits were arranged by the ecumenical officers of both dioceses and on one occasion our diocese actually chartered a ferry and filled it with clergy and laity. On that occasion, led by our then-Bishop, Leslie Brown, himself a keen ecumenist, with experience in Uganda of which he was Bishop before he came to us, we marched in procession, banners flying, through the streets of Bruges to the Cathedral for a service of welcome.

My opposite number there was Father Joris (=George) Fénaux – French/Walloon surname but totally Flemish in culture. He is an extraordinarily kind, generous and warm-hearted, hospitable priest, and was Dean (Deken) of West Flanders, and parish priest of the main church in the seaside town of Blankenberge. On one occasion he took me to meet his well-to-do parents – his father, a carpet manufacturer, had built and endowed an impressive modern church, in (if I remember rightly) Kortrijk, and on a private visit he lent me and my wife a small house he had in the country at Lendelade and entertained us one evening in the famous Grand Place in Brussels. On official visits he took me, and other Suffolk clergy, to a school, a hospital and a printing house and we had useful discussions on various subjects, such as foreign missions, in each others houses. He made it clear that when I attended Mass in his large nineteenth century church in Blankenberge, I was to receive the Blessed Sacrament, and when he stayed with us in Monks Eleigh I reciprocated and he gladly received it from my hands, although this was strictly against the rules. But the Belgian Catholics, like their Dutch neighbours, are well known for their liberal views.

I have, of course, known and met many Roman Catholics, mostly lay people, and never, I think, one whom I did not like. And on many trips abroad in both Catholic and Protestant countries in Europe I have met nothing but kindness and warm fellowship, and thus I have experienced the pain of separation from their Churches. One unforgettable experience must on no account be omitted. Largely through my wife, Anne, who knew and loved France and had taught French (and Italian) before I met her, I came to know France quite well and we had many enjoyable visits there. On one occasion, I think about 1980, we had been staying with friends in Auvergne and from there on our way to stay with others in Alsace our journey took us through Burgundy and it occurred to us we could perhaps break the journey for one night at Taizé. They kindly put us up there in spartan accommodation, and this gave us the opportunity to mix with vast crowds of young Christians, boys and girls, Catholic and Protestant, and to join in worship in one of their beautiful and crowded churches. It was an evening eucharist and I shall never forget that evening – the marvellous chanting and the actual administration of the sacrament using ordinary leavened bread which had, of course, been duly consecrated. We were there less than 24 hours, and it was an unpremeditated visit, but while we were there we were hailed by some other Suffolk people from the small rural parish of Chevington.

Our host in Alsace was René Voeltzel, a professor of Old Testament in the Protestant faculty of divinity in the University of Strasbourg, and the author of a number of books, including *Selon les Écritures* of which he gave me a copy – printed incidentally at the printing press of the Communauté de Taizé. His and his wife Denise's daughter Elisabeth had been *au pair* with us when we lived at Reydon near Southwold. Sadly she and her parents, all dear friends, are no longer living in this world.

There is yet one more ecumenical experience which ought to go on record. It was a ride round the mid-Suffolk village of Wetherden on an eight seater bicycle lent to us by the Stowmarket Young Farmers Club, about 1981. It was a publicity stunt to advertise the Annual (Ecumenical) Sponsored Bike Ride in aid of the Suffolk Historic Churches Trust, of which I was a co-founder. On the eight seats, variously attired, were Eric Devenport, Suffragan Bishop of Dunwich (in a bowler hat and cycle clips); a Salvation Army officer wearing an opera hat belonging to me, fully extended with a Salvation Army hat band round it; a Baptist pastor; a Methodist minister; Father Wilson, the parish priest of the R.C. Church of St. Edmund, Bury St. Edmunds wearing what he called his "car-biretta" with Union Jack attached; and beside him, on one of the two rear saddles, me wearing a Canterbury cap (which I never normally wear) and, as commanded,

Ecumenism on Wheels. Wetherden, Suffolk. 22nd August 1985
Photo: *East Anglian Daily Times*

a cassock. Disaster struck. My cassock got caught in the chain and almost throttled me, as well as doing no good to the cassock. I vowed never again – and kept my vow. However, our photograph appeared in next day's *East Anglian* with a more than usually anguished look on my face – so our object was achieved.

Chapter 9
The Wider World:
The Abrahamic/Monotheistic Faiths

Before embarking on the business of this chapter, there are certain preliminary considerations that need to be addressed. These are:

1. Religious Relativism

Sixty or more years ago, when I was a candidate for Holy Orders studying theology, first at Cambridge and later at my theological college (Wells, Somerset), Britain was not yet the multi-cultural, multi-faith nation it has since become. "Rab" Butler's celebrated Education Act of 1944 provided for definite Christian religious education to be made compulsory in all state schools. In those far off days it was Bible-based Christian theology that we studied, albeit taking fully on board the established findings of up-to-date Biblical criticism/analysis.

The unspoken assumption was that Britain was still basically a Christian country. Such non-Christian minorities as existed, mainly in cities, were comparatively insignificant, and for them and the agnostics and atheists, there was an opt-out clause in the Education Act.

We theological students were aware, most of us, especially those of us conscious of a missionary vocation, that there was a respectable kindred subject then called Comparative Religion. It was not part of our curriculum for the General Ordination Examination but, if we were intellectually adventurous, we may have dipped into the works of its leading exponents such as the Reverend Dr. A.C. Bouquet, an Anglican priest. Or we may have read David Paton's classic SCM paperback, *Jesus Christ and the World's Religions* – still a useful introduction to that vast subject. Also, curiosity may have led us to dabble in the study of anthropology and primitive religion and made us aware of Frazer's *Golden Bough* and, hopefully, Otto's famous *Idea of the Holy*.

Times have changed a lot since then – and not all the changes have

been for the worse! Generally speaking, Britain has given up the
pretence of being a Christian country, although, anachronistically,
England still has an Established Church, theoretically headed by
a singularly gracious, believing, committed Christian monarch.[1]
Oxbridge and a few English universities of more recent foundation
still maintain faculties of divinity, headed by professors of theology.
But the nomenclature is significantly changing, from "Theology"
or "Divinity" to *"Religious Studies"*. The latter term covers the
comparative study of the world's religions (and quasi-religious
philosophies, such as Marxist dialectical materialism), *seen as
alternative choices available to all and sundry, on a basis of equality.*
In other words the rationale underlying this change of wording is
frankly *relativist. The various "religions", including Christianity, are
now seen as competing equals.* Put crudely: "You pays your money
and makes your choice". Also, the numbers of atheists and agnostics
have greatly increased, and those of believing, committed Christians
(of almost all denominations) have declined. An attitude of civilised
detachment is the order of the day.

The same thing has overtaken the parallel field of ethics. The
absolute (our duty to God and our duty to our neighbour) has given
way to the relative. This (insidious?) development coincided with the
onset, decades ago now, of "the Permissive Society"; "I ought," or "I
must," or "I should," giving way to "provided I am not hurting my
neighbour, I will, or won't do such a thing if I want to". Black and
white giving way to various shades of grey. "Situation Ethics" makes
some valid points but we still need the Absolutes, the Categorical
Imperative for guidance. The Ten Commandments are not obsolete.
But they need to be set beside Our Lord's *positive* Summary of the
Law – Thou *shalt* love God and thy neighbour as thyself.

This pervasive and fundamental change of attitude is reflected,
too, in our schools. Instead of straightforward Christian teaching
of doctrine and morals, boys and girls are treated to lessons on the
world's great religions and philosophies. And this is on the implicit
understanding that their still naturally immature intellects will then
or later, enable them to make an impartial, unprejudiced judgment
and choice on which to base their future lives and conduct! We
may ask, what does this expect of their teachers, and their teachers'
teachers by way of intellectual and spiritual integrity? To ask this
question does not entitle us to dodge this same question when it is

---

1. H.M. Queen Elizabeth II, for whom, with her unswerving old fashioned
sense of duty, we have every reason to be deeply thankful. Her Christmas
broadcasts are always stimulating and thoughtful.

put to *us* or to anyone undertaking to "teach Christianity", whether in school, Church, Sunday School or home. Teaching information *about* Christianity, or Buddhism or whatever, is not the same thing as teaching the "religion" itself as a committed believer in it. Children are not fools; they know the difference.

Topically, this all-pervading relativism, often disguised as easy going, broad minded tolerance, and so much part of the very air we breathe these days that to most of us it is imperceptible and taken for granted, was further reflected in the major, historic, (and for the subject of this chapter crucially relevant) British Library exhibition[2] in the summer of 2007, entitled *Sacred Books of the Three Faiths, Judaism, Christianity and Islam.*

It is in the splendid catalogue of this superb exhibition that this attitude becomes apparent, notably in the choice of Karen Armstrong, a militantly secularist Biblical *and* Qur'anic scholar, to contribute the principal introduction. In view of her all-embracing expertise this was probably the natural choice of the Library authorities who organised the exhibition, but even so, is very much a sign of the sceptical, relativist times in which we live.

In her "essay", preceded in the catalogue by warm commendations from Prince Philip, Duke of Edinburgh and the King of Morocco (whose library lent exhibits), Armstrong began by pointing out that:

"By the middle of the twentieth century, many people believed that the Scriptures had been irrevocably discredited" and that "modern scholarship has proved decisively that both the Bible and the Qur'an were human constructs deeply coloured by the conditions of their time . . . Holy writ may once have played a rôle in the development of civilization but, mercifully, humanity had outgrown it." Fair enough so far, one might comment. But then she went on:

> Scripture has, however, made a comeback and once again the Bible and the Qur'an are in the news. Terrorists quote the Qur'an to justify their atrocities" and fundamentalists world wide misuse the Bible to "prove" creation fantasies. This recent preoccupation with Scripture is the result of a widespread religious revival but it represents a literalistic approach that would once have been regarded as exceedingly simple minded . . . If these sacred texts are not scientifically or historically sound, many assume that they cannot be true at all.

---

2. I was unfortunately unable to attend the exhibition but I have a copy of the beautifully illustrated catalogue, which I have studied closely and from which I have learned much.

My comment here is that it is entirely fair game for Armstrong thus to deride fundamentalists both Biblical and Qur'anic. I agree with her there. But it is sad that she totally ignores the illuminating results of so much dedicated and constructive Biblical scholarship, such as that of Dr. N.T. Wright, Bishop of Durham (referred to in an earlier chapter) *and* much wise and prayerful use of the Bible by countless Christians, clerical and lay, in so many Churches, Sunday by Sunday, for some, day by day.

In her "essay" she treats in turn "Torah" (essentially the Pentateuch), "Gospel" and Qur'an as exemplifying her theme of "The Idea of a Sacred Text" and notes, helpfully, the huge variety of interpretative methods, many of them fanciful and far fetched, that have been proposed down the long centuries. Her final conclusions, however, struck one reader as shallow, negative and totally lacking in awareness of a depth and consistency of underlying truth and wisdom which could only derive from transcendent ultimate reality i.e. "God".

In short, it was a pity, given such an historic opportunity, that no suitably qualified enlightened Jewish, Christian and Muslim believers were allowed to bear witness in that fine catalogue to the unique spiritual value and underlying truth still to be found today in these unique and hallowed documents.

Such is the spirit of our age. It is so anxious to seem, and to be, objective, fair and tolerant of all points of view and shades of opinion, that it is in danger of failing to do justice to the precious insights that have come down to us from immemorial antiquity and have stood the tests of time.

This [chapter] is written by a would-be committed, convinced Christian, only too uncomfortably aware of his woeful inadequacy as such, one who is so much a child of the age in which he lives as to have acquired a deeply ingrained habit of trying (relativistically!) to see both sides of every question but who, in spite of this powerful inclination to sit on every (relativist) fence, feels obliged to climb (or tumble?) off it and line up on the side of Christ and his Church, to which he was committed in baptism. In other words, to abjure fashionable and attractive relativism in favour of what he believes to be universally and absolutely true.

2. Inter-faith dialogue

The foregoing does not imply opposition to inter-faith dialogue. On the contrary, I am all for it, provided it goes deeper than a polite interchange of courtesies, compliments and platitudes. Mutual exchange of courtesies is highly important, indeed essential. But if dialogue is to be fruitful, not barren, it must explore frankly not only what the different faiths have in common and points of genuine contact where they can co-operate together in worthwhile projects, but also seek to establish what precisely are the points where they *diverge* and aim to identify the conflicting issues and the reasons for them.

All who take part in inter-faith dialogue must be prepared to listen intently to their opposite numbers, not to take or give offence, but always patiently to "speak the truth in love". If dialogue is conducted on these terms and in this spirit, as with ecumenism, it cannot fail to be constructive. Otherwise it is a waste of time, productive of more harm than good.

And, à propos the main business of this chapter, I would add this. Participants must be entirely honest. I do not attempt to hide the fact that, in dialogue with Jews and Muslims, I would, at the appropriate point, state that, as a Christian, I cannot but believe that, for all the good, positive elements in their respective traditions, their beliefs are both fundamentally flawed. Further, I would have to acknowledge that I long to see us all three united, despite our remaining diversities in secondary matters, in loving allegiance to Christ Jesus as Lord and in communion and fellowship with us Christians in his all embracing Catholic (i.e. universal) and Apostolic (i.e. evangelistic, missionary) Church and in powerful united witness to the *One* Triune God, Father, Son and Holy Spirit.

3. Judaism first: then Islam

The last of my "preliminary considerations" is so nearly obvious and so uncontroversial that it can be expressed very concisely.

Because the Old Testament, the Hebrew Bible, which was the Bible of the historical Jesus the Jew and is that of Judaism today, is, from the Christian viewpoint inseparable from the New Testament and incomplete without it, Jews are much closer to Christians than both are to Muslims. Jews and Christians have the Old Testament in common, whereas the Qur'an (Koran) was allegedly "revealed" to the "Prophet" Mohammed more than six hundred years into the Christian, or Common Era. For this compelling reason, we will be looking at Judaism first, in its relation to Christianity, and at Islam afterwards.

* * * * *

Judaism and Christianity

It can truthfully be said, without fear of contradiction, that Judaism is unique among the world's great religions in that its membership is strictly limited to one particular race, albeit one scattered over the face of the earth, and that it is totally bound up with that race's extraordinary history.

How is an ordinary Gentile Christian to acquire a reliable and sympathetic understanding of something so strange and unfamiliar? Well, of course, to begin with, it is enormously helpful to have Jewish friends and neighbours. But it should encourage any such enquirer to know that there is in existence a slim volume which, in less than 100 pages, sets out to supply that very need. Beguilingly entitled *How to Understand Judaism*, its author is the Reverend Marcus Braybrooke. He is a former Director of the Council of Christians and Jews, and an Anglican clergyman to boot. His is a book I can and do unreservedly recommend. It was published by SCM Press in 1995. If you can buy, beg or borrow a copy, my advice would be to do so without delay and to read it. It is, by the way, an indication of the widespread esteem in which this compact, well-written and aptly illustrated little book and its author are held, that it enjoys the extremely rare distinction, for a non-Roman Catholic publication, of a formal "Nihil obstat" and "Imprimatur", dated 25th October 1995.

I am myself very much in its debt and would confidently expect Jews of all kinds and persuasions to endorse my opinion. The first three sentences of Braybrooke's Preface illustrate what I have said above and inspire a confidence not likely to be disappointed:

> It is a risky undertaking to write about a religion other than one's own. Beyond the proper desire for accuracy and fairness, there is the more difficult task of beginning to feel what it might be like to belong to that religion. Yet, if we do not attempt to do this, we remain outsiders to that which offers the deepest inspiration to our neighbours' lives.

At the risk of being a bore, I will give a brief synopsis of the contents of this book. If you find this a wearisome prospect, just skip the next paragraph, which promises to be a long one!

In the first six chapters Braybrooke deals successively with present day Jewish mobility and identity, now that ghettos are a thing of the past; then with the most distinctive Jewish festivals, Passover and Shavuot (Pentecost) and the manner of their observance; the Jewish Year with its holy days such as Yom Kippur (the Day of Atonement) and Succot (Tabernacles); fast days and special days of remembrance such as Holocaust Day; an important section on the Jewish Home, the Sabbath and food taboos and Kosher regulations; "Rites of Passage" (circumcision, Bar mitzvah, marriage, burial); and a succinct description of synagogues and what happens in them.

Then follow a chapter on the meaning of "Torah" (usually translated "Law") and Jewish literature and another which is a marvellously brief conspectus of Hebrew/Jewish history from Abraham (c.1800 B.C.) to A.D. 1800 [only Braybrooke diplomatically substitutes B.C.E. (= before the Common i.e. Christian Era for B.C.) and C.E. for A.D.]. This is followed by an equally crucial chapter on "Jews in the Modern Period" including, of course, the impact of Zionism, first propounded by Theodore Herzl, 1893, and its progressive implementation at the expense of the resident Arab population, from the inauguration of the "State of Israel" in 1948 through the tragic Arab-Israeli impasse still unresolved. Next is Chapter 10 on Varieties of Judaism – Orthodox, Progressive, Liberal, Humanistic etc. – and finally, the concluding chapter hopefully headed A New Relationship. This is inevitably controversial. All this in 83 pages (double columns) is a miracle of compression – solid, informative reading, but not, I think, indigestible.

Jews and Christians at loggerheads for centuries

As Braybrooke makes clear, the nearly two millennia-old relationship between Jews and Christians has always been a fraught and painful one, ever since the original split, the *exact* circumstances of which remain bafflingly hidden from us in the area of conjecture. In fact the New Testament evidence is more ambiguous, as regards responsibility for Christ's crucifixion, than was generally realised until fairly recently.

It is now coming to be increasingly widely recognised by fair minded Christians that on close and unprejudiced examination, the roots of anti-Semitism are, embarrassingly and tragically, to be found in the New Testament itself, especially in the Gospels. The long and shameful story of "Christian" anti-Semitism and its New Testament origins is accurately summarised in the *Oxford Dictionary of the Christian Church*.[3] This important article supplies the detailed facts of the story, as necessarily told in barest outline by Braybrooke. It deserves to be more widely known.

The evidence is more extensive than a few random scattered references. Consider, if you will, three of the most notorious. First the most chilling: Matthew 27 verses 23-25. The Jewish mob on Good Friday "shouted all the more '*Let him be crucified*' (23).

3. ODCC 3rd edn. (1997) art. Jews, Christian attitudes to. pp. 876f. Also, the Jewish scholar, Hyam Maccoby, pursues the same theme in a detailed and compelling study, *Judas Iscariot and the Myth of Jewish Evil* (The Free Press USA, 1992).

And after Pilate had washed his hands before the crowd saying, 'I am innocent of this man's blood. See to it yourselves', the people as a whole answered, '*His blood be on us and on our children*'" (25). Second, John 18-19 passim, noting especially 19.7 "the Jews answered Pilate: '*We have a law and according to that law he* [Jesus] *ought to die, because he has claimed to be the Son of God*'." And third, words of St. Paul in one of his earliest letters, 1 Thessalonians 2 14-16: ". . . the Jews who killed both the Lord Jesus and the prophets . . .".

These and other, similar N.T. texts were quoted repeatedly down the centuries from the primitive Church to the late Middle Ages to justify hatred, contempt, oppression and actual persecution of Jews by Christians, on the grounds that the Jews were guilty of the unique and appalling crime of "deicide" (God murder) based on a crude interpretation of the fundamental Christian doctrine of God incarnate in Christ – "the Word made flesh". This attitude was encouraged by pulpit rhetoric from many leading Christians, the most distinguished being Origen of Alexandria and St. John Chrysostom. On such grounds as these, all Jews were expelled from England in 1290, and later, successively from France, Spain and Portugal. (They were not readmitted to England until the 1650's.) At various times and places there were forced "conversions" of Jews to Christianity.

Popular anti-Semitic prejudice in this country was fanned by legends such as that of St. William of Norwich in the early twelfth century, and in later times literary stereotypes such as Shakespeare's Shylock and Dickins' Fagin served to keep the prejudice alive. In mid-nineteenth century Britain the unlikely rise to fame and the leadership of the traditionalist Tory Party of the Christian Jew, Benjamin Disraeli, and his success as Prime Minister, must have played its part in softening public opinion on the issue.

Meanwhile savage anti-Semitic pogroms in late-nineteenth century Russia led to mass Jewish emigration, all sanctioned by continuing Orthodox Christian prejudice. The final denouement came with the hideous Nazi persecution of the 1930's and "the final solution" in which six million European Jews were "liquidated". I visited Auschwitz in 1987 and Yad Vashem, the Holocaust memorial/ museum in Jerusalem, in 1992. I shall never forget either. It is dreadful to realise that long centuries of Christian prejudice, hatred and persecution, much of it inflamed by the reading of the Passion narratives of the New Testament, played an indisputable part in this appalling crime.

A New Relationship? In two stages

Marcus Braybrooke heads his concluding chapter "A New Relationship". From the Christian angle, this must be our aim, characterised by a spirit of penitence, charity and honesty. A start has already been made. Braybrooke prefaces this controversial chapter with a quotation of some words of the late Pope John Paul II which are *not* controversial. "Many men and women have worked and are still working today, on both sides, to overcome old prejudices and to secure ever wider and fuller recognition of that 'bond' and 'that common spiritual patrimony' that exists between Jews and Christians."

When he wrote, or said, those words, the Pope was referring to the steps taken since the Second World War to identify and reaffirm those things Jews and Christians hold in common, especially to the work of the Second Vatican Council. That, we are all agreed, is an essential first step in working towards a new and constructive relationship. We shall return to it presently.

Stage One

But there is another, *parallel* first step which has a higher priority still, but brings with it inherent difficulties which must be sincerely addressed, and, if possible, overcome. These difficulties go to the very heart of the Jewish/Christian relationship and, if honestly and frankly faced by both sides, could not help but put it on a new, firmer and healthier footing. The same process, too, could contribute to ecumenical progress, and indeed to the healing of our Christian divisions.

Do not we Christians *owe* the Jews something in the nature of an apology (at the very least), amends, and an explanation for all those past centuries of bitter hostility, contempt, oppression and persecution on the part of our Christian forbears? And what of those passages of *our* Holy Scripture which, there is historically no doubt, contributed so much to the cause of all that terrible, prolonged suffering?

Here is a major problem for us Christians. "Conservative evangelicals", and all manner of "Christian" fundamentalists and biblicists, will never agree to apologise for anything scriptural, since for them the scriptures are "inerrant". And another great difficulty: it is to be feared that many sincere, simple minded Christians, of all denominations, with no awareness of human or Christian *solidarity*, embracing time past and time present, would be likely to object to inclusion in any such suggested act of repentance as so much insincere, unrealistic and unnecessary humbug. (Or am I mistaken?)

Anyway, supposing the evangelists, the writers and compilers of the Gospels, were factually *correct* in assigning the *major* culpability/blame/responsibility to "the Jews"; the Sadducean high priestly party, the Sanhedrin, all who had bribed Judas Iscariot to betray his master to them, and who, on a trumped up charge, supported and incited by the mob, had handed Jesus over to the Roman occupying authority to carry out his execution, what then? Does that constitute some sort of excuse for centuries of cruel antagonism? Does it not make Jews and Romans equally culpable?

But suppose we Christians decide to abandon this historical "blame game" as both inconclusive and at bottom irrelevant? Where does that leave us?

Is there not, after all, only one satisfactory, relevant, and, finally, *true* answer to the question, "Who was/is responsible for the Crucifixion of Jesus?" And it is "All of us, all mankind, past and present." *All* had/have a share in that criminal responsibility. In the end Jesus was left alone, betrayed by Judas, denied by Peter, deserted by all the disciples who "forsook him and fled". We are *all* guilty, Jews, Romans, Christians alike.

There is an old German chorale/hymn, sung sometimes on Good Friday. It is familiar to many of us because J.S. Bach incorporated it in his St. Matthew Passion with the chorale melody, *Herzliebster Jesu*, "Ah holy Jesu, how hast thou offended?" The second verse runs:

> Who was the guilty? Who brought this upon thee?
> Alas, my treason, Jesu, hath undone thee
> 'Twas I, Lord Jesus, I it was denied thee
> I crucified thee.

(Original words by J. Heermann 1585-1647. *English Hymnal*, 70). Some today find this far fetched and offensive. I do not. Do you?

If both Christians and Jews can be persuaded of this principle of human solidarity across time, then we can *all* accept the blame for Christ's crucifixion. (That does not absolve Christians of guilt in persecuting Jews, for which we need to apologise and repent.) Insofar as we are all guilty through our sins and shortcomings for the murder of Christ, Jews and Christians alike, then if we each truly repent of our share in it, we can all claim our share of God's/Christ's forgiveness. By this means can we come to incorporate *together*, through baptism, in solidarity with Him in the new, redeemed, inclusive humanity that he, "the Second Adam", came to inaugurate and personify.

* * * * *

I am racing ahead of myself. Forgive me. What I do seriously propose is that, somehow, we Christians join together to offer our Jewish opposite numbers our humble, contrite and sincere apologies for all the prolonged sufferings we, in solidarity with our Christian forbears, have inflicted upon them in the past. And we invite them to reflect with us on the responsibility for the crucifixion of the One whom we Christians believe came direct from God our Father "to open the Kingdom of heaven to all believers". At the same time I would suggest that we Christians and Jews reflect together on all that we already share, "our common patrimony" (to use John Paul II's words). I will now attempt an outline of what this is. Here are some of the beliefs and values we already hold in common. You can, no doubt, add to them.

1. Belief in God, whose sacred Name is "I AM WHO I AM" (Exodus 3.14). He is our Creator, the origin and source of all that exists, the God not only of Nature, but of History. All His works are good. He made mankind "in his own image" (Genesis 1.26) and gave us "dominion" over all living creatures. Man (Adam) disobeyed God and was expelled from Paradise (Gen. 3.7 and 24). God is our "father" (Psalm 103.13, Hosea 11.1-4) who knows, loves and guides his children. He is just, righteous, holy and merciful (Isaiah 6.1-6). God makes covenants with his "people" (Gen. 9.12-16; 17.7f; Jeremiah 31.31). He has sent his prophets to his people as his spokesmen (Amos 7.14-16; Jeremiah 1.4-10). All mankind owes God worship, obedience and abhorrence of idiolatry.

2. We share God's gift of the Scriptures that Jews call the Law (Torah), the prophets and the writings (Ecclesiasticus/Sirach: Prologue passim especially v.4) and that Christians call the Old Testament. With the Jews we look back to the archetypal figure of Abraham, faithful, obedient servant of God, to whom God promised a great inheritance; to his grandson Jacob, to whom God gave the name Israel; to Moses, the prophet and "friend" of God who led the children of Israel out of slavery in Egypt and through the wilderness and gave them the Law (the Decalogue) at Sinai/Horeb; to Joshua who led and settled them in the promised land of Canaan; to David, the hero Shepherd King and Psalmist of Israel; and to Solomon, his son and successor, legendary fount of wisdom.

3. With the Jews, Christians share the great annual Festivals of Passover and Shavuot (Pentecost). (For Christians they have a rich new layer of meaning.)

4. Jews and Christians alike cherish the God-given ideals of

Home and Family Life and try to uphold the same values of honesty, truthfulness, generosity, compassion and purity, as set forth in the Moral Law embodied in the Ten Commandments (Decalogue), with the duty of loving concern for our neighbours.

Something on these lines, explicit, factual and uncontroversial, agreed and reaffirmed jointly by Christians and Jews as our shared spiritual patrimony, together and concurrently with the Christian apology on the lines suggested above, would, to my mind at least, constitute the First Stage of a New Relationship/Reconciliation.

It seems to me that if something on these lines could be achieved in a sincere, honest and charitable spirit on both sides, embracing the widest possible range of both Jews and Christians (recalling how deeply divided both are among themselves), it would, under God, bring about such an incalculable relaxation in the "atmosphere" and create such a spirit of mutual warmth and good will that Christians and Jews, more united also among themselves, would be ready and even eager to move forward *together* to the next stage in which they could feel able and ready to "speak the truth in love" to one another in the assurance that they would be listened to patiently and with no offence by either side. Am I being too optimistic?[4]

Stage Two: Reconciliation

If my optimism *is* justified, Jews and Christians would by then have sufficient trust and confidence in each other to be ready for plenty of plain speaking. Christians in particular would no longer be afraid of causing offence (provided, of course, that none was intended). The temptations of fashionable relativism, for mealy-mouthed platitudes and smooth talk, would be disregarded.

For all the undoubted good that we share together in our common spiritual patrimony (and it is by no means negligible), Christians surely cannot help seeing in Judaism (whether Orthodox, Reform or Liberal), something tragically incomplete. When, in the fullness of time, heralded by John the Baptist, last and greatest of the Hebrew prophets, YHWH, the Holy God of Israel, came *in person* to his

---

4. The genuinely deep and reciprocal friendship between the present British Chief Rabbi, Sir Jonathan Sacks, and the present Archbishop of Canterbury is an excellent augury. Dr. Sacks was one of the guest speakers at the 2008 Lambeth Conference and his moving speech "from the heart" won him a standing ovation. In the course of it he said that, since the formation of the Council of Christians and Jews in 1942, "Jews and Christians have done more to mend their relationship than any other two faiths on earth and today we meet as beloved friends".

people Israel, "he came to his own, and his own received him not" (John 1.11). "But to those who *did* receive him" [to begin with a handful of Jews and some Gentiles] "to them he gave the power to become children of God, who were born, not of blood, nor of the will of the flesh, nor of the will of man, but of God" (John 1.13f.). The Old Testament/Covenant by itself is incomplete without the New Testament/Covenant sealed in Christ's blood.

The Old Testament is the true story of Adam, unredeemed, "fallen" humanity, Paradise lost. It requires completion in the equally true story of the *second* Adam, who (in the words of Newman's great hymn) "to the fight and to the rescue came". The New Testament tells how the man Jesus, our Redeemer, God's unique "Son", laid down his life for all mankind. Overcoming evil, sin and death by the sheer power of love and goodness, he has "opened the kingdom of heaven to all believers" *(Te Deum)*. Passover thus finds its fuller and *complete* meaning in the Victory of Good Friday and Easter And Shavuot (Pentecost) commemorates, not merely the Giving of the Law, but the fulfilment of the promised gift, not just of "tongues", but of the Holy Spirit of God, our powerful, life giving Guide "into all truth" (John 16.13), our "advocate" (Paraclete) who "stands by" us and leads us (if only we will let him) to "a right judgment in all things" and gives life to Christ's embodiment the Church. The old Israel was confined to the Hebrew race, Abraham's descendants according to the flesh; the new Israel is universal, inclusive, catholic.

Such is the Christian inheritance denied to itself by outworn Judaism, into which inheritance and fellowship we poor inadequate Christians extend a sincere and hearty welcome to all Jews who are prepared to accept God's renewed invitation.

Such, and nothing less, is Stage Two.

The return of God's ancient chosen race would fulfil the hope and longing and rejoice the heart of one who was surely among the very greatest of that race, Paul. In the concluding words of Romans 9-11 he gave free expression to his broken-hearted longing for the conversion of his beloved but erring compatriots.

When, at long last, the fullness of the Jews is gathered in, with their God-given talents they will bring sorely needed energy and enthusiasm to enrich and re-invigorate our divided and languishing Church. My lifetime has witnessed, especially in the fields of art and music, wonderfully talented Jews who found inspiration in Christ and shared so much of His spirit, short of baptism. Jacob Epstein, Marc Chagall and Yehudi Menuhin are but three of the most distinguished. And in the sphere of statecraft Yitzhak Rabin and Shimon Peres in

present day Israel worked valiantly for reconciliation with the long
suffering Palestinian Arabs. Among Jews who, following Paul's
example, were converted to Christ and baptized into Him, two
outstanding men became chief pastors, bishops in His Church, Hugh
Sebag Montefiore, Bishop of Birmingham, and Cardinal Lustiger,
Archbishop of Paris, who died a year or two ago.

*****

If this generation of Christians can find ways, without exerting the
psychological pressure suggested by the words "evangelism" and
"proselytising", of proclaiming, presenting, even (unselfconsciously)
embodying the Gospel of Jesus/Yeshua to those fellow Jews who are
prepared to listen and respond (as their fathers and forefathers, for
understandable reasons, did not) who knows what promise the future
may hold?

*****

Islam in relation to Judaism and Christianity

When we turn to consider Islam, the third of the trio of monotheistic/
Abrahamic faiths, we immediately find ourselves at a serious
disadvantage.

For in the atmosphere prevailing today, the very reverse of calm
objectivity – a world of "War on Terror", the terrorist organisations,
such as Al Qaeda, all emanating from misplaced Islamic ideals and
grievances; a world of suicide bombers, convinced that by inflicting
indiscriminate suffering and slaughter they are doing God's work,
and will be suitably rewarded in heaven; a world of fiery extremist
imams in some English mosques, inciting the younger generation of
Muslims to violence – it is not easy to be relaxedly dispassionate. If
what follows is to be properly constructive, we must make a conscious
effort to put all this on one side, if only temporarily, in order to try to
obtain an unprejudiced view of the *essential* nature of Islam, seen at
its best, not its worst. This is not going to be easy.

Before writing this section, having not the slightest claim to any
sort of expertise in this field, I had recourse to four books which,
together, have provided the background information necessary to
enable a fair and reliable judgement to be made.

The first of these must, by any criterion, be regarded as a minor
classic, and can be recommended without reserve. Originally
published as long ago as 1954 by Penguin Books, and reprinted
many times since, it is simply entitled *Islam*; its author was Alfred

Guillaume, whom we have briefly met before in these pages. (He was the junior of three G's who jointly edited that vast compendium *Gore's Commentary on the Bible*. His responsibility then was the Old Testament and Apocrypha.)

Guillaume, an Anglican priest and an Orientalist with a special interest in Arabic, who had taught extensively in the Middle East, was completely at home and at ease in the Muslim world, where he had a great many friends and an exceptionally balanced and mature judgment. This book of his, one of many, inspires total confidence. His grasp of Islamic history, philosophy and law is impressive.

At present and for some time past, probably the leading *Christian* interpreter of Islam in this country is the current Bishop of Rochester, Michael Nazir Ali. Himself of Pakistani origin and a member of a family which had the courage to convert from Islam to Christianity, his book *Islam: A Christian Perspective* (Exeter, Paternoster Press 1983) usefully supplements Guillaume and I am much indebted to it. Nazir Ali describes his attitude as "sympathetic and critical at the same time". That, as an ideal, sounds just about right to me, and again, I am impressed by the author's erudition, his familiarity with the Muslim culture against the background of which he grew up, and his obvious desire to be fair as well as truthful.

A second, more recent book by the same author, *Conviction and Conflict: Islam, Christianity and World Order*, published in 2006, is in fact Bishop Nazir Ali's Scott Holland Lectures for 2005 in book form. It is no exaggeration to describe this book as indispensable to any serious study of the critical situation in which the world finds itself today. It is totally authoritative in its dispassionate and erudite exposition of the background and causes of Islamic extremism (of which al Qaeda is but one expression), espoused by the present generation of youthful militant terrorists, and which first surfaced in the Iranian Revolution of 1977, for which the West was so completely unprepared. Its second chapter is a masterly exposition of the tangled complexities of the Israeli-Palestinian deadlock which has for so long defied all attempts at a peaceful settlement acceptable to all sides. A salutary reminder this, if one is needed, that until this most intractable of all conflicts is satisfactorily resolved, the world will have no peace.

Finally, because the Qur'an is at the very heart of Islam, I have frequently had recourse to the acclaimed translation by N. J. Dawood, many times revised, and also published by Penguin. Incidentally, on the cover and in the text the translator and publisher retain the traditional Anglicized spelling, Koran. In referring to it, however,

I follow the now generally accepted Qur'an;. Dawood retains the traditional order of the 114 Suras (chapters), beginning with the longest and ending with the shortest. This is essential for ease of reference.[5]

The meaning of the word "Islam" is submission, resignation, or surrender to God ('Allah') and, as Nazir Ali points out at the very beginning of his book, most Muslims would maintain that Islam has always been the religion of the (instinctively) righteous man and that therefore Abraham, and even Adam before the Fall were, in that sense, Muslims. But in actual historical fact, Islam, as a distinctive religion, originated with the self-styled "prophet" or "apostle" of God, Muhammad who was born in what is now Saudi Arabia circa A.D. 570 and died in 632, as virtual ruler of the whole of Arabia.

The "revelations" from God which constitute the Qur'an, were allegedly vouchsafed to him either directly or through the Archangel Gabriel as intermediary. These "revelations", according to Muslim tradition, were originally inscribed upon date-palm leaves, stone, scrolls of leather, tablets or even tattooed upon men's bodies, and/or committed to memory by professional remembrancers whose feats of memorisation were truly prodigious. After the Prophet's death, it was largely the work of his friend, collaborator and successor, the first Caliph, Abu Bakr, reverently to collect them together to preserve them for posterity. It was in fact less than twenty years after Muhammad's death that an authorised version of the Qur'an was established under the third Caliph Uthman. This replaced no less than four rival editions, but these have long since disappeared without trace. The text as we have it now has come down to us virtually unchanged from that day to this. To quote Dawood's introduction: "To this day this version is regarded by believers as the authoritative Word of God" (op.cit. 2006 edn. p. 3). To which we may add the significant words of Guillaume: "In Islam the doctrine of the infallible word of God is an article of faith, and the few who have questioned it have for the most part expressed their doubts in enigmatic language, so as to leave themselves a way of retreat from a dangerous position." (op. cit. p. 55)

So once again, as with Christian Biblicists and with the upholders of Papal Infallibility, *and* some forms of dogmatic atheism, we are up against blind fundamentalism, impervious to reason and fact. The only difference is that, unlike daring *Muslim* critics of the Qur'an,

5. The Victorian translation by Rodwell rearranged the Suras in supposed chronological order, which made reference almost impossible.

we do not have to veil our criticism of the Qur'an in "enigmatic language".

None of the foregoing is to deny the Qur'an genuine elements of greatness and nobility. Apart from its religious and moral value, however that may be assessed, it is unanimously claimed by orientalists in general and Arabic scholars in particular, "as a literary masterpiece in its own right". There are outstanding purple passages such as Sura 24.35:

> God is the light of the heavens and the earth. His light may be compared to a niche that enshrines a lamp, the lamp within a crystal of starlike brilliance. It is lit from a blessed olive tree neither eastern nor western. Its very oil would almost shine forth, though no fire touched it. Light upon light; God guides to His light whom he will . . . His light is found in temples which God has sanctioned to be built for the remembrance of His name. In them, morning and evening, His praise is sung by men who neither trade nor profit can divert from remembering God, from offering prayers, or from giving alms, who dread the day when men's hearts and eyes shall writhe with anguish; who hope that God will requite them for their noblest deeds and lavish His grace upon them. God gives without reckoning to whom he will.

Guillaume writes:

> The Qur'an is one of the world's classics which cannot be translated without grave loss. It has a rhythm of peculiar beauty and a cadence that charms the ear. Many Christian Arabs speak of its style with warm admiration, and most Arabists acknowledge its excellence. When it is read aloud or recited it has an almost hypnotic effect that makes the listener indifferent to its sometimes strange syntax and its sometimes, to us, repellent content. It is this quality it possesses of silencing criticism by the sweet music of its language that has given birth to the dogma of its inimitability; indeed it may be affirmed that within the literature of the Arabs, wide and fecund as it is both in poetry and in elevated prose, there is nothing to compare with it.

It seemed to me essential to give space to this purely literary aspect of the Qur'an, since to a casual reader of a translation even so reputedly good as that of Dawood, it can so easily escape him/her unnoticed. To be brutally frank, such is the sheer inconsequence, the total absence

of any kind of perceptible order or arrangement of subject matter,
to say nothing of mood swings and flat contradictions, that many a
well-intentioned reader, bored and exasperated in equal measure, has
run out of patience and given up in despair. We must not give up, but
grit our teeth and persevere!

Before we examine it critically from a Christian point of view, it
seems essential that we should attempt to inform ourselves of the life
and try to assess the character of the man to whom, allegedly, these
often wearisome and repetitious "revelations" were addressed. This,
too, is difficult because, apart from the evidence of the Qur'an itself
and that of Muhammad's vast political and religious achievement,
we only have the testimony of the markedly hagiographical *Lives*,
written, all of them, by his faithful admirers, to go upon.

Muhammad: His Life and Character

Taking every relevant consideration into account, Guillaume, in his
chapters on the historical background and on Muhammad himself,
his life and times, almost leans over backwards to be scrupulously
fair to "the Prophet".

> At the outset let it be said that Muhammad was one of the
> great figures of history, whose overmastering conviction was
> that there was one God alone and that there should be one
> community of believers. His ability as a statesman faced with
> problems of extraordinary complexity is truly amazing. With
> all the power of armies, police, and civil service no Arab has
> every succeeded in holding his countrymen together as he
> did. All the elements of disunion were present in his lifetime
> but dared not show themselves until his death became known.
> (op. cit. p. 23)

As Guillaume makes abundantly clear at the outset of his long chapter
on Muhammad (op. cit. pp. 20-54), the delicate and challenging
task of the conscientious historian of Islam is to offer a credible
reconstruction of the actual course of "the Prophet's" life, and a just
assessment of his character, by taking the early traditions and the
inevitably hagiographical biographies of his enthusiastic admirers and
sifting the legendary accretions from the underlying hard facts. What
emerges from all the historical evidence, thus critically examined, is
something like this:

Muhammad, an Arab of the Quraysh tribe, was born and soon
orphaned at Mecca, an ancient pagan pilgrimage centre in what is
now Saudi Arabia, about A.D. 570. His mother died when he was

a child and he was brought up by his grandfather and uncle. About 595 he married Khadijah, a merchant woman fifteen years older than himself. She was a devoted wife, who bore him two sons, both of whom died in infancy, and four daughters, two of whom later married loyal followers of the prophet, Uthman and Ali (who both eventually succeeded Muhammad as Caliphs).

Muhammad managed Khadijah's trading caravans to neighbouring Syria, then a Christian country, unhappily within the Byzantine (Greek) empire. His business journeys there brought him into friendly contact with Christians, mostly Monophysite in outlook, and their flourishing monasteries. And at home, in and around Mecca he was often brought into touch with Jewish tribes, who had settled and prospered in Arabia. He was thus familiar with the two opposed "Peoples of the Book", and, to some extent, with their scriptures, in which it is evident he found much to admire and emulate.

There is a persistent tradition, which there is no reason to discount, that on one occasion Muhammad had a strangely disturbing experience, or vision, of two men in white, knocking him down and splitting his belly open and "cleansing" it.

Guillaume says that "he was a man whose common sense never failed him" and dismisses suggestions that he was an epileptic. His early biographers say that it was his habit to leave the haunts of men and to give himself to solitary prayer and meditation. One night, about A.D. 610, while he slept, the angel Gabriel "came to him with a piece of silk brocade on which was written the word 'Recite'." When he asked, "What shall I recite?" the order was repeated three times, while Muhammad felt increasing physical pressure, until the angel said:

> Recite in the name of thy Lord who created
> Man from blood congealed.
> Recite! Thy Lord is wondrous kind
> Who by the pen has taught mankind
> Things they know not (being blind)

When he awoke, these words were indelibly impressed on his mind, and he thought, to begin with, that he must be "possessed". So unwelcome was this idea that he rushed off with the intention of killing himself. On the way he heard a voice from heaven hailing him as "the Apostle of God" and blocking his way to self-destruction. Such was the traditional story of his prophetic call and the origin of the Qur'an. That Arabic word *means* "the recital" and the alleged oracles recorded were in a rough kind of rhyming prose as reproduced above.

Muhammad's prophetic call and his preaching of the almighty power of the one true God, and man's duty of unquestioning obedience, met with hostile derision in his native Mecca, where there was a strong vested interest in the old Arab paganism, centred round the cult object of the Ka'ba where all the local deities, male and female, were represented. Muhammad's own tribe, the Quraysh, opposed and ridiculed him. But he had his staunch supporters. The most outstanding was Abu Bakr, whose daughter, Aisha, Muhammad married following the death of Khadijah. She became his favourite wife. In the years of his final triumphs he had accumulated no less than eleven wives, not counting concubines. According to Sura 4 of the Qur'an, a Muslim man is allowed a maximum of four wives (and this still obtains although monogamy is widely practised in many parts of the Muslim world today). To cover himself, Muhammad obtained a further revelation (Sura 33.50) making the Prophet the sole exception to the general rule.[6]

The eventual outcome of all the Meccan opposition to Islam was the central event of "the Prophet's" life, the celebrated Hijra (or Hejira) of 622, when Muhammad fled, or migrated, from Mecca to Yathrib, as the city of Medina was then known. He had received encouragement in the form of six pilgrims from there to Mecca who had accepted Islam and returned to Yathrib as active missionaries for the prophet. The city quickly rallied to his cause which, in a sense, had been prepared for him by Jewish preaching, and practice, of monotheism.

Guillaume says, "From the outset Muhammad displayed the tact and diplomacy which marked all his dealings with others" (*Islam* p. 39). That, it seems to me, is for once a distinctly questionable generalisation. It certainly applies to his Arab compatriots and enabled him rapidly to build up a solid and impregnable power base in Yathrib/Medina and, before long, successfully to counterattack in Mecca, overcoming the longstanding hostility of his own tribe, the Quraysh.

But it is wildly *in*applicable to his relations with the local Jewish tribes. They had incurred his enmity by refusing to recognise him as a prophet, and ridiculing his alleged "revelations". In the Qur'an, great prominence and honour is accorded to Abraham; and his son Ishmael, by the slave woman Hagar, is recognised as the progenitor of the Arabs, but "the Israelites" and the Jews, as "People of the

---

6. v. M. Nazir Ali: *Islam: A Christian Perspective* pp. 32f. where the facts are set out in detail.

Book", come in for severe criticism.[7] There were three Jewish tribes in and near Medina: they were unpopular because of their economic dominance. Muhammad decided that they must be first crushed and then expelled from Arabia. The first tribe, the Qainuga, who were goldsmiths, were treated less harshly; because their Arab allies interceded for them, their lives were spared, but they were expelled. Another tribe, the Nadir, were forced to lay down their arms and evacuate their settlements. The third tribe, the Qurayza, eventually surrendered unconditionally. The men prisoners were in batches put to death by beheading, and the women and children sold as slaves. 800 Jews were butchered in this way. Nothing it seems to me, can excuse this cold blooded savagery in the name of a God always proclaimed as merciful and compassionate. The Qur'an (sura 47.3) prescribes: "When you meet the unbelievers in the battlefield, strike off their heads and, when you have laid them low, bind your captives firmly. Then grant their freedom or take a ransom from them, until War shall lay down her burdens." No doubt Muhammad could claim that "revelation", such as it is, in support of his brutality. If so, what does that sura, and others like it, tell us about the Qur'an and its religious and moral value, or otherwise, today? Guillaume's restrained comment on this atrocity, after reminding his readers of the modern doctrine of "total war", is: "Nominal Christians and Jews have done similar and worse things in the cause of national, religious or social security, and the fault lies not in religion but in sinful human nature. However, one does not expect such acts from one who comes with a message from the Compassionate and Merciful."

Now that he was no longer a persecuted citizen of Mecca, but the leader of a rapidly growing religious community recognised as possessing divine sanction, it became increasingly clear to Muhammad, the practical man, that there could be no compromise with idiolatry, and that the Arab world must be made to listen to the message of Islam by sheer force of arms if need be. He therefore dedicated himself to the task of mobilising an army of devoted Medinan Muslims under his own command ready for hostilities (jihad). The three small battles that ensued were sufficient to change the course of world history. In the Battle of Badr (624), three hundred Muslims led by "the Prophet" himself routed a thousand Meccans, many of them his own fellow tribesmen. This victory was the

---

7. "You will find that the most implacable of people in their enmity to the faithful are the Jews and the pagans, and that the nearest in affection to them are those who say: "We are Christians". That is because there are priests and monks among them, and because they are free from pride." (*Qur'an*. Sura 5.82)

foundation of all the Islamic successes of the next few years, only to be followed by a reverse the following year at Uhud, where Muhammad was wounded. Muslim morale however was high and following a further success, "the Prophet" in 628 concluded a treaty with the Meccans. Its terms included a truce with the Quraysh, under the terms of which he was freely allowed to proselytise in Mecca and to stay there for a maximum three days. The following year he entered Mecca as a pilgrim, accompanied by a crowd of devoted followers. He circled round the Ka'bah seven times and touched the black stone with his staff. His muezzin went up on the roof of the Ka'bah and called the Muslims to prayer. It was a propagandist triumph. And it must be recognised that it was a crucial part of his achievement that the Ka'bah was purified of the idolatry[8] of which it had been the focus time out of mind and the Pilgrimage (hajj) centred upon it was made mandatory on all Muslims worldwide, once in a lifetime, unless they were incapacitated or unable to afford it. (This still remains a binding obligation (sura 2. 196-200).)

After one last pilgrimage, Muhammad died in 632. Summing up his character, Guillaume wrote: "Trustworthy tradition depicts a man of amazing ability in winning men's hearts by persuasion and in coercing and disarming his opponents"; "he expressly disclaimed miraculous powers"; "he stands out as one of the great figures of history". (op.cit. p. 53) The many stories handed down in tradition, which tell of his generosity and kindness "go far to explain why men loved him". Guillaume concludes his estimate of "the Prophet" by telling two delightful stories to illustrate his kindly sense of humour.

With none of this would we venture to disagree. But, granting all that, may one pose one final, crucial question?

Was Muhammad a genuine Prophet of God?

Was Muhammad right in his repeated claim to be the uniquely genuine Prophet of the one true God? Were the multitudinous "revelations" he claimed to have received, genuinely communicated to him directly by the voice of God? Even to *ask* such a question must, to Muslim ears, sound blasphemous. Yet to my mind, even granting, as we surely must, the undoubted value, the richness even, of so much that is in the Qur'an, it seems to me that this is a fair, indeed the *right* question to put. And it demands an honest answer.

8. The Ka'bah had, pre-Muhammad, been the flourishing centre of the pagan cult of the three so-called daughters of Allah (Al-Lat, Al-Manat and Al-Uzza), as well as other deities.

There can be no doubt that Muhammad himself *thought* he was entirely genuine. He had convinced himself that he, uniquely, had a hotline to God. And it may well be that some of the time he was right in so thinking. There is, we should concede, much in the Qur'an – and not only in the "purple patches" – that is positive, wholesome and constructive, much that is in accordance with the true insights of the Jewish and Christian Scriptures. Our valuable guide, Alfred Guillaume, bears witness once again:

> We have seen how the prophet persisted in the face of heavy odds in preaching the doctrine of the one true God, and the Qur'an shows us what his conception of God was. The formula "compassionate and merciful" is familiar to almost everyone, and though the sufferings of the damned are painted in sombre tones, divine mercy and forgiveness are strongly emphasised. God's power is infinite, as in his knowledge. *Though transcendent and above all similitude, he is nearer to man than the vein of his neck.*[9] Again, though not bound by man's ideas of justice and equity, God hates injustice and oppression, and requires kindness to orphans and widows and charity to the poor. The Muslim is not to fear death, for it is the gate of Paradise; patience and trust are incumbent on him. He must endure with fortitude the troubles and trials of life, and put his trust in God at all times. *This in the briefest possible terms is the moral basis of Islam and only the prejudiced can deny that it has produced, and still produces, men of the highest character and integrity.*[10]
> (*Islam* p. 64)

Even against today's sombre background, I believe that this statement as a whole, and especially the final sentence which I have emphasised, remains as true as when it was written. Unfortunately, though, it is not the *whole* truth.

It is inevitable and entirely natural and right that Christians should read the Qur'an through the framework of their own Scriptures – both the Old and New Testaments – and particularly in light of the Gospel of our Lord and Saviour Jesus Christ. Christians are naturally intrigued by the numerous references throughout the Qur'an to the various characters from Bible stories, from Adam, Noah, Abraham and the Patriarchs, Moses, David, Solomon, and the Queen of Sheba from the

9. My italics.
10. My italics.

Old Testament. Through to appearances from Jesus, his mother Mary, and John the Baptist from the New Testament. Also intriguing are the numerous references through the Qur'an to the Jews as "the People of the Book". What is the explanation and significance of all this?

It will be recalled that Muhammad as a younger man, in the course of his many business trips to (then) Christian Syria had enjoyed fruitful contacts with Christian priests and monks, probably benefiting from monastic hospitality on his journeys hither and thither, as well as with (less friendly) Jewish tribes settled in Arabia. No doubt his lively enquiring mind, formed in Arab paganism, had, over the years before his prophetic call, absorbed and mulled over the exciting if puzzling information he had acquired in this way. Along with profound admiration for the sheer simplicity of uncompromising Hebrew monotheism chiming so well with all his instincts, he was obviously fascinated by the great Bible stories of the Old Testament and made them his own. Most of all, he must have come under the strangely compelling spell of Jesus, son of Mary, although it had puzzling and disturbing aspects that he found quite beyond his grasp.

It is highly significant that, with all the intriguing and sometimes contradictory references to Jesus, son of Mary, in the Qur'an and one extended reference to John the Baptist (sura 19), there is not one single reference to Paul, his conversion and his letters. Muhammad, if he had known of them, which he may well have done, would have almost certainly found them impossible to understand. Likewise, there is no specific reference to particular *Gospels* (why four? He may have wondered) or to *The Acts of the Apostles*, still less to the anonymous *Epistle to the Hebrews*, or *Revelation*. Had "the Prophet" succeeded in fathoming Paul, John and the writer to the Hebrews and taken on board the interlocking mysteries of the Incarnation and the Atonement at the heart of the Christian Faith, the Qur'an would have been completely different, as would the course of world history.

What is remarkable is how close he actually came to the heart of the Gospel, how near to Christian conversion. That can be appreciated by a careful scrutiny of every reference to "Jesus son of Mary" in the text of the Qur'an.

This is not as formidable a task as might at first appear. Not the least merit of Mr. Dawood's fine Penguin translation of "The Koran" (as he prefers to call it) is its comprehensive index. Its references are all to pages in the Penguin. Mine are to suras and verses (approximate in some cases). I have added one "created like Adam". M=Muhammad. I have starred (*) the most striking references.

1. Annunciation. Curiously conflated in M's memory with the annunciation of John's future birth to Elizabeth (3:37-52) (cf. 19:1-36)
2. Created "like Adam from dust" (3:59)
3. Birth, Death and Resurrection (19:33f.)*
4. Covenant with (33:7)
5. Disciples, miracles, death (3:48-58)*
6. Death ("they did not kill or crucify Him but they thought they did") the Day of Resurrection (4:147ff.)*
7. Jesus the Messiah, son of Mary no more than an apostle (5:75) He curses disbelievers (5:79)
8. Sent from God to confirm Torah and to tell of an apostle named Ahmed who shall come after him. [Ahmed=Muhammad] (61:5)
9. Sent from God, to confirm Torah, "given the Gospel" (5:47)
10. Blessed by God and "strengthened with the Holy Spirit, so that you (Jesus) preached to people in your cradle and in the prime of manhood, instructed in wisdom and Torah and in the Gospel, you healed the blind and the leper and raised the dead, was protected from Israelite disbelief and confirmed his disciples in belief. Questioned by disciples: "Can your Lord send down from heaven a table spread with food? He replied Have fear of God" (5:110ff.)* (ref. To Feeding of the Five Thousand?) (5.114)*
11. Given signs and strengthened with Holy Spirit (2:87 and 253 and 5:110)*
12. When Mary's son is cited as an example, people laugh and say "Who is better, he or our Gods?" (43:55)
13. As prophet (2:136, 4:163; 6:87; 61:5)
14. Sonship of God denied. "God forbid that he should have a son" (4:171f. cf.5:115)*

From all these references it can be seen what an extraordinarily garbled, disjointed and confused idea of Jesus Muhammad had got into his head. Although, from some of the references we have glanced at, he seems at times almost to have reached the brink of Christian faith and conversion, the total effect of them all taken together is that he was completely baffled and muddled.

As for the honest answer to our question, was Muhammad a genuine prophet, or spokesman, of the one true God? The answer, at least from the Christian point of view, cannot be in doubt. It must be an unequivocal No. That is not to say that the Qur'an is worthless rubbish! Far from it. It is, in fact, very much a mixed bag, or, to change the metaphor, a curate's egg – good, very good, *in parts*. We have already, with Guillaume, gone out of our way to acknowledge that. The eighth century St. John of Damascus, who experienced Islam at first hand and was not unfriendly to it, described it correctly as a Judaeo-Christian heresy.

What in fact seems to have happened is that Muhammad, essentially good natured, shrewd and in many ways extraordinarily gifted, but inevitably a man of his own time and place with all the limitations that implies, had some genuine mystical experiences – enough to convince him that he was genuinely in touch with Transcendent Reality (Allah). In that conviction he recorded as divine revelations the assorted jumble of thoughts, experiences, and reflections, some good, wise and sensible, some bizarre and unthought out, and some, though comparatively few (let us be candid) thoroughly unwise, unwholesome, untrue, even positively evil. The result was the Qur'an, which unfortunately means that it comes packaged as the infallible word of God!

As such, it is venerated, treasured, read, studied and expounded in homes and mosques by countless millions of devout, unquestioning Muslims across the world from Indonesia and Malaysia, Bangladesh, Pakistan, the former Soviet Central Asian republics, and Azerbaijan in the Caucasus to its birthplace in Saudi Arabia; from Iran, Afghanistan and the volatile countries of the Middle East, the cradle of civilisation, right across North Africa from Egypt to Morocco, from which it is now expanding into Nigeria and Central Africa, and, finally, to its latest outposts in this country and Western Europe. It is not so long since we Christians were boasting that there was no place on earth where the Gospel had not been preached and a Church established. Islam, it seems, has now overtaken us, its rate of expansion phenomenal.

The Challenge of Islam today

In its present mood, as in its beginnings, despite its longstanding internal divisions – Sunni, Shia, Wahhabi – Islam is militant, confident, resurgent. By contrast, Christianity, crippled still by seemingly unbridgeable schisms and weakened by the constant inroads of secularism, stands on the defensive, languishing in low morale in its former strongholds in the West, though resurgent in its extremities, such as China. Vibrant, relentlessly expanding Islam presents us with an urgent and formidable challenge and we are only now waking up to it. Its appeal seems to lie in its superficial simplicity and in the self-discipline it imposes on its faithful in terms of ordered lives of prayer, worship and fasting.

As well as the secret of unity in diversity, we Christians need to rediscover the basic simplicity of *our* faith in Jesus, "son of Mary".

We need to see him clearly as he truly is, "the human face of God", the "second Adam, the Pioneer"[11] and Forerunner of new, redeemed humanity. He invites all mankind, irrespective of gender, race or colour, to fight under his victorious leadership in the never-ending campaign against every form of evil and injustice, in the universal (Catholic) fellowship of his "Body", the worldwide Church, the *real* "salvation army", the *real* "society of friends", Jehovah/YHWH's *genuine* witnesses. We need to see that Church as the new and true Israel of the new Covenant, sealed by his blood in self-sacrifice upon the cross, ratified by his glorious Easter Resurrection; he who has opened the Kingdom of Heaven to all believers. We need, too, to re-learn from our Muslim neighbours that wholesome, ancient discipline of regular, persistent, and realistic prayer and worship, and a thoroughgoing review of all our priorities. There is much we can learn from Islam, and so much to *share with* Islam.

Interfaith dialogue? The Bishop of Rochester is all for it. He devotes two entire chapters of *Conviction and Conflict* to detailed proposals for an agenda (op. cit. pp. 109-159). Of course I defer to him. But I confess that, before reading those chapters, I wrote: "Frankly, there does not seem much scope for fruitful dialogue with the Muslim world. For whereas Judaism simply falls short of the Gospel, Islam via the Qur'an distorts it out of all recognition." And, I added, Muslims are notoriously sensitive to criticism, as we know all too well from the incident of the Danish cartoons of "the Prophet" and the affair of Salman Rushdie's *Satanic Verses*. The Christian response to the Qur'anic distortions can only be patient reliance on the ultimate vindication of Truth. "Great is Truth and it will prevail."

Candidly I can see no reason to change my mind. But, obviously, the Bishop knows best. If there is to be dialogue he is clearly the one to lead it from the Christian point of view. In that case, I wish him well.

Conclusion

When I was young, the old Prayer Book led us to pray three collects on Good Friday. This is the last of the three:

O merciful God, who hast made all men and hatest nothing that thou has made, nor wouldest the death of a sinner, but rather that he should be converted and live: Have mercy upon all Jews, Turks, Infidels and Hereticks, and take from them all ignorance, hardness of heart, and contempt of thy word;

---

11. Hebrews 2.10 and 12.2

and so fetch them home, blessed Lord, to thy flock, that they
may be saved among the remnant of the true Israelites, and
be made one fold under one Shepherd, Jesus Christ our Lord,
who liveth and reigneth with thee and the Holy Spirit, one
God, world without end. *Amen.*

That collect, composed by Archbishop Cranmer, first appeared in
the First English Prayer Book of 1549, where it replaced old Latin
prayers to the same effect.

In the proposed Prayer Book revision of 1928, an alternative
form of the collect was provided. It altered the wording of the actual
Petition to: "Have mercy upon thine ancient people the Jews, and
upon all who have not known thee, or who deny the faith of Christ
crucified", leaving the wording of the rest unchanged.

In the *Alternative Service Book 1980*, following the period of
authorised liturgical experiment, the three Good Friday collects were
wisely retained, using the revised wording of 1928, but substituting
"you" for "thou" and modernising the verbs.

In *Common Worship* (2000) this historic collect was omitted
altogether, along with the second Good Friday collect.

I reprint it here in the form in which it appeared in the ASB, and
commend it for private use, not only on Good Friday, for which it is
eminently suitable, but throughout the year.

Merciful God
who made all men and hate nothing
that you have made:
you desire not the death of a sinner
but rather that he should be converted and live.
Have mercy upon your ancient people the Jews,
and upon all who have not known you,
or who deny the faith of Christ crucified,
take from them all ignorance, hardness of heart,
and contempt of your word,
and so fetch them home to your fold
that they may be made one flock under one shepherd
through Jesus Christ our Lord.

Chapter 10
The Fitch Ecclesiometer

Following those lengthy excursions into the wider Christian world, all that remains to be done is to return to our main theme in the light of our findings, and to record them. I had intended to achieve this in one final chapter, but, as an aide memoire, I now propose to preface that with what follows. (From that you may think this is going to be no more than vain repetition and decide to skip it, and turn to the next. I very much hope you won't.)

Following this page is a diagram to illustrate the main features of my Ecclesiometer. It won't be altogether new to you because I have, admittedly with some reluctance, given away most of its secrets in the earlier chapters.

The entire diagram, putti and all, represents, however crudely, the Christian Faith, under attack as it has been from the beginning – and the human approach to it. For our present purposes I have simplified it by leaving out the system for recording ecclesiometrical readings. (Had I not done so, it would have had the appearance of a dart board with numbered concentric circles round the bull's eye in the middle.) Here there are only two, one being the "bull's eye", which, were it in colour, would be the brightest golden yellow. With its radiant effulgence it stands for the ineffable Ultimate Reality, God, uniquely revealed to mankind in his incarnate "son" Christ – hence the traditional form of his name IHS (Jesus) at the point of intersection, His Cross and Resurrection. This is the epicentre of our Faith, on which, significantly, the four approaches, High, Broad, Low and Narrow converge. The way along the straight lines leading directly to the central point of the Victorious Crucified Paschal Lamb is (you note) obstructed by the zigzag centrifugal obfuscations of evil temptation (which some would call "the world, the flesh and the devil"). But, you will also note, God's messengers, the cherubim, are

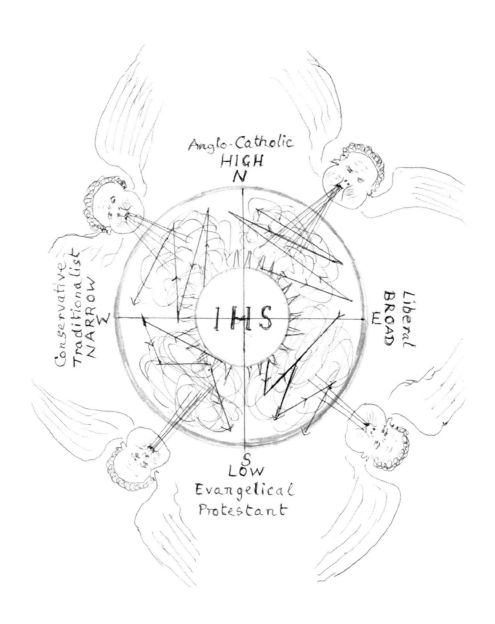

Fig. 2   The Dial of the ECCLESIOMETER

puffing with all their might the centripetal breath of the Spirit, the glorious Grace of God.[1]

God created humankind "in his own image", endowing us with freedom of will, independent of Him. Neither the Grace of God, nor the machinations of evil, chaos and anarchy, are irresistible, because we are not automata, but autonomous human beings. Here the old medieval axiom holds good: "Gratia non tollit naturam, sed perficit"- the grace of God does not destroy (or supersede) nature, but perfects it, i.e. accords it its full potential.

The two radial axes, North to South and East to West, both represent Truth, approached from different angles – North to South as Revelation, East to West by way of Reason and Tradition. The putti, or cherubim, act (automatically; *they* have *no* freedom of will) on behalf of their Master, the invisible Father Creator of the Universe; they are represented as puffing the gentle breeze of the Spirit, the Grace of God. (Ezekiel 37 v. 9f.). The zigzags of Evil Temptation are incapable of straightforward motion; they can only deviate,[2] however subtle their attack. Centripetal/centrifugal – the choice is ours. The benign Grace of God has given us a real, if limited, freedom of will, and is ever at hand to help us find, and keep, the right direction.

Some unresolved problems

I now have to own up to two areas of as yet unresolved uncertainty. The first of these is that I have only *provisionally* assigned proper quarters to three categories of Anglicans. The first two of these are, I think, on the fringe of Anglicanism, both, in their own ways, symptomatic of the current flight from (God-given) Reason; (i) "Charismatics", Pentecostalists, sometimes called "happy clappies". In the 18th century, the Age of Reason, they would have been termed "enthusiasts": as witness Bishop Butler's rebuke to John Wesley: "Sir, enthusiasm is a horrid thing, a very horrid thing." The word, then, had quite a different connotation to what it has today – viz.

---

1. The percipient art historian may have noticed a possible, more than chance, link between this crude diagram and the splendid classical 18th century altarpiece of Framlingham Church, Suffolk. Its centrepiece is the Glory of God, represented by the Hebrew tetragrammaton.

2. Here a verse by Belloc has some relevance:

The Devil, having nothing else to do,
Went off to tempt my Lady Poltagrue
My lady, tempted by a private whim,
To his extreme annoyance, tempted him.

In ed. Michael Roberts: *The Faber Book of Comic Verse* (Faber 1942) *pretension* to a *special* manifestation of the Holy Spirit. Ronald Knox analysed it in his *magnum opus, Enthusiasm* (OUP 1950); (ii) Flat Earthers, Rock Bottomers, Dents (opposite extreme to "Spikes") – terms of endearment for varieties of Hard Fundamentalism. I have *provisionally* assigned them (both species) a place among the Narrow Churchmen, who may not welcome them, feeling perhaps that their true location is with the Low Church: they, again, may not receive them with open arms. I would welcome advice and expressions of opinion on this matter.

The third category of Anglicans is the Christian Socialists. I inadvertently overlooked them earlier. I think, first, of Charles Kingsley, F.D. Maurice, Tom Hughes and Barham Zincke (rector of Wherstead, Suffolk) and others who, with them, pioneered "the social gospel" in the mid-Victorian era, when it was distinctly unfashionable – *all honour to them*. With them, a little later, I suppose, should be included Mackonochie, Lowder and other very High Church and devoted slum priests – later still including the stalwart Father Joe Williamson of Stepney who ended his ministry at Alpheton and Shimpling in remotest Suffolk. Kingsley and Hughes would have found a congenial lodging with the Broad Church; not so the Anglo-Catholics, of course.

But, to adapt a famous saying of Arthur Balfour:[3] "We are all [Christian] Socialists now", and it has long been almost *de rigeur* for our Anglican "top brass" to align themselves, no longer, as of old, with the Tory Party of Church and Crown, still less with the Liberal stronghold of Nonconformity and its famous "conscience", but with the Labour Party – as witness Archbishop Williams, who elegantly described himself as "a hairy Leftie" (in contrast, perhaps, to his role model, William Temple, a smooth Leftie): Jacob and Esau please note. Where do these present day worthies belong? With the Christian Social Union and the Industrial Christian Fellowship in mind, I ventured to group them *provisionally* with the High Churchmen. Comments please.

But my main area of uncertainty, due to my (lamentable, but total) ignorance of technology, concerns the crucial matter of ecclesiometrical rating – crucial, because of course, that is the main *raison d'etre* of the ecclesiometer. There is no problem about the principle of it.

3. Arthur James Balfour (1848-1930), Conservative Prime Minister 1902-5, and author of *A Defence of Philosophic Doubt* (1879) and *Foundations of Belief* (1895). A communicant member of both the Church of England and the Church of Scotland, he was perhaps the *most* brilliantly intellectual of our Prime Ministers. He was created an earl in 1922. The Balfour Declaration favouring Palestine as a "home" for Zionist Jews was named after him.

Archbishop Fisher

Although his "shade" is blissfully unaware of it, the credit for establishing its basic mathematical principle must go to Geoffrey Fisher, Archbishop of Canterbury from 1945 to 1961. He has already been mentioned more than once in these pages. My old mentor, Charles Smyth, who was a boy at Repton when Fisher, whom he greatly admired, was a very young Headmaster, was fond of telling how, as a boy, he watched Fisher courting Rosamond his future wife, daughter of a housemaster, as they skated in graceful circles on the ice.[4]

The point here is that Fisher liked to describe himself as a central churchman. What I think he meant, subconsciously at any rate, was that he was a natural blend of all four quarters, High, Low, Broad and Narrow. That struck me as the *ideal* for Anglicans – indeed for all Christian believers. It is the *real* meaning of the Via Media. The exact ratio of each of the four quarters to each of the others will naturally vary with the individual but they will *all* at least be present in his mind, converging on the centre where stands the Cross of Christ.

The Ideal Ecclesiometrical Rating

So that is the principle on which I have written this essay, and designed the ecclesiometer, and it is borne out by experience. *Every one* of the extremely varied selection of outstanding clerics I have known, or in the very few cases where I have not known them *personally*, have had opportunities to hear and to observe and whom I have mentioned in these pages, has come, or comes, well within this category. In *all* without exception "churchmanship" was, or is, decently unobtrusive, more or less imperceptible. Applying this to the dial of the ecclesiometer, it seemed to me to give an ideal rating, North and East, of 50-50, i.e. 50N 50E (That is how a reading, based on the two axes, should be recorded.)

Some Practicalities

As I have said more than once, being lamentably ignorant of such matters, I am perfectly content to entrust the technology to an expert

---

4. My son tells me that the late Roald Dahl, brilliant writer for children, when also at Repton, took a very different view of Fisher, accusing him of sadistic flogging. The only time I saw Fisher, in the 1950s, he looked to me exactly like Harry Secombe's impersonation of the benign, cherubic Mr. Pickwick. I find it hard to see him as a sadist. It may be more than a coincidence that Fisher, Smyth and I were all prepared for the Ministry at Wells Theological College.

in that field. In the advanced state of electronics I am assured that there would be no difficulty, and that, on the business side, we could reach an equitable arrangement, fair and acceptable to both of us. Should any reader be interested, let him or her get in touch with me and if I have not already made other arrangements, provided he or she can satisfy me about his or her qualifications, there should be no problem.

Earlier on I gave some thought to the commercial aspects of marketing what I would insist on calling the Fitch Ecclesiometer. It occurred to me that, once launched and proved efficient, it would prove indispensable to bishops, patrons (including the Crown) and all parsons seeking new pastures. Further, that a special contract might be negotiable with *Crockford's Clerical Directory*, who could discreetly insert the current reading for each entry – indeed General Synod could prepare legislation requiring all clergy, male and female, to be tested ecclesiometrically at regular intervals (say once every so many years). Skilled ecclesiometrists would require a short course of instruction, perhaps at a technical college. Indeed, the prospects are limitless.

Chapter 11
Beyond a Joke

Readers who have stayed the course thus far may well be asking themselves, "Is this all an elaborate joke or are we meant to take it seriously?" To answer the second half of the question first, I reply, "Yes, please *do*. Take it with the *utmost* seriousness."

In response to the first half, I will come completely clean. The idea of the Ecclesiometer, which I would like to think original, came into my head years ago. I toyed with it without putting anything on paper, but it occurred to me that it might have its uses one day. Then, again long ago, years after the publication (1950) of Stephen Potter's *Lifemanship*, that minor masterpiece came my way. Naturally, I couldn't help putting that infuriating word "Churchmanship" alongside Potter's inspired "Lifemanship", and having a bit of harmless fun with it. But it was not until 2003 that, with the onset of old age and deteriorating eyesight, I made up my mind to try and put the whole thing on paper before I "go hence and be no more seen."[1]

My first attempt was not a success. It was an unhappy blend of superficial frivolity and rather heavy seriousness and gave the impression that I was trying to be too clever, and falling clumsily between two stools. As it was, what I had written was clearly not fit for publication.

I gave the matter further anxious thought, did more reading, sought and received some useful advice, and eventually decided to try again, this time treating the subject with the seriousness which, by this time, I realised it deserved, but without abandoning the light touch. What you have in your hands is the result. It has taken me, altogether, several years and much cogitation, but has kept me out of worse mischief!

---

1. Psalm 39 verse 15. Prayer Book version.

About the Ecclesiometer (which I am now happy to assure you doesn't exist outside my imagination), the idea of it increasingly took hold of me and I almost began to wish that it really did exist. The theory of ecclesiometry as I worked it out in detail on our labourious circuit of the imaginary dial, not only *seemed* to me increasingly plausible, but I came to believe that it actually is 100% valid. I would much like to know if you agree; or is this just another case of the manufacturer believing in his own product?

Having thus convinced myself and (I hope) you, the reader, that there really is something in this essentially four square view of Christian faith/commitment underlying the Anglican concept of "Churchmanship", let us now try to define more precisely than we have before, *exactly* what this "something" is. If only we can agree a fair definition to replace those unsatisfactory ones we noticed at the beginning of this essay, it will at least enable us to get rid of those tiresome inverted commas. (I hope it will enable us to do rather more than that!) Here, then, is the definition I propose: if you can improve it, so much the better.

Churchmanship finally defined, analysed and evaluated

The peculiarly Anglican concept of Churchmanship is the deliberate identification by an Anglican of one or more of four distinct, separable, but essentially complementary and interlocking aspects of orthodox Christian belief/faith/commitment, seen and emphasised by that Anglican as being of supreme importance over against the others, and used as a label or description for him/herself.

These four complementary aspects are:

(1) Conversion, whether sudden or gradual, leading, via repentance and baptism, to lifelong faith/commitment to God in and through Jesus his incarnate "Son", to the Gospel of whose uniquely saving life, teaching, death, resurrection and exaltation, and to the gift and guidance of his Holy Spirit, the Bible bears unique, true and authentic witness. (Low Church/Evangelical)

(2) This same Christian faith/commitment realised as involving also binding, lifelong active membership of Christ's living mystical "Body", i.e. His universal/catholic, historic and missionary/Apostolic Church, with its threefold ministry, and all its sacramental privileges, duties and responsibilities, personal (membership one of another in Christ) social and financial. (High Church/Anglo-Catholic)

(3) Unrestricted openness to the sure guidance of the Holy Spirit of Truth, Reason and Love in every field of contemporary knowledge,

experience, science and learning (including Biblical scholarship and analysis) in order to enable and equip Christians to present and proclaim the unchanging Gospel intelligibly, credibly and effectively in and to the secular world we inhabit and for the love of which the eternal God gave himself without stint in the person of his "Son" Jesus, and continues to give himself in the person of His Holy Spirit today, and in the fellowship of his Church. (Broad Church/Liberal)

(4) Without contradicting anything in (1), (2) or (3), in *this* quarter especial stress is laid upon the transcendence, holiness, majesty and mystery of God the *Ultimate* Reality, and on Christ and the Holy Spirit the *Proximate and Immanent* Reality, and therefore upon the reverence due to Holy Scripture as well as the respect and honour due to all that is of permanent value in past and present Christian Tradition and our Christian heritage of art, music, architecture and literature. This type of Churchmanship often finds useful expression in a call for Restraint to curb the perceived excesses of Liberal openness (3); just as *that* quarter (3) sometimes finds expression in denouncing the opposite tendencies to excessive caution, timidity or hidebound conservatism in (4). (Narrow Church/conservative traditionalist)

The holding together, in tension and balance, of all four of these complementary aspects of our Christian faith/commitment is Central Churchmanship, the attainable ideal for all.

Conversely, each of these four aspects or basic types of Churchmanship, while true in themselves when held in this tension and balance with the rest; when isolated, separated, and over-emphasised over against the others, they all suffer distortion and cause needless friction.[2]

Widening circles

So far in this concluding chapter, after calling my own bluff on Ecclesiometry, I have been at pains to redefine and restate, as precisely as I could, and then to defend my (perfectly serious) thesis on Churchmanship and its solution in terms of *principled Central Churchmanship* as the *ideal* for all Anglicans worldwide.

In my Preface I was rash enough to hint at a wider scope for this thesis than as a peace making tool for the C. of E. That, of course, was the theme of chapters 7, 8 and 9. There we looked in turn, in ever widening circles, first at our own worldwide Communion; then at the ecumenical scene; and, finally, in the sphere of world

2. This is memorably illustrated in C.S. Lewis's classic *Screwtape Letters* and is commonly experienced in everyday Church life. We all do it!

religions, at the possibilities of fruitful dialogue between the three related Abrahamic, monotheistic faiths, Judaism, Christianity and Islam.

In all three spheres we found that there was scope for dialogue aimed at mutual understanding and the removal of obstacles between the various participants. But in the first two we also found that, in both, we reached a point where the conversations were broken off and further progress seemed impossible.

In the case of the Anglican Communion this was due to the unilateral action of the conservative evangelicals losing patience with the peacemaking efforts of their Anglican colleagues, and hiving off, under the banner of GAFCON, to a much cosier dialogue of their own, where agreement was easy, thereby boycotting the much larger setting of the traditional ten-yearly Lambeth Conference. There these divisive issues were freely debated in the helpful style of an African indaba and in the context of intensive Bible study. No bones were broken. But the GAFCONites were left with an uneasy conscience.

In the ecumenical field great – and unexpected – progress was made in the middle years of the last century towards healing the wounds of the Reformation and envisaging and accomplishing the visible reunion of Christ's divided Body, the Church. Then, in the 1980's and 1990's, all came to a grinding halt. This time it was a deep-seated reaction in Rome itself against the *aggiornamento* initiated by Pope John XXIII and the Second Vatican Council, bringing with it a return of the old intransigence of the days of Pius XI and Pius XII.

There is more in common between these two disappointments than might seem. Both are due to different forms of rigid dogmatism which effectively blocks and excludes the refreshing wind of the Holy Spirit, in favour of, in the first case, Biblical "certainties", and in the other, of "infallible certainties". (In both cases probabilities are preferable.)

As to the interfaith scenario, there was no breaking off conversations. There is general agreement that interfaith dialogue is good and wholly desirable, especially between the three monotheistic faiths, and in present circumstances. If this is to be fruitful, it requires an almost infinite degree of patience, forbearance, and readiness to listen and genuinely to learn.

The obstacle encountered in all these scenarios is one form or another of fundamentalism. In the case of Judaism, the Christian's partner in dialogue must be the *liberal* Judaism represented by people like Chief Rabbi Jonathan Sacks and Rabbi Tony Bayfield. Dialogue with *Orthodox* Jews like those of the notoriously fanatical

Mea Shearim district of present day Jerusalem is a non-starter. They and their like worldwide are fanatically fundamentalist with tightly closed minds.

By and large, the same is true of most Muslims in their attitude to the Qur'an. But there are hopeful signs of a cautiously more liberal and critical attitude developing in some quarters. This must be the hope of the future for fruitful interfaith dialogue with Islam. In the meantime, as we wait patiently for these hopeful shoots to develop further, we must do our utmost to keep lines of communication between Muslim, Jew and Christian open.

A remarkable and too little known example, at the purely *secular* level, of the degree of not only peaceful co-existence and toleration, but of mutual cordiality and understanding which is *achievable*, is to be found in the unlikely context of present day West Bank Israel in the shared Arab-Jewish community of Neve Shalom Wahat al Salam (Oasis of Peace) between Jerusalem and Jaffa. And that owes its inspiration and existence to a *Christian* priest, the Italian Dominican Father Bruno Hussar (1970).[3] It is a tragic fact that the Arab-Israeli conflict is rooted in *"religious"* prejudice on both sides.

* * * * *

Because of this conviction of mine of the evil of fundamentalism of any and every kind I want to include in this last chapter a thoroughgoing examination of the *true* (as opposed to the false and misconceived fundamentalist view of the) relationship of our Christian Bible to the Holy Spirit.

The Bible and the Holy Spirit in the Church

In what follows I am totally indebted to an article by my teacher, mentor and dear friend, the late Professor C.F.D. Moule, who died in 2007 aged 98, universally admired and respected for his outstanding Biblical scholarship and as a singularly modest, unassuming Christian. This article was originally given as a lecture under the aegis of the Faculty of Divinity and the Department of Education in the University of Cambridge, and published in Epworth Review in May 1981. It was reprinted in Moule's *Forgiveness and Reconciliation* (SPCK 1998) pp. 211-224 under the title *The Holy Spirit and Scripture*. This lecture deserves to be *read, re-read and pondered* by *all* Bible readers.

In the lecture C.F.D.M. set out to pinpoint what is really "distinctive

3. I visited Neve Shalom in 1992 and saw for myself. More information available from British Friends of NSWaS, Premier House, 112 Station Road, Edgware, Middx. HA8 7BJ.

and indispensable" about the Bible, at the very heart of the Church's life, and in relation to the Holy Spirit.

He began by considering the widespread claim or assumption that "the Bible is inspired" by God the Holy Spirit, and commented that it "concerns a problem that is anything but simple and moves in a veritable minefield of prejudice and shibboleths." The statement "The Bible is inspired", he pointed out, "cannot help to define its distinctiveness", what is unique about it, adding "I wonder whether any distinctive meaning can be attached to such a statement." At this point C.F.D.M. pleaded, "Do not misunderstand me." He was not denying that God's Holy Spirit speaks through Scripture. He does, of course, but not through Scripture alone. Who is going to deny that the Spirit speaks through poets, artists and composers? (He might have added scientists, and mathematicians). "I can see no particular gain therefore," he wrote, "in calling the Bible inspired when one is searching for what is *distinctive* of it." We recognise when a person's normal powers are somehow divinely enhanced and say (s)he is inspired, but such inspiration is not confined to religious themes. Moule candidly confessed that he found it hard to believe that "the more pedestrian writers in the canonical scriptures, instancing the Book of Ezra, were, in this sense, inspired at all" adding "inspiration in this general sense of the heightening of human powers above the normal gets you nowhere if you are looking for a definition of what is special about the Bible."

Is it then a special *kind* of inspiration, and if so, what kind? Observing that those who attribute *special* inspiration to the Bible are usually found to be talking, not of inspiration at all, but of *infallibility*, C.F.D.M. wrote that what they want to believe is that the writers were overpowered by God and made the mouthpiece for messages straight from Him – that the fallible mind and imperfect character of the human agent were not allowed to hinder the authentic message from heaven. They were overridden by the divine. "Where is the evidence that this was so?" he asked, adding, "I know of none."

He went on to make the crucial point that if one believes in God as personal, it follows that "He would not and could not treat a person like an instrument". But he admitted that some writers, both Jewish (e.g. Philo of Alexandria) and Christian (e.g. Athenagoras) have asserted that He *does*. But, wrote C.F.D.M. "it seems to me totally out of character with the God a Theist acknowledges" and quotes a modern writer, John Ziesler, "God does not threaten man's humanness or freedom or integrity. He guarantees them." And he adds that Christians can never forget their conviction that God's ultimate utterance to us is not a statement but a Man.

"Thus," he went on,

> a conception of inspiration as the mechanical prevention of
> error is not only an illegitimate stretching of the meaning of
> the word; it is a sub-personal, sub-theistic conception of God:
> least of all is it compatible with a fully Christian understanding
> of God and of the Word made flesh. Inspiration does not mean
> infallibility and infallibility does not seem to be God's way,
> and even if it were, how could we profit by it?

This, of course, brings Moule up against the inevitable quotation of
2 Timothy 3.16 "All Scripture is inspired by God", literally "God-
breathed" (theopneustos). His answer is threefold: (1) theopneustos
may mean "*out*breathing by God" – in any case we are no nearer
infallibility; (2) the term "Scripture" in 2 Tim. 3.16 refers to part only
of the Old Testament – the Old Testament canon was not yet fixed
and the New Testament canon had not been formulated; and (3) the
clinching argument: "It is in any case poor logic to say that the accused
is not guilty because he says so." The argument is circular. (I dealt with
this in relation to Nicky Gumbel's Alpha Course in Chapter 2.)

C.F.D.M. then reiterates that in denying that "inspired" is a term
that has any useful or legitimate application to Scripture when we are
trying to locate its *distinctiveness*, he is not for a moment denying
that the Holy Spirit may and does speak through Scripture or that
Scripture is inspir*ing*. "I am not denying any of the great things that
God does for us in Scripture. He does speak to us through it. Scripture
does "find" us as Coleridge said. It contains passages of stupendous
grandeur, it probes the conscience, kindles the soul, exalts the spirit.
The Bible knocks us down and lifts us up. It is, to a high degree,
inspir*ing*."

In his search for what is uniquely distinctive about the Bible,
C.F.D.M. then turns from "inspiration" to the canon of Scripture.
"Must it not be allowed that the canon was an inspired choice?"
The canon – the list of books comprising the Bible – is the list of
those books deemed by the Church Catholic to constitute the norm
for faith and practice. He quotes Article Six of the Thirty Nine:
"Holy Scripture containeth all things necessary to salvation, so that
whatsoever is not read therein, nor may be proved thereby, is not
to be required of any man that it should be believed as an article of
the faith or be thought necessary to salvation." "That is not to say,"
comments Moule, "that everything outside Scripture is incorrect,
nor everything in Scripture correct, but that the Church recognises
this body of writings as the norm and standard of the Faith beyond

which (in matters of controversy) nothing is to be deemed essential. Was it not the Holy Spirit that led the Fathers to this momentous decision about what constituted the entire Bible?" We must surely answer "Yes" but once again not in any *distinctive* way. C.F.D.M. could think of no evidence that the Church's choice was safeguarded in some special way, over and above ordinary human precautions, against a mistaken judgment. The documents were established by their own antiquity and authenticity, and this is endorsed by critical scholarship. This was a perfectly "natural" process; no evidence of it being a special case.

"My main point," he wrote, "is that in none of the directions in which we have looked does there seem to be any clear reason for discerning a conspicuous or recognisably distinctive work of the Holy Spirit protecting selectors and interpreters from error or guaranteeing authentic transmission. Is there then some other way in which a distinctiveness may be defined or to which a doctrine of Spirit is relevant?" To both questions Moule answers, "Yes."

He then offers an analogy. A crater in Arizona is believed to have been formed by the impact of an enormous meteorite. The character and size of the meteorite is only discoverable by the scientific work of geologists, meteorologists and other experts. The "impact" *we* are studying is what is called "the Christ event". *Our* "crater" is the stamp of that impact in the earliest Christian literature and any other relevant data. This includes the Jewish scriptures, "the matrix of the Christ event". Part of the crater is the very emergence of a canon of the Scriptures. Thus Scripture's *distinctive* function is a *historical* one; it is the primary evidence for the Christ event – the main part of our evidential crater. The geologists' methods of examining the successive layers and deposits is duly represented in the New Testament critics' procedures. What are we to say about the Person at the centre of these events that caused this impact? "What the Scriptures point to is a self-authenticating reality which lends to the Scriptures the distinctiveness we seek."

Moule writes:

> It always seems to me that the genesis of the Easter belief, the reaching, that is, by certain of Jesus' followers of the conviction that Jesus was alive after the crucifixion (alive with permanent, irreversible, eternal life) – simply cannot be adequately described without using religious terms – terms of divine revelation. The secular historian cannot deny that the friends of Jesus did (rightly or wrongly) come to that preposterous

conclusion. If he is determined to acknowledge as real nothing outside the secular historian's field, he can suggest that this was due to hallucination or to deductions from already held religious beliefs or to superstitions and imaginative enthusiasm for a hero and a leader. But none of these suggestions (to my mind) is anything like adequate to account for the facts. It is positively more plausible and (I believe) more honest for the historian to admit that he can find, within his own terms of reference, no adequate explanation of how the friends of Jesus reached that conviction. If so, he must be ready to acknowledge that the evidence points beyond the frontiers of history to some religious conclusion, a conclusion in terms of revelation. Jesus, we have to say, showed himself alive; God raised him from among the dead. His supposed aliveness corresponds with reality. This is the distinctive statement. The historical evidence cumulatively, including both the Scriptures themselves and the fact that the Christian Church selected them point, it seems to me, to one who was not only a great magnetic, supremely powerful man of superb integrity, but to this person's being, in an unparalleled way – in a *distinctive* way – one with God. Not like our meteorite (for here the analogy completely fails), entering the earth's atmosphere from outside, colliding with the ground, and flying into a thousand fragments. No. Jesus clearly belonged to human kind and came from within. Yet, all the time, he belonged also, in an unparalleled way, to what I can only call "the beyond". And the mark has been left, embedded in the evidence, by the impact. This is a paradox; but it is one from which I see no way of escape.

C.F.D.M. goes on:

Now, if so, then the whole of Scripture, not miraculously safeguarded against error, but critically examined, points to the impact of one who is both within and beyond the world of human affairs. That is its distinctive character. Nothing can take its place for throwing a brilliant point of light on the mysterious appearing of God in Christ. Scripture performs its distinctive function when it brings us to God through Jesus Christ.

Moule concludes his lecture by asking his audience

to consider what happens when the Bible – in its entirety – is allowed to perform this one proper and distinctive function, that is, of confronting the readers with a portrait of Jesus

Christ and with the events that show that he lives and is with
them. The Bible (he says) is then at the very heart of the
process by which Christians draw near to the living God and
He to them. It is by constant study of the Bible that the people
of God are held to their historical roots, and held also to faith
in Christ, crucified, raised from among the dead, and alive
for evermore – the Christ through whom we draw near to
God and He draws near to us. In this steady holding of the
Church to the *fait accompli* under Pontius Pilate and to its
constant consequences, the Bible is distinctive, paramount,
and indispensable. Its character as the primary evidence
for the beginnings of Christianity and as a uniquely early
and authentic presentation of Christ is what lends it its
distinctiveness. But we cannot effectively use (or rather be
used by) this access to the living God through Jesus Christ to
which the Bible admits us unless the Spirit of God is among
us and within us making our minds alert and fortifying our
resolve to obey him in what we are shown. The ministers
of the Christian church are ordained expressly as ministers
of the Word and the Sacraments which means, I think, that
all clergy are theologians: it is their professional duty and
responsibility to communicate and interpret the knowledge
of God. And in both sides of their professional task the Holy
Spirit of God is at work in them, and in their communities:
otherwise they will toil in vain. God's presence as Spirit is
the *sine qua non*.

The Scriptures lead us to the Son – the living Son of God
and in the presence of God, Father, Son and Holy Spirit, we
are in a position to discern his will and find the moral strength
to follow it. It is no part of the function of Scripture to give us
moral direction. Scarcely any of the pressing moral problems
of the present day are so much as mentioned there. If, as
does happen on occasion, some clear insight or compelling
directive does come straight from what is written, that is a
bonus. But it is not anything to be surprised or distressed at if
the Bible does not guide us so.

The Bible is not itself so much a compass or a chart, as
direction for finding the Pilot, and he it is who will be to
us both compass and chart, and will steer us through the
shoals. He is God's living Utterance. Putting it in terms of
an elementary diagram, we are not to expect moral guidance
normally to come straight along the base of the triangle,

from the Bible to our predicament. Rather we are to look
to the Bible to help us ascend the gradient up the side of the
triangle to the living God through Jesus Christ; and it is from
there down the third side of the triangle that we may look for
guidance to come if we seek it seriously and realistically in
obedience to the Holy Spirit and with the help of the experts
in the relevant sciences and skills.

I make no apology for printing here such a full summary of Professor
Moule's[4] stimulating lecture. For it is totally relevant to the threat of
schism posed by the dissident bishops boycotting Lambeth 2008. It
should be urgent required reading for all of them, guaranteed to make
many think again.

I do, however, need to apologise for daring to add the comments
which follow – my own.

The historical approach

As will have become only too obvious to my sorely tried readers, my
bias and my approach throughout this book have been historical. I
cannot help that. Since my earliest days my absorbing and overriding
interests, as, later, my academic training were those of an historian.
So it comes naturally to me to approach the Scriptures as historical
documents, with all that that implies, and to see the people and events
and the stories to which they introduce their readers in the light of
history. Bound up with this, of course, is the historical geography and
topography of what we have come to call The Holy Land. On top of

---

4. In my time at Cambridge there were three prominent clerical dons, all
of them with the Christian name Charles. They knew each other well and
were, I think, critical friends, but were commonly regarded as representing
three sharply contrasting churchmanships. Most senior was Charles Raven,
Regius Professor of Divinity and Master of Christ's College, an outstanding
naturalist as well as a fine theologian. He was a quintessential Broad
Churchman. Next in age was Charles Smyth, distinguished ecclesiastical
historian. As Dean of Chapel of my college, Corpus Christi, he was a
preacher of highly polished sermons and a wit. He was a Conservative High
Churchman. Most junior of the three was Charlie Moule, a young Dean of
Clare and future Lady Margaret's Professor of Divinity – an unmistakable
Evangelical (Liberal). I was influenced by all three, taught by the last two
who became good friends of mine over many years, as they were of each
other. I was an admiring attender of Raven's lectures and sermons but did
not know him personally. What is particularly interesting for the readers
of this book is that all three Charleses were, in my terms, sound *Central*
Churchmen – though Raven might have had difficulty in recognising
himself as such!

all this, has then come a range of other relevant studies, linguistic, ethnographic, anthropological, etc.

But at the same time I am very much aware of the *limitations* of history and all that goes with it. The Scriptures are very much more than historical documents. What they have to tell us is timeless, transcendent, permanent. But at root, historical documents they remain, and they require to be seen and understood in that light *before* we can fully see and understand them in the light both of today and of Eternity. (That incidentally is why I find the brilliant reconstruction of the life of the historical Jesus, and his death and resurrection, by Bishop Tom Wright so absorbing, exciting and important. It complements the work of his friend (and mine) Charlie Moule, but is not yet complete.)

Before closing this section, I just want to add this. When teaching confirmation candidates about the Bible, I have occasionally used an analogy which seemed to me to have some advantages. Probably others used it too, despite its limitations. I said that the Bible was in some ways like the title deeds which go, or used to go, with an old property. To prove rightful ownership, you had to be able to trace the title back a long way – the law has changed in recent years, so this has to some extent grown out-of-date. With ownership of an estate, or an old farm, the title deeds might go back to the Middle Ages and be of great interest. The Bible in that sense is the title deeds of the Christian Faith and Church. I hope this keys in with Charlie Moule's lecture.

The Ecumenical Dimension

This matter of the Bible and its unique importance for Christians, so thoughtfully expounded by Charlie Moule, is, of course, not just one for Anglicans but has a resonance for Christians everywhere. The perplexing problem of homosexuality and the question of the weight to be given to the references to it in both Testaments has been variously assessed in the course of the controversy. No sensible Christian believes that it should be ignored or discounted simply because it is now at least two millennia old. But the passage of time and the findings of the modern age of science cannot be ignored either. Nor can the swing in public attitudes and opinion from abhorrence to easygoing tolerance. Sensitive and sensible Christians take all these factors into prayerful consideration when seeking the guidance of the Holy Spirit of Truth and Love, the spirit of the living Lord Jesus. He can be relied upon to lead us eventually into the truth of this difficult matter, provided we have not already closed our minds. We should be wrong to foreclose the matter in the meantime. Rowan Williams's lecture *The Body's Grace* is highly relevant.

Not by any means for the first time have Anglicans served as guinea pigs for the rest of divided Christendom. As in the debate over the ordination of women, we conduct our controversies out in the open for all to witness. That must be the intention of Divine Providence! In which case it is for us not to lose patience but to put our trust in the Lord and leave the outcome in *his* hands.

Here is another consideration. I have written as though Churchmanship was a peculiarly Anglican invention, and it certainly looks like that. But the four distinctive emphases I have analysed correspond to universal phenomena:

> Every boy and every gal
> That's born into this world alive
> Is either a little liberal
> Or else a little conservative.

And if that is true ecclesiometrically, as well as politically, latitudinally, the pull between the Corporate and the individual is equally valid longitudinally.

The Roman Catholic Church is highly disciplined and presents to the world a solidly monolithic appearance. But this is only a façade. Behind that impressive exterior appearance of unity, there is plentiful evidence of a healthy diversity of outlook. Hans Küng is not the only liberal, we may be sure. I referred once to the late lamented Adrian Hastings's powerful advocacy of women priests (and bishops) in his book *The Theology of a Protestant Catholic*. Liberation Theology was not confined to South America. The ultramontane reaction personified in the suave figure of Benedict XVI will not last for ever. There is an urgent liberal agenda awaiting his successor. And if that is true of Rome, the same could be said for the Protestant world.

Ongoing Ecumenism

When the Ecumenical Movement recovers its nerve and, under new (Papal?) Leadership resumes its onward march, as, God willing, it will, some such analysis as that presented here may well commend itself, the notion of Churchmanship representing a healthy *balance* between opposing emphases true to its historic roots and the slogan "Unity in diversity".

I promised to end this final chapter on a more cheerful, positive note. Here it is.

An Alternative to Churchmanship

As a concept, Churchmanship is at worst confrontational, an expression of the partisanship first manifested in Corinth and deplored by St. Paul. "Is Christ divided?" he asked, and Christ himself had warned his contemporaries that a household or kingdom divided within itself is doomed to destruction. (Mark 3.25). Our Church is painfully experiencing the truth of that, in the deeply entrenched partisanship we call Churchmanship. It is possible to rise above this destructive factionalism by embracing *all* the artificially separated aspects of Christian belief and discipleship in what we have called the *ideal* of Central Churchmanship.

But there is, and always has been, an alternative, or perhaps complementary method of seeking to resolve the controversial issues that from time to time crop up to perplex and divide Christian people. In contrast to confrontation it is often described as consensus. But for Christians that word must be handled with care. For consensus, as such, as a way of reaching agreed decisions on controversial subjects, is applicable to politics, ethics and every field of human debate. Reaching "a common mind" on any subject, after free, frank and probably prolonged discussion is admirable, but not in itself a guarantee that the decision reached is right, though likely so to be.

But when, after earnest prayer for guidance by God's Holy Spirit, a controversial matter is fully and openly debated, we have, it is true, no guarantee of infallibility, but the *assurance* that, provided we are prepared to follow, the Holy Spirit will lead us, slowly perhaps and gradually, but surely, into truth. So long as we do not identify all decision making by consensus, reaching a common mind, with the guidance of the Holy Spirit, we shall not go far wrong.[5] The traditional Latin term for this is *consensus communis fidelium.*

The first Church Council, held in Jerusalem c. A.D. 50, sent an encyclical letter by Paul and Barnabas in which the Council's agreed decisions were introduced with the famous words: "It seemed good to the Holy Spirit and to us..." (Acts 15.28). That is a good precedent. In that case all present at the Council had reached a common mind, a consensus, which they had reason to believe was "the mind of Christ". This method, following such a precedent, is sensible, civilised, honest, open and profoundly Christian.

---

5. Religious affairs journalists have coined a contemptuous phrase, "typical Anglican compromise" (TAC for short) for indiscriminate use whenever Anglicans agree. In some circumstances it may be appropriate. Consensus in the Spirit, as described above, is emphatically not one of them.

Recent examples of this kind of approach have met with a mixed response. The document *Issues in Human Sexuality* published by the English House of Bishops in 1991 featured largely in Chapter 7 above. I thought it admirably fair and balanced but it met with a rough reception in some quarters of the Church of England. Years later at the beginning of the new millennium the then-Bishop of Oxford and three senior colleagues, all with differing standpoints on the homosexuality debate, were commissioned to produce a study guide, eventually published in 2003 under the slightly confusing title *Some Issues in Human Sexuality*. The four bishops discharged their commission with commendable thoroughness, disguising the differences between their standpoints, with such exemplary fairness that at least one reader, having dutifully read the very substantial document from cover to cover, emerged at the end of it blinded by too much science and at a loss what to think.

The Church of England, it has to be said, is particularly good at this sort of thing. Another example, recently to hand, is a Report of the Doctrine Commission of the General Synod of the Church of England called *Being human: a Christian understanding of personhood illustrated with reference to power, money, sex and time* and was published, like *Some Issues,* in 2003. It is not easy reading but amply repays the effort to master and absorb it; plenty of practical wisdom is provided on subjects which intimately concern us all. It no doubt owes much to the then-Chairman of the Doctrine Commission, the former Bishop of Ely and sometime Regius Professor of Divinity at Cambridge, Dr. Stephen Sykes. And it stands in a distinguished line going back to the prototype *Doctrine in the Church of England*, the Report of the Commission on Christian Doctrine appointed in 1922 but which did not publish its then famous, now forgotten, Report until 1938, the predecessor of many such. One is entitled to wonder how much of the distilled wisdom in works such as these filters down to the ordinary Church public.

Whatever the answer to that conundrum, true consensus in the Holy Spirit, whether by way of Churchmanship shared or heads put together in Council, Synod or Committee, provided it is genuine, and preceded, accompanied and followed by patient, trusting persistence in prayer in the widest ecumenical context, cannot fail to be rewarded.

Conclusion

With all this in mind, I can think of no better way to bring this essay to a fitting conclusion than by drawing attention to a noble prayer for unity introduced, I believe, into the Sovereign's Accession Day Service in the Book of Common Prayer in the reign of King George I (1714-1727), when England was threatened with the prospect of a Jacobite uprising. Its relevance is no longer even remotely political, but purely, in the true sense, ecclesiastical, across all that at present divides us as Christians one from another.

A Prayer for Unity

O God, the Father of our Lord Jesus Christ, our only Saviour, the Prince of Peace; Give us grace seriously to lay to heart the great dangers we are in by our unhappy divisions. Take away all hatred and prejudice, and whatsoever may hinder us from godly union and concord: that, as there is but one Body, and one Spirit, and one Hope of our Calling, one Lord, one Faith, one Baptism, one God and Father of us all, so we may henceforth be all of one heart and one soul, united in one holy bond of Truth and Peace, of Faith and Charity, and may with one mind and one mouth glorify thee, through Jesus Christ, our Lord. *Amen.*

Acknowledgements

The author and publisher are deeply grateful for permission to reproduce extensive copyright material from the following:

Archant Suffolk, for their kind permission to reprint the photo "Ecumenism on Wheels".

Church Times, for their kind permission to reprint excerpts from Rowan Williams' *Reflections*.

HarperCollins Publishers, for their kind permission to reprint selections from George Cary's *Know the Truth*.

Penguin Group UK, for their kind permission to reproduce the cover of *Lifemanship*, as well as for the right to reprint selections from *Islam*.

SPCK, for their kind permission to reprint selections from C.F.D. Moule's *Forgiveness and Reconciliation*.

Every effort has been made to find and contact the copyright holders for all other relevant materials. If any such party should notice their property reproduced here without permission, please contact the Lutterworth Press, and we will be happy to rectify the situation.

Bibliography

Addleshaw, G.W.O., *The High Church Tradition*, (Faber 1941)

Anglican-Roman Catholic International Commission: The Final Report, (Catholic Truth Society and SPCK 1982)

Bates, S., *A Church at War: Anglicans and Homosexuality*, (I. B. Tauris 2004)

Being Human: A Christian understanding of personhood illustrated with reference to power, money, sex and time, A Report of the Doctrine Commission of the C. of E., (Church House 2003)

Bockmuehl, M., ed., *The Cambridge Companion to Jesus*, (Cambridge Univ. Press 2001)

Braybrooke, M., *How to Understand Judaism*, (S.C.M. 1995)

Carey, G.L., *Know the Truth*, (Harper Collins 2004)

Chadwick, H., *The Early Church*, (Penguin 1967)

Chadwick, O., *The Reformation*, (Penguin 1964)

Chadwick, O., *Michael Ramsey: A Life*, (Oxford Univ. Press 1990)

De La Noy, M., *The Church of England*, (1993)

De Rosa, P., *Vicars of Christ: The Dark Side of the Papacy*, (Corgi 1989)

Dix, G., *The Shape of the Liturgy*, (Dacre Press 1945)

Duffy, E., *The Stripping of the Altars: Traditional Religion in England c.1400-1580*, (Yale Univ. Press 2nd edn. 2005)

Duffy, E., *The Voices of Morebath: Reformation and Rebellion in an English Village*, (Yale University Press 2001)

Edwards, D.L., and Stott, J.R.W., *Essentials*, (Hodder 1988)

The Fullness of Christ: the Church's Growth into Catholicity. A Report to the Archbishop of Canterbury, (SPCK 1950)

Furlong, M., *The C. of E. the State its In*, (Hodder 2000)

Gore, C., Goudge, H.L., and Guillaume, A., eds., *A New Commentary on Holy Scripture*, (SPCK 1932)

Guillaume, A., *Islam,* (Penguin 1954)

Gumbel, N., *Questions of Life,* (Eastbourne Kingsway 1993)

Habgood, J., *Confessions of a Conservative Liberal,* (SPCK 1988)

Habgood, J., *Faith and Uncertainty,* (Darton, Longman and Todd 1997)

Hastings, A., *A History of English Christianity 1920-2000,* (SCM 2001)

Hastings, A., *The Theology of a protestant Catholic,* (SCM 1997)

Hick, J., ed., The *Myth of God Incarnate,* (SCM Press 1997)

Higham, F., *Catholic and Reformed: A Study of the Anglican Church 1559-1662,* (SPCK 1962)

Holloway, R., *Doubts and Loves. What is Left of Christianity,* (Edinburgh. Canongate 2002)

Hooker, R., *The Laws of Ecclesiastical Polity,* 2 vols., (Dent Everyman 1907)

Issues in Human Sexuality. A Statement by the House of Bishops of General Synod, (Church House 1991)

Jenkins, D., *The Calling of a Cuckoo,* (Continuum 2002)

Knox, R.A., *Enthusiasm,* (Oxford Univ. Press 1950)

Koran, The, trans. N.J. Dawood, (Penguin, revised edn. 2006)

Küng, H., *Infallible?,* trans. E. Mosbacher, (Collins 1971)

Küng, H., *On Being a Christian,* trans. E. Quinn, (Collins/Fount 1978)

Mascall, E.L., *Pi in the High,* (Faith Press 1959)

Maxstone Graham, Y., *The Church Hesitant. A Portrait of the Church of England,* (Hodder 1993)

Moorman, J.R.H., *A History of the Church in England,* (A. and C. Black 1953)

Moule, C.F.D., *The Origin of Christology,* (Cambridge Univ. Press 1977)

Moule, C.F.D., *Forgiveness and Reconciliation,* (SPCK 1998)

Murphy O'Connor, J. *1 Corinthians. People's Commentary,* (Bible Reading Fellowship 1999)

Nature of Christian Belief, The Statement of the House of Bishops of General Synod, (Church House 1986)

Nazir Ali, M. *Islam. A Christian Perspective* (Exeter. Paternoster Press 1983)

Nazir Ali, M. *Conviction and Conflict. Islam, Christianity and World Order,* (Continuum 2006)

Objections to Christian Belief, (essays by D.M. Mackinnon, H.A. Williams, A.R. Vidler and J.S.Bezzant), (Constable 1963)

Livingstone, E.A., ed., Oxford Dictionary of the Christian Church (3rd edn. Oxford Univ. Press 1997)

Pawley, B.C., *Anglican-Roman Relations and the Second Vatican Council*, (Church Information Office 1964)

Peacocke, A.R., *Creation and the World of Science*, (Bampton Lectures 1978), (Oxford Univ. Press 1979)

Polkinghorne, J., *Science and Christian Belief: Theological Reflections of a Bottom Up Thinker*, Gifford Lectures 1993/4, (SPCK 1994)

Potter, S., *Lifemanship*, (Penguin 1962)

Powell, M.A., *The Jesus Debate*, (Oxford. Lion 1998)

Priestland, G., *The Case against God*, (Collins 1984)

Punch, The Reverend Mr. Pictorial Record of a Sixty year's Ministry, (Mowbray 1956)

Ramsey, A.M., *The Gospel and the Catholic Church*, (2ⁿᵈ edn. Longmans 1958)

Randall, K., *Evangelicals Etcetera, Conflict and Conviction in the Church of England's Parties*, (Aldershot Ashgate 2005)

Robinson, J.A.T., *Honest to God*, (SCM 1963)

Shortt, R., *Rowan's Rule: the biography of the Archbishop*, (Hodder & Stoughton 2008)

Smyth, C., *Simeon and Church Order*, (Cambridge Univ. Press 1940)

Some Issues in Human Sexuality, (Church House 2003)

Stott, J.R.W., *The Cross of Christ*, (Inter Varsity Press 1986)

Vermes, G., *The Changing Faces of Jesus*, (Penguin 2000)

Vermes, G., *Providential Accidents*, (SCM 1998)

Vidler, A.R., *Christian Belief*, (SCM 1962)

Vidler, A.R., *The Church in an Age of Revolution*, (Penguin 1961)

Waugh, E., *Two Lives: Edmund Campion and Ronald Knox*, (Continuum 2001)

Welsby, P.A., *A History of the Church of England 1945-1980*, (Oxford Univ. Press 1984)

Williams, H.A., *Some Day I'll Find You*, (Beazley 1982)

Williams, R., *The Body's Grace*, (LGCM 2002)

Wright, N.T., *Christian Origins and the Question of God:*
    vol. 1 *The New Testament and the People of God*, (SPCK 1992)
    vol. 2 *Jesus and the Victory of God*, (SPCK 1996)
    vol. 3 *The Resurrection of the Son of God*, (SPCK 2003)

Wright, N.T., *The Original Jesus: The Life and Vision of a Revolutionary*, (Oxford Lion 1996)

Yallop, D., *In God's Name*, (Cape 1984)

Biblical References

Index

Printed in the United Kingdom by
Lightning Source UK Ltd., Milton Keynes
139919UK00001B/1/P

9